CURRENT SOCIETAL CONCERNS ABOUT JUSTICE

CRITICAL ISSUES IN SOCIAL JUSTICE

Published in association with the International Center for Social Justice Research, Department of Psychology, Washington University, St. Louis, Missouri.

Series Editors: **MELVIN J. LERNER** and **RIËL VERMUNT**

University of Waterloo   *University of Leiden*
Waterloo, Ontario, Canada   *Leiden, The Netherlands*

CURRENT SOCIETAL CONCERNS ABOUT JUSTICE

Edited by

Leo Montada
University of Trier
Trier, Germany

and

Melvin J. Lerner
University of Waterloo
Waterloo, Ontario, Canada

PLENUM PRESS • NEW YORK AND LONDON

Library of Congress Cataloging-in-Publication Data

On file

ISBN 0-306-45395-9

©1996 Plenum Press, New York
A Division of Plenum Publishing Corporation
233 Spring Street, New York, N.Y. 10013

10 9 8 7 6 5 4 3 2 1

Printed in the United States of America

Contributors

C. Daniel Batson, Department of Psychology, University of Kansas, Lawrence, Kansas 66045

Susan Clayton, Department of Psychology, The College of Wooster, Wooster, Ohio 44691

Karen S. Cook, Department of Sociology, Duke University, Durham, North Carolina 27708

Faye J. Crosby, Department of Psychology, Smith College, Northampton, Massachusetts 01063

Shawn Donnelly, Department of Sociology, University of Washington, Seattle, Washington 98195

Russell Hardin, Department of Politics, New York University, 715 Broadway, New York, New York 10003

Elisabeth Kals, Fb I - Psychologie, Universität Trier, D-54286 Trier, Germany

Melvin J. Lerner, Department of Psychology, University of Waterloo, Waterloo, Ontario N2L 3G1, Canada

James R. Meindl, School of Management, State University of New York at Buffalo, Buffalo, New York 14260

Dale T. Miller, Department of Psychology, Princeton University, Green Hall, Princeton, New Jersey 08544-1010

Leo Montada, Fb I - Psychologie, Universität Trier, D-54286 Trier, Germany

Susan Opotow, Graduate Program in Dispute Resolution, University of Massachusetts–Boston, Boston, Massachusetts 02125-3393

Rebecca K. Ratner, Department of Psychology, Princeton University, Green Hall, Princeton, New Jersey 08544-1010

Barbara Reichle, Fb I - Psychologie, Universität Trier, D-54286 Trier, Germany

Karen J. Thompson, School of Management, State University of New York at Buffalo, Buffalo, New York 14260

Janet Todd, College of Education, University of Kentucky, 245 Dickey Hall, Lexington, Kentucky 40506-0017

Judith Worell, College of Education, University of Kentucky, 245 Dickey Hall, Lexington, Kentucky 40506-0017

Preface

What role does justice play in the formation of public opinion and the scholarly debates about social problems? Does the perception of injustice force problems to appear on the political agenda? Does the perception of an injustice give momentum to social change? Or are violations of self-interest or threats to one's material welfare the more important factors? Or are empathy-driven concerns for the needy and the disadvantaged motivations to solve societal problems? What is known about the role justice concerns play in leadership? In several chapters of this volume, justice concerns and justice motives are viewed in relation to other concerns and motivations; welfare, self-interest, altruism. It is argued that the consensus of political theorists converges on mutual advantage as the main criterion of acceptable solutions to solving societal problems. In economics, self-interest is considered the driving force and provides the criterion of acceptable solutions. Sociological and social psychological exchange theories share these basic assumptions. Thus, questions are raised and answered concerning how justice and these other important motives appear in the analyses of societal problems and the search for solutions.

Moreover, in addition to the issue of conflicting motives—self-interest, altruism, justice—it is commonly recognized that the definition of what is just and what is unjust is open to question. In public as well as in scientific dialogues, diverging views about justice have to be integrated or decided upon. These conflicting concerns are true for all current societal problems selected as issues to be addressed in this volume: protection of natural ecology and resources, unemployment, gender inequalities in the household and at the workplace, and the intergenerational contract. Thoughtful analyses of these societal issues and theoretical approaches to the relations among motivations and value orientations that often compete with justice motives provide the focus for the chapters in this volume.

Acknowledgments

The Fourth Conference on Social Justice Research at Trier, Federal Republic of Germany, provided the occasion to select the issues and authors for this volume. These biennial conferences are organized by the International Center for Justice Research. The conferences offer a forum for the presentation and discussion of new developments in all fields of justice research. The conference, which took place in Trier in 1993, was sponsored by the ADIA Foundation, the Deutsche Forschungsgemein-schaft\German Research Foundation, the Fritz Thyssen Foundation, and the Universitaet Potsdam. The preparation of the manuscript was sponsored by the Ministerium fuer Wissenschaft und Weiterbildung des Landes Rheinland–Pfalz. We are grateful to all these institutions, to the authors for their contributions, to all reviewers for their valuable and insightful comments, and especially to Maria Haas, whose extraordinary and creative efforts enables both the conference and this volume to become a reality.

Contents

**Chapter 8   Justice and Leadership: A Social
               Co-Constructionist Agenda** **137**

James R. Meindl and Karen J. Thompson

**Chapter 9   Victims without Harmdoers: Human
               Casualties in the Pursuit of Corporate
               Efficiency** **155**

Melvin J. Lerner

1

Doing Justice to the Justice Motive

Melvin J. Lerner

Is it still true, if it ever was, that "Justice is one of the most highly respected notions in our spiritual universe. All men—religious believers and nonbelievers, traditionalists and revolutionaries—invoke justice, and none dare disavow it." (Perelman, 1967, p.3).

Most of the contributions to this volume offer credible challenges, or at least serious qualifications, to this oft-cited assertion of the pre-eminence of justice. For example, in the course of a most impressive and highly erudite analysis of theories of distributive justice Russell Hardin arrives at the observation that "backed to the wall by the real world, virtually every moral and political theorist is a mutual advantage pragmatist." That is a strong statement, refreshingly absent of any of the typical scholarly qualifications, of "by and large," or "under many circumstances" "there is a tendency for." And, as he points out later "the core concern of mutual-advantage theories is to allow for making our world better for us , not only fairer. One of the justifications (oops!) for elevating the pragmatic to the pre-eminent position in political and moral dialogues is that much of what happens under the name of justice occurs in institutional contexts and the participants are inevitably fallible. So if justice can not be fully realized, and most people recognize that, then the only alternative is to engage in actions which are guided by pragmatic considerations of mutual advantage. And if, when, it comes down to it, it would be silly, foolish, to follow rules of justice when that

Melvin J. Lerner • Department of Psychology, University of Waterloo, Waterloo, Ontario, Canada N2L 3G1

Current Societal Concerns about Justice, edited by Leo Montada and Melvin J. Lerner. Plenum Press, New York, 1996.

would jeopardize our common welfare. What an eminently reasonable, sensible position . But where does that leave justice. the "justice motive"? Is it true, in fact that political theorists, more or less enlightened and concerned people, are basically pragmatists, of some sort, but especially involving principles of mutual advantage...welfare always "trumps" justice concerns.

Karen Cook's contribution to this volume is highly consistent with Russell Hardin's approach to justice and mutual advantage. In her analysis of intergenerational relations, not surprisingly, she takes as her starting point the assumptions of Emerson & Cooks version of exchange theory. From that perspective all relationships are governed by the participants rewards and costs. People persist in relationships when their exchanges are relatively profitable compared with what they might obtain elsewhere. Justice enters in to the system only to the extent to which it becomes part of the rewards and costs. Cook's analysis of the dynamics involved in intergenerational relations includes an extension of the social exchange model whereby the participants are involved in a form of "chain generalized" exchange. Although the younger generations engage in clearly unprofitable direct exchanges with their elderly parents, they continue because they anticipate later reciprocity for themselves and their offspring. The individual participants are actually involved in an extended exchange with others, the collectivity, including the next generations. But where is the justice in all this? According to exchange theorists, what is driving, or at least guiding, the participants acts, e.g. family members taking care of infirm granny, is the expectation that in so doing they themselves will be better off in the long run. Is that what justice is all about? If so, then there is no need for people to decide whether mutual advantage "trumps" justice since they are one and the same thing, with different labels. Justice is not only removed from its position of pre-eminence, in this case it becomes psychologically epiphenomenal, just another label for costs and benefits.

Many of the other contributors, assume a familiar somewhat modified version of these exchange theory assumptions that cast justice as an instrumental part of the public dialogues concerning the distribution of resources.

For example, Susan Clayton, examines the role of fairness in the environmental debates from three justice perspectives, distributive, procedural, and macro. As a consequence of her analyses including relevant data generated from several of her studies, she recognizes that the participants in these debates can often seem to consciously manipulate the models of justice they employ in self-serving ways. Then turning to the open forum as the arena in which these alternative justified positions can be debated she finally recommends that "we should think through the effects of any policy and evaluate it from a number of different justice perspectives. Then we can make decisions that really will maximize the collective welfare rather than bowing to the tyranny represented by a single, absolute definition of what is fair." Once again, without any doubt, collective welfare trumps justice in the public dialogue, possibly after "being backed to the wall."

Susan Opotow, also effectively documents the limited scope that justice has in peoples lives . In this chapter dealing with environmental issues, she presents a powerful reminder of the fact that rules of morality, including justice, apply only to those who are included in one's community. People are able to ignore the rights and welfare of those who are perceived as "them," or infra-human with psychological impunity. The creative extension to this observation provided here considers the implications of excluding other forms of life and the inanimate components of the environment from the moral community. There are voices in the environmental debate that describe the destructive consequences to the common welfare of these forms of exclusion. And since there are various sectors of vested interests Opotow describes the dynamics underlying the rules of inclusion and exclusion. In this manner it becomes clear that people's decisions of whom , or what, to treat justly or unjustly are highly influenced by other values and goals. Given the extent to which important aspects of the human, living, and inanimate features of the environment may be excluded from consideration on any given occasion. The concern with justice then must be a rather narrow and highly vulnerable component of people's lives, vulnerable in the sense of being shaped or trumped by other concerns including personal or mutual advantage.

Elisabeth Kals poses central issues of ecological justice: Pollution behavior has some immediate advantages for polluters (economic and others). Those who have the advantages are quite frequently not the ones who have to bear the multiple impediments by pollution. Those who avoid pollution have immediate disadvantages and, quite frequently, they have no personal benefits for their behavior. So, we have problems of distributive justice with respect to the benefits by production and consumption causing pollution and the distribution of costs and impediments caused by pollution. Environmental policies can be evaluated by considering their effect on such distributive injustices as well as by considering their congruence to basic values and rights such as the right to personal and economic freedom or the right to live in a sound ecology. Kals presents data out of two large scale multivariate studies investigating predictors of proenvironmental commitments and the readiness to carry them out. Derived from a heuristic model, an extended list of supposedly relevant predictor variables was tested including basic value orientations, perceptions of general risks by pollution, personal suffering by pollution, perceptions of causation, efficacies and responsibilities, and appraisals of (in-)justices in various environmental policies. One of the stable main results is the following: Proenvironmental commitments (at least for global in contrast to local protection goals) are motivated morally instead of by self-interest in the sense of protecting one's own health. However, self-interest in the sense of personal freedom to economic endeavours and to consumption as well as in the sense of economic welfare turned out to be a powerful antagonist of moral and justice considerations. But Kals' studies done on large heterogeneous German samples demonstrate that the latter motivations are widespread and with many people sufficiently strong to compete successfully with self-interest and economic welfare. The subjectively rated justice of policies as well as preferred basic rights turned out to be potent predictors of proenvironmental commitments and personal renunciations of pollution causing consumption.

That so often appears to be the case. That may be why Faye Crosby, Janet Todd, and Judith Worrell, were challenged to seriously exam whether feminist psychologists dedication to social change and gender justice has recently declined as the movement has "matured." In their chapter they report, in considerable detail, the fascinating findings of a survey of female professors of psychology who describe themselves as feminists and who teach in women's colleges, coeducational colleges, and universities in the United States. The results of their study confirm their hypotheses that, contrary to what some have claimed, the feminist movement is "alive and flourishing" working within as well as outside the social and political systems "to increase the "civil rights of all women." But why the need to defend the viability and effectiveness of the feminist movement ? There are probably several answers to that question, but one may be that there is a generally held view that people often do not live up to, or act upon, their stated values, including the concern for social justice. To be sure, the concern may be there, and it may be quite genuinely held, but, it is commonly understood that people have to realistically assess in each instance the personal costs and benefits associated with acting upon their concerns for justice, including women's equality. Is it not generally assumed, as in exchange theory, that when the costs become too high or the benefits lower than other alternatives than the commitment to justice will be set aside? Interestingly enough, that turned out not to be the case with these feminist psychologists. But most people suspected that it had.

Barbara Reichle, too, addresses the issues of the inconsistency between peoples expressions of commitment to justice and their behavior. In her chapter she focuses on the inconsistencies between peoples professed beliefs about principles of justice in marriages - the "ought" and what actually occurs -the "is"- their relationships.. She describes very informative findings on the way couples in close relationships deal with the distribution of duties, privileges, costs and benefits in her chapter. In particular she is concerned with how considerations of justice, both procedural and distributive appear in the way couples deal with these issues. The questions of justice are critical since, as she points out, the societal context maintains serious inequities associated with gender. Among the important questions she raises and then provides informative answers for, is whether the couples recognize discrepancies, whom do they blame for them, and what are the emotional and interpersonal consequences of these reactions concerning the causes, and extent of injustices? She documents the relationship between partners experiencing injustice in their relationship and the stress they experience as well as the longevity of the relationship. Conceivably then the tolerance of inconsistencies between what occurs in a relationship and what the partners believe ought to be the distribution of duties, rights, and privileges that is especially found among women, is again functional...it allows them to maintain a relationship that considering all the costs and benefits is to their mutual or personal advantage. Once again justice comes out as a nagging, irritating, potentially destructive interference with the welfare of all concerned. Would they not all be happier if they simply ignored the inequities in the relationship? Would that not be to their mutual benefit?

Frankly, the picture of justice that seems to be emerging is much different than described in the opening quote. People may not dare to publicly disavow justice, but they seem certainly ready to sneak around it so that it does not cause them grief, or find ways to use to their personal or collective benefit. Or, otherwise simply abandon it, when it appears more profitable to do so.

Batson and Meindl, in their chapters offer interesting systematic variations on this emerging theme of justice as a limited, if not limiting, consideration in the way people go about distributing resources and dealing with conflicts. Meindl for one firmly locates justice considerations as part of the social construction processes that occur in organizations, and probably everywhere else for that matter. Building on his highly cited previous work on the social construction of leadership and followership, he offers the intriguing hypotheses that distinctive kinds of leader-follower constructions are linked to either distributive or

procedural justice concerns: Transactional domain of leadership is associated with the exchange of goods and services, while the Transformational domain, dealing with creative issues of values and visions, is most
clearly associated with procedures. How, what, leads people to construct
a particular form of leader-follower relation is not entirely spelled out,
but clearly those events are not justice dominated? Once again justice is
an instrumental device, and in fact in the third kind of leader-follower-
ship construction, Charismatic, justice has no place whatsoever. It is
instead replaced by a sacred set of values where "the normative operation of the justice motive is suspended" in the service of some higher
good. This time the trumping is not done by mutual advantage, but by a
higher purpose.

Batson, also relegates justice consideration to much more limited
secular role in people's lives. In fact, after identifying the theme of
justice, as well as justice theorists, as highly amenable to self-serving
constructions of what justice is all about in any particular context, he
then proposes that empathy based altruism is a much more reliable value
in peoples lives and one that in his experiments easily trumps justice,
every time. In the end of his compelling and delightful chapter, however,
he does concede that justice, at least in concert with altruism, can
provide some incentive for people to act decently or constructively for
the common good. But, if we take his admonitions seriously, justice
motive by itself is thoroughly unreliable and easily corrupted by other
more self-interested desires...such as scientific eminence, no doubt.

So, even contentious Batson allows that under some special circumstances the commitment to justice can provide people with the motivation to act in virtuous , decent ways, to eliminate suffering and maintain
social order. And that is where Montada leads us in his chapter. He takes
on the most pressing and demanding contemporary issue of long term
unemployment. After describing the harm it does to people he then
moves on to the question of what can be done about it. Because, after all.
by almost any definition of justice, and with or without the guiding hand
of empathy based altruism, it is clear that most of the widespread
suffering caused by this long term unemployment happens to innocent
victims. They do not deserve the deprivation, and degradation that is
inflicted upon them by the systemic changes occurring in Western
economies. And of course, there is no easy solution to this nest of
problems, because quite realistically, helping one set of victims may
clearly jeopardize the welfare of many other citizens. Finally, Montada
turns to earlier work he and his students had done on "existential guilt"
to find some hints as to how solutions may be developed. They demonstrated the pervasiveness of people's genuine resentment over unjust

inequalities...and amazingly they found that this reservoir of justive based resentment appears without the aid of empathy inducing instructions. Is it possible, then, that people do actually care about justice, but if so why is that not more evident all the time?

Lerner, in his chapter, adds to the documentation of the injustices caused by the contemporary practise of "corporate restructuring." In addition to the suffering of those directly victimized, he identifies the survivors who are allowed to keep their jobs, the managers who design and implement the restructuring and the younger generations who are about to enter the labor market as equally, if not more victimized in the process. In describing the counternormative, and entirely unexpected prevalence of guilt among the managerial staff following a restructuring, he employees the recent work of Shweder, and Epstein to suggest that people have two senses of justice. One is consciously held conventionally rational and guided by self interest, while the other is pre-conscious, "introspectively opaque" and has the immediacy and emotional compelling quality of moral intuitions. Considerable prior research on the justice motive leads to this important conclusion about what people "think" about justice and how it fits in their self-interested lives, and how people actually function, and feel especially when confronted with instances of injustice. These two senses of justice operate according to different rules, and both influence people's lives but in specifiably different ways and to different degrees on specifiable occasions. Lerner suggests : You may think, as most people do, that you are self-interested, and that justice is easily used or subverted in the service of other goals...but that may not be the case at all. Your emotions, and in many cases your acts, actually reveal that you remain strongly committed to very simple rules of justice and highly vulnerable to any signs of injustice. But at the same time you believe you and others are motivated by self-interest, that is more or less rational.

But is that possible? Could people actually care deeply about justice while often, typically, not recognizing it? Is it possible that appears to be the subverting, avoiding, "trumping" of the justice motive, may be, in fact, manifestations of a conflict between people's personal commitment to justice in its various forms, and the way they have been taught to think about and describe their own and others motivations?

Miller's chapter provides a compelling portrayal of why people, including social psychologists, may believe everyone is primarily and continually concerned with their own self-interest. At the outset he presents considerable evidence to the effect that this collectively held belief is a "myth" in the sense that people's important decisions are often quite contrary to what self- interest would require. While at the same time, people believe that it is normatively common and, even more important, considered desirable in our society to pursue individual profit. He then provides additional evidence that people typically are suspicious of others' acts that are not obviously self-invested and may well disguise their own behavior, try to publicly present their own acts, in the same egocentric light. And of course, as he then demonstrates, one critical effect of this collective representation and pervasive "myth" is that it creates a reality, by influencing people's self-reports, expectations, and public acts.

So, there we are: Does justice matter at all in people's lives. If so, how, when, and in what ways? After reading the chapters in this volume you will be in a much better position to decide the answers to those and many other important questions.

The chapters in this volume are excellent exemplars of the recommendation that: "Our first task must thus be to analyze scientifically the concept of justice. This like a prism which breaks down white light into its elements, will permit us to distinguish the variety of its meanings and uses." (Perelman, 1967, p.6).

References

Perelman, Ch. (1967). Justice. New York: Random House.

2

Distributive Justice in a Real World

Russell Hardin

1. Introduction

Most of moral theory has traditionally been about individuals and addressed to individuals (Hardin, 1989a). But most of what matters in life seems to depend on institutions, including the institutions of the modern economy that makes the average person in advanced industrial states splendidly wealthy, institutions that are dearly sought in much of the rest of the world. Much of the most interesting moral theory in recent decades has been focused on institutions, at least in principle—there is often no serious account of any institution, there is merely recognition that institutions must be in place if moral outcomes are to be achieved. A serious institutional morality must take institutions into account at the outset, in the very foundations of the theory.

Among the contemporary body of institutional moral theories is the efflorescence of theories of justice. The best known theory of justice in our time is that of John Rawls (1971). Although this theory is fundamentally about institutions (and their relation to distribution), the theory is clearly unsatisfactory as a general moral theory. First, it is unsatisfactory because distributive justice is inadequate as a moral concern. There are other concerns that may sometimes trump justice. And second, Rawls's theory is unsatisfactory because it still requires an articulate account of the ways relevant institutions work and can be made to work. Without

Russell Hardin • New York University, Department of Politics, 715 Broadway, New York, New York 10003

Current Societal Concerns about Justice, edited by Leo Montada and Melvin J. Lerner. Plenum Press, New York, 1996.

such an account, we cannot even judge whether any actual society approaches Rawlsian justice. Nevertheless, the shift in moral theory from individual-level to institutional-level argument is compelling. Moreover, Rawls's theory is not necessarily unsatisfactory as a theory of distributive justice—many would insist that it is the best such theory going.

Rawls's theory is an effort to accommodate fairness and welfare considerations, which are not directly commensurable. He takes fairness, defined by equality, as the central motivating concern. Rawls recognizes and perhaps accepts the sociological claim of the classical economists that genuine equality can only be achieved by reducing the status of all to some common denominator (Okun, 1975). The result would be loss of incentive to be very productive, so that the egalitarian society would be generally impoverished. If this were the sociological implication of equality, we might find it unappealing. But the prospects could be even worse than this. With general equality and the resulting lower productivity of the society, the typical person might be worse off than even the worst-off person in an unequal, productive society. As David Hume, F.A. Hayek, and many others suppose, we might make the poorest better off by letting those who are able go on to reap far better than equal rewards.

Rawls wishes somehow to find an acceptable compromise between equality and productivity—the economist's big trade-off between equality and productive efficiency. His solution is to resort to a particular claim of fairness. What a society produces is largely a result of the way that society is organized; it is not merely the sum of what all individuals would do under any circumstances. Therefore, because the total product is determined socially, the reward to individuals for the social product should be determined socially. Rawls supposes that a fair determination, which any rational person would accept, is to allow all inequalities that produce better lives for those who are worst off. If a system that allows some very few to be billionaires produces enough to allow raising the wellbeing of the worst-off class to the highest possible level, then the apparent inegalitarianism is fair. Why? Because the worst off and the best off both benefit from the system as compared to any alternative system.

"Well-being" and "welfare" may be inadequate terms to capture what Rawls wishes to equalize. He includes certain political rights as well as standard welfare concerns. Unfortunately, his cluster of concerns seems to have several dimensions and it is not easy to define a notion of equality to cover all these dimensions. Rawls's fairness is therefore murky if not thoroughly incoherent. Value pluralists such as Joel Feinberg (1975) and Thomas Nagel (1977) insist on multi-dimensionality.

This is essentially an open question for Rawls' s theory because he has not worked out articulately how the elements of wellbeing fit together. I will assume that his notion of fairness is nevertheless a simple one that can be applied. If it is not, then the general conclusions below follow even more transparently.

The great appeal of Rawls's theory for moral theorists is that it combines two major streams of thought, one based on fairness and one based on mutual advantage. Among its conspicuous failings, depending on what is your preferred moral stance, are that it neglects simple beneficence, commitment to specific moral principles other than fairness and mutual advantage, and commitment to values based in community or religion. In the last of these neglects, Rawlsian justice is deliberate. In the great tradition from Locke forward, Rawlsian liberalism denies political standing to specific religious values. More generally, Rawlsian theory is similar to every other systematic theory in neglecting some plausible concerns while taking others seriously.

The central problem for a systematic theory of justice is how to fit it with other concerns, especially concerns that sometimes compete with justice. We could say that justice always trumps, as in the silly claim that we should do justice though the heavens should fall, as discussed below. For a theory of distributive justice, we must even be concerned with how it fits with a theory of criminal justice or justice as order. And throughout we must be concerned to make it work with plausible real-world institutions.

2. The Structures of Moral Theories

Moral theories fall into two somewhat artificial modal categories. Many are primarily theories directed to personal behavior in face-to-face and small-number interactions. And many, while partly personal, are distinguished by their strong commitment to social and political concerns. Twentieth-century moral theory in the Anglo-Saxon world was almost entirely personal in the seven decades before Rawls's *A Theory of Justice*. The turn to personal morality afflicted theories as different as Kantianism and utilitarianism. Immanuel Kant himself had addressed issues of international peace and jurisprudence, although these were not genuinely extensions of his moral theory, which is entirely at the individual level. More critically, early utilitarians had been conspicuously concerned foremost with institutions and governments. Indeed, utilitarianism was arguably the reigning moral theory of law in the

Anglo-Saxon world until the rise of rights-talk in the last couple of decades (Hart, 1979).

One might say of a social or political theory that it was morally inadequate or merely a partial theory because it fails to deal with issues of personal morality, as Rawls's theory of justice might be thought to fail to deal with lying or weakness of will. I will not raise such issues here but will focus only on problems of the incorporation of collective or political concerns that seem beyond justice. *The focus will be entirely on political theories and the concerns that drive such theories.*

There is one other kind of moral theorizing that ranges from the personal to the institutional levels. It is an alternative position that has a long history in moral philosophy, although it has been less well argued or received in political and legal philosophy. This kind of theorizing—it cannot be called a theory—is *intuitionism*, in which the theorist has direct intuitions that certain specific substantive principles are right or wrong. For example, some people just happen to know that abortion or lying is right or wrong. There may be no further principle that stands behind these intuitions, which must include a substantial collection of independent claims about different classes of problems. Intuitionism has most conspicuously invaded political philosophy in intuitionist rights theories (Nozick, 1974). But it also stands behind many arguments for procedural justice (not merely fairness, but specific procedures), retributive justice, corrective justice, and collections of right and wrong laws. And it probably stands behind the bulk of social scientific work on actual norms and morality. For example, a large fraction of the social psychological literature on these problems focuses on ad hoc norms or specific principles that do not cohere with each other, that seemingly come via intuition that is more or less untutored.

In practice, intuitionists are anti-theorists. Nothing deflates the enterprise of theory quite so effectively as the assertion of absolute knowledge that defies the need of theoretical argument or of any kind of proof. In general, I think substantive moral intuitions are of no value, but I will not argue that here (Hardin, 1988, pp. 178–191). The critical question to ask of them is where they come from. They were once commonly held to be god's implants in the human mind. Their messy incoherence, their diversity across times, places, and classes, and their sometime silliness argue against this possibility even for the religious believer. They might be learned social conventions or incoherent inferences from other principles. If we reject intuitionism, we reject large parts of moral theory. For example, commonplace rights-talk is vitiated by its grounding in little more than direct intuition that some collection of claims, usually including ownership of property, are moral rights.

Theories may be grounded in formal intuitions that are compelling, and from these and various facts, including sociological facts, we may infer substantive conclusions. But we cannot directly intuit the rightness or goodness of such conclusions. Criticisms of moral theories can therefore take only two forms. We can criticize a theoretical claim as incoherently derived from the theory's basic principles. Or we can criticize the basic principles of a theory (Hardin, 1993). For an example of the former, one might argue that an absolute prohibition against telling a lie no matter what the circumstances does not follow from Kantian first principles (as Kant [1797] thought it did). For the latter, one might criticize the concern with welfare that drives utilitarianism or the concern with transcendental rationality that drives Kantian theory. In what follows, I will focus only on problems of incoherence and will not debate basic principles.

There are at least three formal intuitions from which several coherent theories are derived. The best known of these is some version of utility or welfare added across individuals to yield a total, as in classical utilitarianism. The least well known is an ordinal variant of this: the mutual-advantage principle of Hobbes (Hardin, 1991) and contemporary ordinal utilitarians, including many standard economists who no longer accept additive, interpersonally comparable utility (Hardin, 1988, chapter 3). While traditional utilitarianism was essentially a morality of beneficence, mutual-advantage theories have no place for beneficence. Between these two in broad understanding is fairness, which has a long history, but which was made articulate and relatively coherent only recently by Rawls. Mutual-advantage theories and Rawlsian-fairness theory must seemingly both be stated in ex ante terms. They both focus on the nature of the world in which we might live, not on the actual rewards we receive.

Theories in these classes have difficult problems that sometimes seem devastating. All face severe measurement problems, although the demands on additive-welfarist theories is especially severe. Mutual advantage theories are inherently indeterminate in some applications even for the kind of issues they ostensibly apply to (Hardin, 1989b). Mutual advantage might rank A over B and C over D but have nothing to say about the ranking of A and C. It can be indeterminate (not merely indifferent) for the latter, just as the Pareto rules in economics can be indeterminate. The Pareto comparison can say that some outcomes are all better than where we are, but it might not be able to say which of them is best in the sense of being Pareto superior (or mutually advantageous) to the others. Finally, Rawlsian fairness may be incomplete in the sense that there are classes of problems that it does not cover.

Many other principles are occasionally touted and one or of them might eventually play central roles in moral theory. But they are not yet well or coherently elaborated and, although they sound in principle attractive to many people, they are not very workable. These include autonomy, as in the views of many contemporary Kantians; the maximal extent of rights consistent with extending the same rights to others, as in the French revolutionary constitution, in John Stuart Mill, and in many contemporary libertarian accounts; substantive rationality, as in the views of many contemporary Aristotelians; and rational agency, as in the work of Kant and Alan Gewirth (1978).

Historically there have also been strictly procedural theories, such as contractarianism, according to which what we contract jointly to do is right. The impracticality of actual contracting has killed classical contract theory. In its place have risen rationalist variants, as in the ostensible principles of "reasonable agreement" and "discourse theory." Both of these implicitly suppose that there is a truth to be found through debate and discourse, a truth on which we would all agree if only we could first find it. Despite its current vogue, I think such theory is wishful thinking. Debate and discourse are likely all too often to lead us better to understand that we do not agree, cannot agree, will not agree.

There are non-distributive principles that loom large among the historical theories of justice. If Rawlsian distributive justice is inadequate as a general political-moral theory, these other principles are even more so. Briefly consider one major class of theories: procedural justice. A theory of procedural justice may have distributive implications. Procedural justice can easily fit with great inequality, as it does in libertarian theories. Procedural justice might be important not only normatively but also sociologically. For example, the perception of procedural justice may contribute to law-abidingness by encouraging people to accept their treatment by courts or the justice system (Tyler, 1990). And fair rules that protect the rights of the innocent, such as fair punishments, may increase the willingness of the community to cooperate in the law enforcement effort (Akerlof & Yellin, 1994). But procedural justice lacks content and yields no criticism of bad results produce by correctly following procedures.

In addition to non-distributive theories, there are distributive principles of justice that differ from Rawls's. Straight egalitarianism is clearly different empirically if sociological conditions are such as to induce greater production from some by offering them unequal rewards. And an Aristotelian notion of justice as reward by merit is strictly distributive but according to principles quite different from those of Rawls. Such reward by merit requires that reward be commensurate with merit. One who accepts contemporary, quasi economic understandings of value and its construction cannot take Aristotelian notions of merit seriously. The legal analog of reward by merit is corrective justice, in which I compensate you for a harm I have done out of the gains I got from harming you. Quite apart from the analytical difficulty in the theory of value already noted, corrective justice fails because there can be net loss of wealth all around from criminal or tort actions. For example, a thief might break and enter before stealing—the breaking would be a dead loss. There would then be no way for the thief to make right the victim's loss through mere Aristotelian corrective justice. More grievously, a murder or rape cannot be corrected. Similarly, in tort law, corrective justice is often misfit, as when my tortious action is to smash your car.

3. Coherence

Most so-called theories, as opposed to mere commentaries, on morality must be consistent and complete for the range of their application. In actual fact, no extant theory may meet these demanding conditions fully. Classical additive utilitarianism is, in principle, complete and, because it has only one dimension on which to measure value, it is also coherent. For the latter reason, mutual-advantage theories are also in principle coherent. But, because they are sometimes indeterminate, they may not be complete. (Perhaps the world to which we apply the theory is best fitted to an indeterminate theory.) Rawlsian distributive justice, however, is compounded of two quite different elements: fairness and mutual advantage. Because these need not cohere, we might expect Rawlsian distributive justice not to cohere.

One might suppose that the joining of Rawls's different values must logically fail or that it must require an independent third principle to balance mutual advantage against fairness when they conflict. But this presumption is wrong. Fairness and mutual advantage are combined analytically without any need for balancing them. If mutual advantage can apply, it does—automatically and, at that point, without conflict with fairness. First we do fairness, perhaps insisting on perfect equality. Then, we apply the mutual-advantage principle to this state of equality, starting with the worst-off class (in this case, everyone, because all are equal). Perhaps there are many mutual-advantage moves available. We discard all those which can be improved by yet another mutual-advantage move. Now we choose that one in which the worst-off class is best off (or one of the more than one if there are more than one).

There may still be a problem of multi-dimensionality in the items that constitute the well-being over which fairness ranges but, if fairness and mutual advantage are each uni-dimensional, then we can combine the two without an overarching third principle for making trade-offs and without addition along a single dimension. There is no failure of logic. Equality is always trumped by mutual advantage if possible. Indeed, mutual advantage is a necessary condition on Rawlsian justice, in the following sense. If we have a putatively fair distribution but a mutual advantage move to another distribution is possible, we must make that move before we have Rawlsian distributive justice.

There is one plausible flaw in this device. When we are comparing one state of affairs to another and saying that the worst-off class in the first state is better off than the worst-off class in the second state, we need not be comparing the *same* worst-off class in each state. The worst-off class in one state could be one occupational group, what that in another state could be a different occupational group. Hence, the device is exclusively ex ante, because ex ante we are deciding on the fates of unidentified people.

All three of the major principles for ordering society are plausibly coherent, at least internally. But, if one of them is not complete, then its overall coherence must be judged in conjunction with its fit with whatever theory is added to make it complete. Again, classical utilitarianism is clearly coherent because it is plausibly complete. Rawlsian distributive justice, however, does not appear on its face to be complete, nor does it seem likely that Rawlsians would think it is or should be complete. Indeed, distributive justice is only half of the usual notion of political justice, the other half of which is criminal justice and justice as order more generally.

Let us make a first pass at the coherence of a combination of Rawlsian distributive justice and criminal justice. (To finish the analysis, we will have to bring the theory to bear through plausible institutions, as discussed in the next two sections.) The evident starting point for both is some principle of fairness. If they follow the same principle of fairness, then we should expect them to fit coherently together. In Rawls's theory, at this point we would be able to argue that, if the worst off would be made better off by introducing some inequality, then the inequality is justified. That is, Rawls makes a strong concession to mutual advantage when it does not interfere with distribution at the bottom. But this concedes too much. One way to make the worst-off class even better off is to treat them more leniently in the criminal justice system, especially if their victims often enough include those in better-off classes. Or, we could be more lenient only to those of the worst-off class who offend against those in better-off classes.

If our principles of distributive justice drive the argument at its most fundamental level, we are stuck with this odd conclusion that criminal justice should be somewhat less than abstractly just, that it should be subordinated to concern with distribution. This is clearly a possible intellectual and moral conclusion, and perhaps it is what we should conclude. But it is jarring and we should not accept it without further ado. It merits extensive discussion before it can merit adoption. Perhaps this result follows from the complexity of Rawls's underlying value, which is wellbeing defined as a collection of concerns with autonomy, self respect, wealth, and so forth. Perhaps if this relatively under-articulated value theory were more fully worked out, we could see that distributive justice requires principles of criminal justice that are fair across individuals rather than across groups. But since Rawls's principle of distributive justice is inherently a principle across groups, it seems likely that it must conflict with any principle that ignores groups.

Incidentally, the apparent conflict between Rawlsian distributive justice and standard principles of criminal justice is jarring not simply because it runs against a primitive intuition we have about the law. Rather, it is jarring because it seems to represent an internal contradiction in the notion of fairness. After all, the usual principles of criminal justice and Rawls's principle of distributive justice are both derived from what seems to be the same formal intuition about fairness. Either that formal intuition is incoherent or one or the other of these two putative deductions from it is inconsistent with it. Arguably, the inconsistency is in Rawls's deduction because Rawls lets quasi welfare considerations constrain fairness. It is in this move that he brings in considerations across groups. Unfortunately, pure fairness may have analogous drawbacks in criminal and distributive justice.

In sum, although Rawlsian distributive justice may be internally consistent in principle, it may not be consistently joined to a parallel theory of justice as order. Perhaps this is because the principle of fairness of Rawlsian distributive justice is not the same as the principle of fairness in criminal justice and justice as order more generally.

4. Institutional Fallibility

One of the most important considerations in actual institutions is their fallibility. They may be misdesigned or, more ordinarily, they may be staffed with less than perfectly functioning agents. They therefore often bring about results that fit poorly with their mandates. One might say it is part of the epistemology of an institution that it is fallible, sometimes in ways individuals are fallible, sometimes in ways in which institutions are distinctively and incorrigibly fallible. A well designed institution is one that reduces the incidence of failure—but it typically can only reduce, not eliminate, this incidence.

If institutions are fallible—inherently, predictably fallible—then that fact should enter into our principles for designing them. Of course, among the chief of the principles for designing institutions of criminal justice is our general theory of justice and political morality more generally.

Charles Beitz supposes that an institutionally designed egalitarian voting scheme might actually leave someone in a less than equal voting position. Arguing from the structure of Rawls's more general theory of justice, Beitz (1989) concludes that this person would then have no further recourse to get the seeming injustice of the voting scheme corrected if the scheme is the best that can be done under the just theory of democratic participation. Similarly, Rawls's theory of just distribution offers no further corrective to the worst-off class once the institutions of justice have been properly designed. In these two cases, it seems that there is nothing further for the individuals to do or to claim against the larger society or its institutions. Why? Because the institutions are ideally designed and they achieve the best that can be achieved so that there is no further principle for corrective action.

But this is not the universal problem when institutions go awry, when they fail to meet the theory. What should individuals do when they think that the state is fallible and that it has brought about or allowed the wrong result? They should do just what they should do in general when they think the law is wrong. They should sometimes violate the law even knowing that the authorities may sanction them for their violation. It can be right for me to break a law that it would be right for the state to enforce (Hardin forthcoming a). Similarly, in some underlying sense of justice, it could be just for me to violate the distribution that an institutional principle of justice fallibly mandates.

Justice as order is a mutual-advantage theory and should therefore fit easily enough with fundamental mutual advantage arguments. Some defenses of criminal law are essentially defenses from justice as order. Others, such as theories of corrective justice or retributive justice, are not typically either theories of distributive justice or of justice as order (mutual advantage). These theories therefore have the logical (and likely) possibility of conflicting with theories of distributive justice and with mutual-advantage theories. And theories of distributive justice have the possibility of conflicting with theories of mutual advantage, although Rawls's theory appears to accommodate limited arguments for mutual advantage without incoherence. But I wish to argue something even more forceful and telling than this merely logical problem. Theories of distributive justice, retributive justice, and corrective justice (the last may be incoherent in any case) must generally *give way* to mutual advantage *in a real-world justification*. In abstract theory one might argue against this conclusion. But in practice the conclusion seems unavoidable. This is the reverse of the relation between fairness and mutual advantage as argued above for Rawlsian distributive justice, in which the mutual-advantage principle only modifies egalitarian determinations.

Why is practice so harsh for theory? Recall the once commonplace claim that we should do justice though the heavens fall. The claim is silly in two quite different ways. First it is silly even to suppose there is a connection between whether the heavens fall and whether we do justice. Second it is silly to suppose that, if we read the claim as merely pompously metaphorical, even if grievous harm will follow from doing justice we should always nevertheless do justice and let the harm follow. This is often seen as an issue in the pluralism of values. But reality is harsher than this.

Suppose our theory of justice is anything other than merely mutual advantage. It follows that mutual advantage considerations must potentially conflict with justice. Now consider an actual justice system that is grounded in our theory of justice. Although we might not be certain of any particular case—except, perhaps, in the current wave of retrospective DNA tests—we are very nearly certain in principle that our courts occasionally do grievous injustices. I might nevertheless think it best that we have our fallible criminal justice system, even at the risk that it wrongly punish me, because, ex ante, I expect to be generally better off with such a system than without one. If everyone shares my view, then the system is mutually advantageous even though it might occasionally be unjust. Moreover, we might think it is not merely mutually advantageous—it is hugely advantageous, so much so that we think it justified to trade its advantages for its injustices. Nobody but a rationalizing Pollyanna could suppose any actual working system of criminal justice does not occasionally produce unjust results. Anyone who nevertheless supports an actual system of criminal justice therefore supports letting mutual advantage considerations trump justice considerations. Backed to the wall by the real world, virtually every moral and political theorist is a mutual-advantage pragmatist.

Mutual-advantage theories are almost inherently institutionalist. (This claim is qualified by "almost" because David Gauthier [1986] has presented a mutual advantage theory that is ostensibly not institution-alist but personal.) For example, it may not be to our mutual advantage to refrain from murder. But it likely would be to our mutual advantage to have a relatively effective state regime against murder. What makes it advantageous to me to be coerced not to murder or steal is that virtually all others find it advantageous to themselves—under the regime of state coercion—not to murder or steal on the condition that all be threatened with sanctions if they do murder or steal. Hence, there is mutual advantage in having a relevant legal regime.

The core concern of mutual-advantage theories is to allow for making our world better for us, not only fairer. Strangely, it may be easier to argue for the mutual advantage of a legal regime than to argue from any other perspective for its justice. To argue for the justice of a practical regime per se against murder, for example, requires that we construct it to achieve only—or almost only—correct convictions. At some point, of course, failure to convict any innocent person is tantamount to not convicting any guilty person either, hence tantamount to having no regime at all. We must, on our principles of justice, decide on a trade-off between convictions of the innocent and convictions of the guilty. If we do this, then at some point we are, again, arguing from mutual advantage rather than from justice.

Most theories of justice are not argued in ways that make this inference perspicuous. But a theory of mutual advantage could, in principle, easily handle the trade-off. I am better off at the point at which my losses from no regime outweigh the union of my gains from a regime (in the conviction of those who are guilty and deterrence of those who might be guilty) and my losses from it (in the mistaken conviction of me or others whom I would rather have protected). In actual application, the theory may not be so easy to work out, because our social scientific account of the effects of various regimes may not be very good.

The heavy burden for a pure theory of distributive justice is to *accommodate principles of criminal justice through fallible institutions* that will predictably take action against the innocent on occasion. If such a theory cannot do this, it must inherently rule out practical criminal justice. If we insist on the perfect fairness of never convicting the innocent, we may have such faulty results that we all suffer. And if we insist on the equality of results that pure distributive fairness might seem to require, we would also achieve far more dismal results than if we constrain our application of the fairness principle in our collective interest.

5. Other Pragmatic Constraints

One way for Rawlsian distributive justice to be made to include a theory of criminal justice would be, as noted, to allow criminal verdicts to fit into the range of what is to be distributed. A member of the worst-off class would receive a lighter sentence for a particular crime than would a member of a better-off class. This move might be pleasing to hard-nosed egalitarians. It would reverse the more likely practice in our own law and the quite open norms of medieval European law, in which penalties for crimes were correlated inversely with status: the higher the status, the lower the penalty.

Where would mutual advantage stand on a status-based criminal law? If we are to choose between a medieval system, in which penalties varied enormously depending on social status, and a universalistically fair system, the principle of mutual advantage cannot be determinate unless sociology and psychology could show that we would all benefit from one over the other—a prospect that might seem implausible. Despite its superficial implausibility, however, it could be sociologically true that those in upper status positions would benefit enough from the society of egalitarian law for it to be in their interest to choose egalitarian law over caste law. Why? Because those of lower status might be far more productive and cooperative under a regime of fair law, enough so as to benefit those of higher status even after yielding their legal privileges. This result might be dependent on whether the law was relatively effective at suppressing illegal activities and on whether there were status differences in the effectiveness of law.

Perhaps the largest practical problem in a system of justice, however, is the combination of ordinary institutional and organizational problems with limits to individual rationality and commitment. These presumably lie behind the problem with extant systems of justice that they occasionally go awry and punish the innocent. Among these problems, one that seems to have got very little attention looms very large. Although a system of justice might readily be characterized as fitting some theory—mutual advantage, Rawlsian distributive justice, procedural justice, or retributive justice—its officers might follow very different principles, including their personal interest. Part of the problem of designing a good system of justice therefore is to design one that will work with the human material at hand. And part of the problem of arguing a good theory is to construct it to work well in the hands of actual humans.

This was a central issue for James Madison and others in the drafting of the United States Constitution—to structure government so that it would work reasonably well even with knaves in office.

6. Concluding Remarks

Unless it is applied ex ante, the principle of mutual advantage is woefully conservative in many contexts. It allows only those changes that hurt no one or that fully compensate all those who are harmed by the change. Ex ante, all might be expected to benefit from, say, technological change—although we can be sure that ex post some will have lost, as peasants and farmers, Luddites, and modern high-tech firms such as IBM have done. Mutual advantage applied as from today could hold the world hostage to a backward dictator or social class. But ex ante it is so broadly pleasing that the greatest of fairness theorists has accepted it fully in his theory of distributive justice. Since utilitarians also find it compelling, it may be currently the most widely accepted principle in western moral and political philosophy. It may not be sufficient to resolve all issues—it is too radically indeterminate for that—but neither fairness theorists nor utilitarians would ever violate it.

There is a potential intellectual problem in the focus on mutual advantage. Historically, that has been the focus of philosophers now considered conservative. And, indeed, if the principle of mutual advantage is not viewed ex ante but in medias res, it is inherently conservative, because it commends only those policies that do not make the wealthy (or anyone else) worse off. Mutual advantage in medias res is seemingly the political theory of many contemporary libertarians and it, in the form of an initial unanimity rule, was once enunciated as the necessary starting point for any theorizing about policy (Buchanan & Tullock, 1962). But even mutual advantage ex ante is associated primarily with conservatives such as Thomas Hobbes (for Hobbes, justice is merely a positive term—it is what government achieves).

Henry Sidgwick accused Hume of having restricted vision, because Hume neglected distributive justice and discussed only justice as order. In fact, before the radical utilitarians, distributive justice was only sometimes of concern. The very term meant, perversely to the modern ear, reward by merit, as in Aristotle's concern with giving the persons with the best relevant characters the offices of leadership. Occasional appeals for egalitarianism, as in the writings of John Winstanley (1652) during the English revolutionary period, were often grounded in an appeal to a particular kind of life, especially agrarian subsistence farming. This was a kind of life that was eventually doomed and that could have brought equality only by violating the possibilities of mutual advantage. Unfortunately for the long debate over mutual advantage and other theories of justice, the non-conservative tradition has often been hobbled by bad social science or has been anti-social-scientifically romantic.

Rawls has done political theory the great service of bringing the egalitarian and mutual-advantage principles together into one theory, where their effects can be debated constructively without dismissively lumping them into ideological out-boxes turned it opposite directions. For this and for his institutional turn in moral theory, we should be grateful to Rawls. Unfortunately, much of the response of philosophers to Rawls's work—even much of his own later commentary on these issues—has been retrograde effort to push us back to individual-level morality and out of the world of institutions in which we live. With the push of social scientists, perhaps this retrograde effort can be blocked. Utilitarian economists had kept up the interest in institutional arrangements while philosophers neglected it through much of this century. But utilitarian economists were—I think wrongly—lumped into the ideological world of, supposedly, Hobbes, where they could be ignored by those with egalitarian leanings. Again, today, perhaps we can count on social scientists to keep us on track in the effort to understand justice and its workability by treating workability as important and independent of ideology.

References

Akerlof, G., & Yellin, J.L. (1994). Gang behavior, law enforcement, and community values. In H. J. Aaron, T. E. Mann, & T. Taylor (eds.), Values and public policy (pp. 173–209). Washington, DC: Brookings.

Beitz, C. R. (1989). Political Equality: An essay in democratic theory. Princeton: Princeton University Press.

Buchanan, J. M., & Tullock, G. (1962). The calculus of consent: Logical foundations of constitutional democracy. Ann Arbor, Mich.: University of Michigan Press.

Feinberg, J. (1975) Rawls and intuitionism. In N. Daniels (ed.), Reading Rawls: Critical studies of a theory of justice (pp. 108–124). New York: Basic Books.

Gauthier, D. (1986). Morals by agreement. Oxford: Oxford University Press.

Gewirth, A. (1978). Reason and morality. Chicago: University of Chicago Press.

Hardin, R. (1988). Morality within the limits of reason. Chicago: University of Chicago Press.

Hardin, R. (1989a). The contemporary crisis in ethics. In The world community in post-industrial society. The confusion in ethics and values in contemporary society and possible approaches to redefinitions (Vol. 3, pp. 191–131): Seoul, Korea: Wooseok Publishing Company

Hardin, R. (1989b). Political obligation. In A. Hamlin & P. Pettit (eds.), The good polity (pp. 103–119). Oxford: Basil Blackwell.

Hardin, R. (1991). Hobbesian political order. Political Theory, 19, 156–180.

Hardin, R. (1993). Blackmailing for mutual good. University of Pennsyvania Law Review, 41, 1787–1816.

Hardin, R. (Forthcoming a). My university's yacht: Morality and the rule of law. In R. E. Barnett & I. Shapiro (eds.), NOMOS 26, The rule of law. New York: New York University Press.

Hardin, R. (Forthcoming b). Institutional morality. In G. Brennan & R. E. Goodin (eds.), The theory of institutional design. Cambridge University Press.

Hart. H. L. A. (1979). Between utility and rights. In H. L. A. Hart (ed.), Essays in jurisprudence and philosophy (pp. 198–222). Oxford: Oxford University Press, 1983.

Kant, I. (1797). On a supposed right to tell lies from benevolent motives. In T. K. Abbott (ed.), Kant's critique of practical reason and other works on the theory of ethics (pp. 361–365). London: Longman's, 1909, 6th edition.

Nagel, T. (1977). The fragmentation of value. In T. Nagel (ed.), Mortal questions (pp. 128–141). Cambridge: Cambridge University Press, 1979

Nozick, R. (1974). Anarchy, state, and utopia. New York: Basic Books.

Okun, A. M. (1975). Equality and efficiency: The big tradeoff. Washington, DC: Brookings.

Rawls, J. (1971). A theory of justice. Cambridge, Mass.: Harvard University Press.

Tyler, T. R. (1990). Why people obey the law. New Haven, Conn.: Yale University Press.

Winstanley, J. (1652). The law of freedom in a platform or, true magistracy restored. New York: Shocken. 1973.

3

The Power of the Myth of Self-Interest

Dale T. Miller and Rebecca K. Ratner

Self-interest is the cardinal human motive, or so many of the most influential theories of human behavior would have us believe. Theories as diverse as evolutionary biology, neo-classical economics, behaviorism, and psychoanalysis all assume that people actively and single-mindedly pursue their self-interest, whether it be embodied in reproductive fitness, utility maximization, reinforcement, or wish fulfillment (Schwartz, 1986). On the other hand, much of the most interesting social science research of the last twenty years points to inadequacy of self-interest models of behavior (for reviews, see Batson, 1991; Etzioni, 1988; Kohn, 1990; Lerner, 1980; Mansbridge, 1990; Sears & Funk, 1990; Sen, 1977; Tyler & Dawes, 1993). We now know that people often care more about the fairness of the procedures they are subjected to than about the material outcomes these procedures yield (Tyler, 1990), that they often care more about their group's collective outcomes than about their personal outcomes (Dawes, van de Kragt & Orbell, 1988), and that their attitudes toward public policies are often shaped more by their values and ideologies than by the impact these policies have on their material well-being (Sears & Funk, 1990).

One perspective missing in the debate over the sovereignty of self-interest has been that of the layperson. This is an unfortunate omission since an important aspect of a culture's ideology is its depiction of human motivation (Miller & Prentice, 1994). In cultures steeped in

Dale T. Miller and Rebecca K. Ratner • Department of Psychology, Princeton University, Green Hall, Princeton, New Jersey 08544-1010

Current Societal Concerns about Justice, edited by Leo Montada and Melvin J. Lerner. Plenum Press, New York, 1996.

liberalism and the ideology of radical individualism, the assumption that self-interest is a powerful motive can be expected to have wide currency. And whether or not self-interest is as powerful as collective representations claim that it is (and should be), its prominence in these representations ensures that it will have powerful consequences. Biological fact or not, self-interest is—to use Durkheim's (1982) phrase—a social fact. In the present chapter, we explore the power of the myth of self-interest, showing both that the layperson holds an exaggerated belief in the extent to which self-interest motivates behavior and that this widely shared misconception has important social psychological consequences.

1. The Layperson's Belief in the Power of Self-Interest

We begin by describing four studies that explore people's belief in the motivational power of self-interest. These studies were designed to test the hypothesis that people overestimate the power that self-interest exerts on others' attitudes and behavior. The format in all the studies was basically the same: each study assessed both the *actual* extent to which a self-interest motive guided people's behavior in a particular situation and people's *estimates* of the extent to which behavior in that situation would be guided by a self-interest motive. The first two studies (Miller & Ratner, 1995; Studies 1 and 2) assessed the actual and expected impact of group membership on attitudes toward issues that affect group members. The next two studies (Miller & Ratner, 1995; Study 3; Miller, 1975) examined the actual and estimated impact of financial incentive on people's willingness to engage in a pro-social action. In combination, these studies allow us to assess whether people overestimate the power of two different types of self-interest: 1) personal stake as a function of group membership and 2) personal gain as a function of monetary reward.

1.1. Estimated Impact of Gender on Support for Abortion Coverage

In the first study, we examined both the actual and estimated impact of gender on undergraduates' attitudes toward abortion coverage under a new health plan. Who should care more about access to medical coverage for abortions, men or women? Given that access to abortions may have a greater impact on the lives of women than men, one might predict that women would care more. But do they? And how do people's beliefs about which gender cares more correspond to reality? We asked undergraduate psychology majors (61 males, 60 females) to answer four questions concerning their attitudes toward full abortion coverage under a new Clinton-sponsored health plan (Miller & Ratner, 1995; Study 1). Subjects were asked whether they thought a new plan should include full coverage of abortions, what they thought the opinion of the average male psychology student was, and what they thought the opinion of the average *female* psychology student was. In addition, subjects were asked which sex they thought would benefit more from a plan that covered abortions.

As expected, over ninety percent of the subjects indicated that they believed that a health plan that provided abortion coverage would benefit women more than men. Furthermore, subjects predicted that the attitudes of their male and female peers would reflect this perceived difference in self-interest. Specifically, subjects estimated (on 7-pt. scales) that females' attitudes toward the plan would be more favorable than males' attitudes (M = 5.7 vs. M = 4.4). Despite the subjects' predictions—but consistent with the research of Sears and his colleagues (Sears & Funk, 1991)—gender did not predict support for the policy. The attitudes of both males and females toward abortion coverage were moderately positive and did not differ (M = 4.5 vs. M = 4.4). Subjects thus estimated that gender would have a significantly greater impact on attitudes toward abortion coverage than it actually did. On the basis of these results, it appears that laypersons are ardent (if misguided) self-interest theorists—or at least they substantially overestimate the impact that having a stake in an issue has on people's attitudes.

1.2. Estimated Impact of Racial Status on Concern for Minority Needs

In a second study, we examined the accuracy with which people estimated the impact that a student's racial status would have on his or her attitudes toward racial issues. We asked undergraduates (68 majority students, 53 minority students) to answer a series of questions about their University's commitment to the needs of its minority students (Miller & Ratner, 1995; Study 2). Subjects were asked to indicate whether or not they thought minority students' needs on campus were being met satisfactorily, to estimate the percentage of minority students who thought that needs of minority students were being met satisfactorily, to estimate the percentage of majority students who thought that the needs of minority students were being met satisfactorily, and to indicate what effect an improvement in the circumstances of minority students would have on their own quality of life.

We assumed that the treatment of minority needs would be perceived to be of greater consequence to minority students than to majority students; indeed, minority students did express a stronger belief that their quality of life would improve if the general situation of minorities on campus improved. The estimates of both minority and majority students reflected this perceived difference in vested interest. Subjects estimated that only a small fraction of the majority students (31%) would feel that minority needs were not being met satisfactorily but that the preponderance of minority students (68%) would have this concern. However, examining the actual responses that subjects gave, we see that subjects' racial status did not significantly predict their attitudes toward minority needs: almost as many majority students as minority students (54% vs. 61%) indicated they felt that minority students' needs were not being met satisfactorily. Like the abortion study, this study reveals a strong tendency for subjects to overestimate the impact that having a stake in an issue has on people's attitudes.

1.3. Estimated Impact of Payment on Willingness to Donate Blood

We now describe two studies that assessed the real and estimated impact of another form of self-interest—monetary incentive. The goal of these studies was to examine whether subjects could correctly predict the impact that financial incentive would have on their peers' willingness to engage in pro-social behaviors. In the first study, we presented psychology undergraduates with notice of a Red Cross blood drive that allegedly was coming to their campus in several weeks (Miller & Ratner, 1995; Study 3). Subjects were told that the Red Cross had asked the researchers to provide an estimate of how many students would be willing to donate blood and what factors might make volunteering more attractive. All subjects were asked (in counterbalanced order) both whether they would be willing to donate blood for free and whether they would be willing to donate blood for $15 In addition, subjects were asked to estimate the percentage of students in their psychology class that they thought would be willing to donate blood for free and for $15.

Consistent with the assumption that the decision to give blood is determined more by values and ideology than by personal material consequences, subjects' expressed willingness to donate blood was only slightly affected by financial incentive: 73% said they would donate blood if paid and 63% said they would donate if not paid. Once again, however, subjects estimated that vested interest (in this case, financial gain) would have a significantly greater impact on behavior than it actually did. In fact, subjects estimated that almost twice as many students would agree to donate blood for $15 as would agree to donate blood for free (61% vs. 32%). It is interesting to note that subjects not only overestimated the elasticity of blood donation to financial incentive, but also underestimated the general willingness of students to donate blood. Across the two payment conditions, the percentage of subjects actually willing to donate blood was 68%. In contrast, subjects estimated that only 47% would donate. In sum, subjects both overestimated the impact that financial incentive would have on blood-donating behavior and underestimated the extent to which their peers, irrespective of incentive, would be willing to donate blood.

1.4. Estimated Impact of Payment on Willingness to Participate in Future Experiments

An experiment conducted by Miller (1975) provides further evidence that people overestimate the impact of monetary reward on behavior. Subjects who had participated in a 45-minute experimental task for course credit were asked if they wished to participate in additional psychology experiments for payment. There were three key conditions in the experiment. In one condition, subjects were offered a flat rate of $2 for each 45-minute experiment they signed up for. In a second condition, subjects were offered a flat rate of $3 for each 45-minute experiment they signed up for. In a third condition, subjects were presented with an opportunity to assist a needy victim in addition to making money for themselves through experimental participation. In this condition, subjects were told of charity work that the Psychology Department allegedly was doing in connection with a community organization that provided for family needs in the local area. Subjects in this condition were informed that, for each 45-minute experiment they participated in, they would receive $2 with an additional $1 being donated to the community organization. Subjects in all conditions were asked to complete a form, stating how many future sessions they would be willing to participate in (for a maximum of 20 sessions).

Consistent with the results of the blood-donor study described above, the actual impact of financial compensation on the number of experimental sessions subjects agreed to sign up for was negligible. The results revealed that the difference between the $2 and $3 flat-rate conditions was nonsignificant and small (M = 7.25 vs. M = 7.58). On the other hand, the opportunity to help a victim in addition to making money for themselves dramatically increased the volunteer rate. Subjects told that each session volunteered would yield $1 for a victim in addition to $2 for themselves volunteered for an average of 11.91 sessions—a number that significantly exceeded not only that volunteered for a flat rate of $2 but also that volunteered for a flat rate of $3.

There obviously is little support in the results of this study for the view that people are solely, or even primarily, self-interested agents. But do these results diverge from what the layperson might predict? To answer this question, Miller (1975) approached another group of subjects from the same population. These subjects were presented with a description of one of the three payment conditions and asked to estimate the number of sessions they thought the average subject would volunteer for. As predicted, subjects mistakenly predicted that monetary incentive would have an over-riding influence. First, subjects assumed (incorrectly) that people would volunteer for more sessions when offered a flat rate of $3 than when offered a flat rate of $2 (M = 15.70 vs. M = 1 1.33). Second, they assumed (also incorrectly) that the arrangement in which $1 was donated to a victim and $2 were given to the subject would yield the lowest (rather than the highest) number of volunteered sessions (M = 8.30).

1.5. Summary

The results that we have described converge on a simple and striking point: People hold an exaggerated view of the power of self-interest. In all four studies, subjects significantly overestimated the impact that self-interest would have on others' behavior and attitudes, whether self-interest was defined in terms of group membership or financial incentive. In the first two studies, subjects overestimated the impact of their peers' sex on their attitudes toward abortion coverage and the impact of their peers' racial status on their opinions about the treatment of minorities on campus. In the second two studies, subjects overestimated the impact of monetary gain on their peers' willingness either to donate blood or to participate in additional psychology experiments. We cannot claim, of course, that self-interest always plays as small a role in shaping attitudes and guiding behavior as it did in the present studies, but we suspect that, even when it plays a more powerful role, laypersons will still tend to overestimate the impact that it has.

2. Paths by Which the Myth of Self-Interest Exerts Power

What are possible consequences of this "myth of self-interest"? Consider challenger Ronald Reagan's memorable line from the 1980 U.S. presidential campaign: "Ask yourself, are you better off today than you were four years ago?" Consistent with the customary small observed correlation between self-interest and political attitudes, the correlation between self-interest (defined by personal financial situation) and voting in the 1980 U.S. presidential election was a scant .08 (Sears & Funk, 1991). This would seem to indicate that people were not asking themselves Reagan's question; or at least, if they were, they were not acting on their answer to it. In the 1984 Presidential election, however, the correlation between self-interest and voting behavior was a more substantial .36 (Lau, Sears, & Jessor, 1990). One interpretation of this change is that the tenor of the selfinterest-celebrating rhetoric of Reagan's first term contributed to the social construction of voting behavior (and perhaps many other aspects of social life) as something that selfinterest does and should dominate. Supporting this interpretation are surveys that showed that people actually did come to endorse the legitimacy of self-interest more during the 1980s—a period known, after all, as the "me-decade" (Wuthnow, 1991). If exposure to self-interest rhetoric can influence voting behavior, what other aspects of social and political life might it also influence? In the sections that follow we sketch four possibilities.

2.1. We Normalize Behavior Congruent with Self-Interest and Pathologize Behavior Incongruent with Self-Interest

Rhetoric and public discourse linking self-interest with rationality serves to normalize self-interested behavior and pathologize non-self-interested behavior. Consider first the case of negative or undesirable behavior. Undesirable behavior that is motivated by self-interest tends to be viewed as more normal than undesirable behavior not motivated by self-interest. People comprehend behavior that is self-interested; they may not like it, but they comprehend it. One manifestation of the tendency to pathologize non-self-interested behavior is the greater punishment people mete out to those convicted of crimes that cannot be explained by a self-interest motive—for example, thrill killings or other so-called wanton acts of violence (Miller & Vidmar, 1981: Vidmar & Miller, 1980). The tendency to pathologize non-self-interested crimes may also be part of the psychology behind the recent U.S. Supreme Court ruling that declared it permissible to give stiffer sentences for hate crimes—crimes committed against people merely because of their membership in a social category. We take this ruling to mean that if you assault someone because you want the star or cross around his or her neck you merit a lighter sentence than if you assault him or her because you hate people who wear stars or crosses. A self-interested crime may be a crime but at least it's normal—boys will be boys and criminals will be criminals. But a hate crime, that is a different matter—that is not natural. It is difficult to resist drawing a clear moral here: If you commit a crime, make sure you provide a self-interested account for it.

The case with desirable behaviors is even more interesting. It might seem that the performance of a desirable behavior that cannot be traced to self-interest would produce an especially flattering impression of the actor. But the present analysis suggests this may not always be the case. Behavior incongruent with self-interest—like any behavior that violates expectations—will not only surprise and puzzle observers, it frequently will dismay them as well. We found evidence of this in a study which asked subjects to indicate how strange they would find each of a number of instances of social activism. The first set of scenarios consisted of six actions that a person could take in advocating a pro-choice position on abortion (e.g., writing a letter to a daily student newspaper, volunteering for a pro-choice organization, arranging for a pro-choice speaker to come to their university). Subjects were first asked how strange the various actions would seem if the actor were a woman and then how strange the various actions would seem if the actor were a man. In the second set of scenarios, subjects were asked to consider four actions a person could take in advocating gay rights (e.g., organizing a student group to protest the presence of the Reserve Officer Training Corps [ROTC] on campus because of military policy toward gays). Subjects were asked first how strange the scenarios would seem if the actor were a heterosexual student and then how strange the scenarios would seem if the actor were a gay or lesbian student. As predicted, in virtually every case the scenarios depicting the actions of a nonvested actor were rated as more strange than the same scenarios depicting the actions of a vested actor. Subjects said that they thought all of the "pro-choice" actions presented would seem more strange if the actor were a man than if the actor were a woman. Similarly, subjects indicated that they thought all but one of the four "pro-gay" actions would seem more strange if the actor were heterosexual than if the actor were gay or lesbian.

The claim that people often look askance at nonvested actions will no doubt surprise many social psychologists, as research has demonstrated that lacking a vested interest in the cause one is promoting often renders one a more effective spokesperson for that cause. For example, a heterosexual spokesperson arguing for gay rights has been found to be more persuasive than a gay spokesperson arguing for the same cause (Clark & Maass, 1982), and a man arguing for abortion rights has been found to be more persuasive than a woman presenting the same arguments (Maass, Clark & Haberkorn, 1982). These studies indicate that judgment or opinion divorced from vested interest can inspire greater trust: a nonvested source seems less biased. However, we believe that the situation is different in the case of more effortful action: Political or social action divorced from vested interest will tend to evoke less, not more, trust. To illustrate this psychological dynamic, consider how college students would react to the knowledge that a heterosexual student organized a rally to protest the presence of an anti-gay organization on campus. Based on the results described above, we can assume that they would find this strange and perplexing. Not only would the organizer have violated an expectation (that people do not expend effort for causes in which they do not have a personal stake), but he or she would also have violated the dictates of "rational self-interest." What is more, the students can be expected to communicate, both subtly and not so subtly, their dismay to the organizer.

Interestingly, the contribution of avowed self-interest to credibility appears even more critical in the legal domain. The U.S. Supreme Court has found that to qualify as having legal standing for judicial review, it is necessary for a person to show that he or she has suffered or will suffer some injury, economic or otherwise (Sierra Club v. Morton, 1972). Moral outrage, without demonstrable personal injury, is not sufficient grounds for legal action.

2.2. We Experience Discomfort When We Take Action Incongruent with Our Self-Interest

Collective representations that exalt self-interest stand as prescriptive standards and, as such, induce discomfort in people when they act inconsistently with those representations. We not only judge others' behavior to be deviant when it seems inconsistent with self-interest; we judge our *own* behavior to be inappropriate when it lacks a self-interested basis. Evidence that people feel uncomfortable acting without self-interest can be found in one of the most famous experiments in social psychology: Festinger and Carlsmith's (1959) induced-compliance study. This study tested the hypothesis that when people engage in actions that are discrepant from their attitudes—and they perceive there to be no justification for the discrepancy—they will experience cognitive dissonance. As an aversive state, cognitive dissonance is presumed to motivate those experiencing it to reduce it, which they can do by bringing their attitudes into line with their behavior. (In this experiment subjects were induced to tell a naive subject that an exceedingly boring experiment they had just participated in was, in fact, very interesting.) At this point, we draw the readers' attention not to the account of dissonance arousal or dissonance reduction, but to the recipe the researchers used to test their hypothesis. How would one create a dynamic that was sufficiently powerful to induce people to act counter-attitudinally but was not perceived to be sufficiently powerful to do so? Once again, if people acknowledged its power there would be no dissonance.

The dynamic that these researchers, and all those who followed, used is one that exploits what Goffman (1956; 1961) refers to as social etiquette. Although the experimenter offered the subjects compensation for their lie ($1 in the "insufficient" justification condition vs. $20 in the "sufficient" justification condition), what really induced subjects to comply with his request to lie to the other subject was their wish to avoid challenging the experimenter's construal of the situation, in particular his apparent view that what he was asking the subject to do (help him out by leading the next subject to think the experiment was interesting) was an appropriate request. Rather than causing a scene by challenging the face of the experimenter, subjects agreed to tell a lie. But compliance with the dictates of social etiquette apparently was not perceived to provide sufficient justification for their action; subjects modified their attitudes in a direction that made their action less discrepant when they were given a mere $1 for the lie, although not when they were given the more ample $20.

Large financial compensation was not necessary to induce compliance in Festinger and Carlsmith's experiment (and we doubt it would have been sufficient without the social etiquette pressure) but it did provide an acceptable account. The credo of radical individualism, with its view of people as rational, autonomous, and socially unencumbered agents, imbues self-interest (but not social etiquette) with sufficient perceived power to produce counter-attitudinal behavior. Our collective representations do not accord social politeness the motivational power it apparently has. In our culture it is not permissible to comply in the induced-compliance paradigm solely out of a desire to protect our face or that of the experimenter.

Now complying with an experimenter out of respect for social etiquette may not seem particularly noble—it certainly is not an act of compassion—but it does reflect an important fact about members of

Western culture: we are much more social than either neoclassical economics or our collective representations seem comfortable with. In regard to the latter point, it is interesting to note that whereas dissonance effects such as postdecisional regret are commonly found in Japanese samples, induced-compliance effects are rare (Shinobu Kitayama, personal communication, July 28, 1992). One intriguing possible explanation for this anomaly is that Japan's emphasis on interdependence over independence leads the Japanese (unlike Americans) to view social etiquette as sufficient to induce counter-attitudinal behavior (Miller & Prentice, 1994).

Additional support for the hypothesis that people feel uncomfortable taking actions inconsistent with their self interest comes from Tyler, Huo and Lind 's (1993) investigation of people's inclination to pursue claims for personal injuries. Consistent with a rational choice model, Tyler et al. found that people's decision as to whether or not to pursue an injury claim was influenced much more strongly by their expectations of financial gain than by their expectations of fair treatment. On the other hand, people's reported feelings of satisfaction with the claiming process were influenced much more strongly by the experienced fairness of their treatment than by the degree of financial gain. These results led Tyler et al. (1993) to raise the provocative question of why people would persist in making choices primarily on the basis of instrumental concerns when their post-choice reactions suggest that they should be as, if not more, sensitive to issues of fairness and respect. Consistent with the present analysis, these authors point to the normative pressure people feel to base their decisions on expected value. People are willing, in their words, to "... abandon their own experience in favor of the conventional wisdom that outcomes should predominate" (p. 30). Ironically, the myth of self-interest is apparently so powerful that it can even lead people to willingly adopt decision strategies they know will not maximize their satisfaction.

Finally, it appears that people's discomfort with acting in non-self-interested ways can be increased by exposure to self-interest rhetoric. In an intriguing set of studies, Frank, Gilovich, and Regan (1993) sought to determine if exposure to the self-interest model embraced by neo-classical economic theory would increase the extent to which people behaved in self-interested ways. They examined this question by assessing students' responses to two ethical dilemmas (e.g., Would you return a wallet with $100 in it? Would you report a billing error?) at both the beginning and end of the semester. Students were either members of one of two different micro-economics classes or a class unrelated to economics (astronomy). Of the economics classes, one was taught by an instructor who specialized in game theory (a field that takes self-interest as axiomatic), the other by an instructor who specialized in economic development in Maoist China. Whether or not economics has special appeal to the more self-interested among us, Frank et al.'s (1993) results suggest that studying economics can itself foster self-interestedness. Over the course of the semester, the responses of students in the game theorist's class increased in self-interestedness more than did those of students in the other economist's class; these students' responses, in turn, increased more in self-interestedness than did those of students in the control (astronomy) professor's class. Providing further support for the hypothesis that self-interestedness can be increased through rhetoric that links self-interest with rationality, Brunk (1980) reported that exposing political science students to the rational choice model of voting behavior (which emphasizes the irrationality of voting) decreased the students' inclination to vote.

In sum, the assumption that it is normal and rational for self-interest to dictate behavior may lead people to feel uncomfortable taking actions that are inconsistent with self-interest. Individuals seem less comfortable telling a lie for social reasons than for financial reasons. Individuals seem less comfortable with decisions based on procedural fairness considerations than with ones based solely on outcomes. And individuals seem less comfortable engaging in non-self-interested behavior—such as returning a wallet or reporting a billing error—once they have been exposed to the "it's rational to be selfish" rhetoric of neo-classical economic theory. Whatever people's inclination to transcend the dictates of self-interest, they appear to feel uncomfortable doing so.

2.3. We Fear Social Isolation When We Take Actions Incongruent with Our Self-Interest

A third path through which the myth of self-interest may influence behavior involves the perception of social support. If people overestimate the impact of self-interest on others' opinions, they will underestimate the support they have for those opinions of theirs not anchored in self-interest. To examine the proposition that people underestimate the commonness of their non-self-interested positions, we return to the minority-needs and blood-donor studies described earlier (Miller & Ratner, 1995; Studies 2 and 3). In these studies, subjects were asked for their attitude toward the target issue as well as for their estimates of the attitudes of their peers. As reported previously, subjects in both of these studies estimated that vested interest would be more strongly linked to attitudes than it actually was. Because these studies asked subjects for their own attitudes as well as the attitudes of others, they also speak to the question of how subjects' estimates of peer support are influenced by the apparent consistency of subjects' attitudes with their vested interest.

Consider first our study of minority and majority students' attitudes toward the circumstances of minority students on their campus (Miller & Ratner, 1995; Study 2). The extent to which subjects assumed that the attitudes of their same-race peers were similar to their own depended greatly on whether their own attitude was consistent or inconsistent with their vested interest (as indexed by group membership). Those whose attitudes were consistent with their vested interest (minority students who were dissatisfied and majority students who were satisfied that minority needs were being met) predicted a high number of like-minded peers (76% and 78%, respectively). Those whose attitudes were inconsistent with their vested interest (minority students who were satisfied and majority students who were dissatisfied) predicted significantly fewer like-minded peers (45% and 40%, respectively). Subjects clearly estimated much greater consensual support for their attitudes when those attitudes seemed consistent with than when they seemed inconsistent with their vested interest.

A similar pattern emerged in our blood-donor study (Miller & Ratner, 1995; Study 3). Subjects' estimates of the commonness of their response (to volunteer or to not volunteer) depended significantly on the congruence of their response with the incentive structure. When the incentive structure was most favorable to volunteering ($15 was offered), subjects who agreed to volunteer estimated that 70% of their peers would do the same; when the incentive structure was least favorable to volunteering (no pay), subjects who declined to volunteer estimated that 78% would do the same. Once again, the consensus estimates of those who acted inconsistent with vested interest were significantly lower; subjects who declined to volunteer for money estimated that only 57% of their peers would do as they did, and those who agreed to volunteer for no money estimated that only 39% would do the same.

In summary, irrespective of how insensitive their own behavior was to the incentive structure, subjects assumed that the behavior of others would be highly sensitive to it. Indeed, when their own behavior violated the dictates of self-interest, subjects appear to largely ignore the diagnostic value of their own behavior in predicting the behavior of others. One inevitable consequence of this misjudgment is that people will underestimate the consensual (peer) support they have for their position when that position is inconsistent with their self-interest. This latter underestimation, in turn, will provide people with another reason for not acting on attitudes inconsistent with their self-interest—they will anticipate that their peers will not share their attitudes or be acting similarly. The thought that one may be the only person without a vested interest to take a particular action can be expected to serve as a powerful deterrent to the taking of that action, irrespective of one's desire to take it (Marks & Miller, 1987; Noelle-Neumann, 1986).

2.4. We Justify Our Behavior in Terms of Self-Interest

Another manifestation of the power of the myth of self-interest is found in people's eagerness to explain their behavior in terms of self-interest. The justification of behavior in terms of self-interest is perhaps most remarkable when the behavior is pro-social in nature. Robert Wuthnow (1991), in a recent book entitled *Acts of Compassion*, examines how people talk about their motivations for helping others. According to Wuthnow, although people engage in many acts of genuine compassion, their vocabulary for talking about their motives in these cases is extremely impoverished. The language people seem most comfortable with in explaining their acts of compassion is one that emphasizes self-interest. People's accounts for giving to charity generally emphasize pragmatic or instrumental reasons: "It gave me something to do." "I liked the other volunteers." "It got me out of the house." People seem loathe to acknowledge that their behavior may have been motivated by genuine compassion or kindness. Indeed, the people Wuthnow interviewed seemed to go out of their way to stress that they were not "a bleeding heart, a goody two-shoes, or a dogooder." Just as the social sanctions evoked by the appearance of high intelligence leads (or at least lead) many women to "play dumb," it appears that the social sanctions evoked by the expression of pure compassion leads many members of contemporary Western cultures to "play selfish."In light of Wuthnow's findings, it would appear that accounts for actions that emphasize self-interest, rather than serving to diminish the actions, actually normalize them—they license them. This line of argument suggests a very different interpretation of certain familiar rituals. Consider the interviewer's standard opening question to activists: "Why did you get involved in this cause?" This question frequently elicits, and seems designed to elicit, statements of vested interest. But rather than serving to discredit the nobleness of the activists' behavior, these revelations may serve primarily to diminish the potential perverseness of their behavior. Self-interest provides a sufficient account for what might otherwise seem inexplicable.

The claim that people will misrepresent compassion as self-interest is quite extraordinary because social scientists from Harold Lasswell (1948) on have told us that people are motivated to conceal self-interest and will endeavor to present their behavior as reflecting a concern with the public good even when it is actually motivated by self-interest. Despite the conventional wisdom that if you scratch an altruist you may find an egoist, it may be that the opposite is actually more common: Scratching a self-confessed egoist may often reveal an altruist. Interestingly, the claim that people—at least Americans—often conceal their more noble sentiments under the guise of self-interest is not new. Over a hundred years ago, the French social philosopher, Alexis deTocqueville, observed that: "Americans ... enjoy explaining almost every act of their lives on the principle of selfinterest ... I think that in this they often do themselves less than justice, for sometimes in the United States, as elsewhere, one sees people carried away by the...spontaneous impulses natural to man. But the Americans are hardly prepared to admit that they do give way to emotions of this sort. (1835/1969, p. 546)."

We turn now to more direct evidence of the prommence of self-interest in behavioral accounts. The first relevant finding comes from a comparison of people's accounts for their voting preference at different temporal points. Sears and his colleagues have found that the relation between self-interest and voting behavior is much higher in exit polls than in either pre-election or post-election surveys (Sears & Lau, 1983). The claim that people "vote their pocket book" may not be well substantiated by actual studies of voting behavior (Feldman, 1984), but it receives strong support in people's accounts for their votes in exit polls (see also Stein, 1990). Whether people distort their votes in the direction of their self-interest or vice versa, it appears that people who have just cast a vote are motivated to tell a story that closely links their vote with their self-interest. A similar finding emerges from the accounts of U.S. Whites opposed to busing as a means of achieving racial integration. Research revealed that there was little relationship between self-interest and attitudes toward busing: Whites who had children in the school system and who were at risk of having their property values diminish were no more likely to oppose busing than those without these vested interests. Yet White's accounts for their opposition to school busing tended to focus primarily on utilitarian arguments—concern for their children's safety, diminished property values, inconvenience to kids and so forth (Sears & Funk, 1990).

In sum, whether explaining pro-social or anti-social action, people seem incapable of—or at least uncomfortable with—explicating any philosophy other than self-interest. The fact that people feel compelled to account for their altruistic acts with self-interested stories provides another route by which self-interested motivation can be acquired—people may come to believe what they say (Bem, 1972). And if people take their myth-inspired "self-interested" accounts to heart, they can be expected to engage in behaviors more congruent with self-interest in the future (Darley & Fazio, 1980; Fazio, Effrein, & Falender, 1981).

2.5. Summary

This section has outlined four paths through which the myth of self-interest may exert power over individuals' behaviors. The assumption that vested interest has a major impact on attitudes may lead people (1) to normalize others' behavior congruent with self-interest and pathologize others' behavior incongruent with self-interest, (2) to experience discomfort when their own behavior is not self-interested, (3) to fear that taking actions incongruent with self-interest will make them a social isolate, and 4) to justify their own behavior in terms of self-interest.

3. Implications of the Myth of Self-Interest for Social Justice

Our analysis of the myth of self-interest suggests a novel perspective on the common finding that self-interest, while not predicting attitudes very well, does predict behavior quite well. Before examining this perspective, however, consider three studies that found stronger relationships between self-interest and behavior than between self-interest and attitudes. First, a study by Regan and Fazio (1977) reported no relation between undergraduates' attitudes to the circumstances of a campus housing shortage at Cornell University and whether or not the students were personally inconvenienced by the shortage—all students expressed considerable hostility. However, Regan and Fazio (1977) did find a strong relationship between self-interest and behavior: undergraduates' willingness to take direct steps to alleviate the problem was highly positively correlated with whether or not they were personally inconvenienced by the current policy.

Sivacek and Crano (1982) reported a study that yielded a similar pattern of results. In the fall elections of 1978 Michigan voters were asked to decide whether the legal drinking age should be raised from 18 to 21 years. Sivacek and Crano asked Michigan State students—some of whom would be 21 before the change and some of whom would have to wait more than 2 years—two questions: (1) How do you feel about this proposal? (2) Would you be willing to join the group "Students against proposal D" and make calls to generate support for a no vote? The researchers found that, although those students with a vested interest in a no vote were no more opposed than students without a vested interest, the former were much more likely to take social action than were the latter.

Green and Cowden (1992) found a virtually identical pattern when they reanalyzed two "busing" surveys conducted in the mid-seventies. Initial analyses of these surveys revealed little or no relation between self-interest and social attitudes; for example, Whites with children in the school system were no more likely to oppose busing than Whites without children in the school system. In their reanalysis, Green and Cowden (1992) examined the relation between self-interest and political action, as indexed by subjects' responses to a question that asked them to indicate the extent of their involvement in antibusing organizations. The results of this latter analysis were dramatic: Those whose self-interest was threatened by busing were much more likely to take action. For example, parents of school-age children were much more likely than non-parents to have participated in anti-busing organizations.

One interpretation of the stronger relation between self-interest and social action than between self-interest and social attitudes focuses on the different thresholds that must be reached to express an attitude versus take an action. One might not need a vested interest in a cause to express an attitude supporting it, but one might require a level of motivation that only having a stake in the issue can provide to convert a supportive attitude into a supportive action. As Green and Cowden (1992) have argued, the prospect of behavioral involvement (unlike the request for an opinion) forces people to consider cost, and hence prompts self-interest reflection. In their words, the potential political actor must first ask him or herself, "Is it worth it?"

3.1. The Source of Social Inaction: Lack of Incentive or Lack of Justification?

Green and Cowden's claim that survey research underestimates the "political wallop" of self-interest is certainly plausible. But we suggest that there also may be another reason why the link between self-interest and behavior is stronger than that between self-interest and attitudes.

Rather than viewing those with a vested interest as benefiting from a facilitative push toward action, it may be more (or at least as) appropriate to view those without a vested interest as suffering from an inhibitory pull away from taking action. Specifically, we think it possible that those without vested interest are inhibited from acting not only because they lack an incentive, but because they lack a justification. People may fear they will be stigmatized if they take actions for which they lack a clear incentive, possibly even suspecting that they will be the only person of their non-vested status taking those actions. By this account, the question the political actor needs to answer is not "Is it worth it?" but "Is it appropriate?" For example, a non-parent who showed up at an antibusing event might risk prompting queries such as "What are you doing here? You don't even have any kids," or "It's not your kid who is being bused, why do you care?" Returning to Green and Cowden's results, could one really expect a non-parent, no matter how opposed to busing he or she was, to join an anti-busing organization with the name "Mothers for Kerrigan"?

We explored this line of reasoning by examining the impact that the name of a political organization had on male and female subjects' willingness to support a cause in which their sex allegedly either did or did not have a vested interest. Specifically, Princeton undergraduate subjects were told that a local organization was protesting a Federal budget change that would take money away from research on a medical disease that primarly affected either men or women. As expected, the presentation of the issue left virtually all subjects opposed to the budget change. The organization ostensibly seeking students' help was called "Princeton Opponents of Proposition 174" in one condition and "Princeton Men and Women Opposed to Proposition 174" in another. The question of interest was whether the latter (inclusive) framing would disinhibit nonvested subjects (men who read that women were at risk and women who read that men were at risk for the disorder) and increase their willingness to take action in support of their attitudes. Indeed, we found that nonvested subjects were more willing to help the local group by writing a statement in support of their opinion when the organization's name included the phrase "Men and Women." As predicted, the name of the organization had no effect on vested subjects' willingness to write a statement. These results strongly suggest that at least one reason why nonvested individuals may be inhibited from converting their supportive attitudes into supportive actions is that they feel it is "not their place" to act.

3.2. Committing Altruism under the Cloak of Self-Interest: The Exchange Fiction

If people feel uncomfortable acting altruistically, they will be attracted to those circumstances that, while providing them with an opportunity to act altruistically, conceal from others and themselves the fact they are doing so. Under the cloak of self-interest, people can act compassionately without fear or discomfort. Holmes, Miller, and Lerner (1995) tested the hypothesis that financial incentive can sometimes *disinhibit* altruistic behavior by providing people with psychological cover for their altruistic behavior. The design of their study was inspired by the following question: Why do charity organizations so often offer potential donors some product (e.g., light bulbs, address stickers, magazine subscriptions) for their donations? More precisely, why should the net contributions elicited by product-for-donation exchanges exceed those contributions elicited by strict charity appeals? Holmes et al. (1995) hypothesized that the offer of an exchange creates a fiction which permits people to act on their impulse to help without committing themselves to either a public or private image as a "do-gooder." If people get something for their donation—even something they do not need or want—they do not need to ask themselves a series of potentially threatening questions, such as "Why did I help these victims and not others?" or "Why did I help these victims when others would not?"

To test the *exchange fiction* hypothesis, Holmes et al. dispatched a group ot experimenters to approach students on a university campus with one of various charity appeals. The design was complicated and only the most relevant conditions will be discussed here. The key manipulations were the seriousness of the victims' need and the presence or absence of an exchange. In the moderate-need condition, the representatives presented themselves as working for the local "Perceptually Handicapped Society" which allegedly was "starting a training program for handicapped children about 7 to 10 years of age who have problems performing many normal activities." In the high-need condition, the representatives presented themselves as working for the local "Society for Emotionally Disturbed Children" which allegedly was "starting a training and remedial program for handicapped and emotionally disturbed children who have severe problems in coping with most normal activities." The appeal for donation either did or did not include the offer of an exchange (a decorator candle) for the subjects' donation.

The pattern of donation rates supported the hypothesis that subjects who wish to help will often be encouraged to do so when they can do so under the cloak of self-interest. In the no-exchange condition, the donation rate increased only slightly from the moderate to high need condition (M = 34 cents vs. M = 41 cents), while in the exchange condition the donation rate increased over threefold (M = 33 cents vs. M = $1.31). Two aspects of these results bear attention. First, by examining only the no-exchange condition, one would conclude that the variation in the victim's need produced no difference in the sympathy of the subjects. Second, by examining only the moderate-need condition, one would conclude that the product employed in the exchange—the candles—had little appeal itself. The sale of the candles only made a difference when combined with the opportunity to help those victims who aroused strong sympathy.

The results confirmed Holmes et al.'s (1995) prediction that subjects would be more willing to give money to help the handicapped children when they were allowed to act as though they were engaged in a "fair" economic exchange. We see here the social mechanism on which the exchange fiction is based: People pretending to care about candles and bargains so that they can care for other people. Tax deductible charities possibly benefit from a similar psychological process. When people receive something (e.g., a small tax deduction) for their assistance, they do not have to feel like a do-gooder. They can construe their action as something to feel good about, but not as something that is inconsistent with collective representations of what constitutes acceptable forms of motivation. From the perspective of the present analysis, it is the mere existence of a tax-deduction, not its size, that is critical in eliciting greater donation rates. To the extent that a tax-deduction provides the "excuse" rather than the "incentive" for giving, all that is important is that one be offered.

In a related vein, recent psychological analyses of volunteerism (Perloff, 1987; Snyder, 1993; Snyder & Omoto, 1992) have argued that emphasizing the link between volunteerism and self-interest may be an effective means of increasing and sustaining the former. One reason this is likely to prove an effective strategy is that it will provide people with the license to act on their sympathies. Lacking a self-interested account, people may feel they lack the moral authorization to act. As Kurt Lewin (1951) observed many years ago, when confronted with people behaving in undesirable ways (e.g. not volunteering), it is generally more effective to remove obstacles that inhibit them from taking the desired action than to provide them with additional reasons for taking the desired action.

4. Conclusion

The myth of self-interest inhibits people from taking social action inconsistent with self-interest. This is not to say that people are always, or even typically, inclined to take action inconsistent with vested interest. If taking action inconsistent with self-interest would yield actors personal outcomes less desirable than they feel they deserve, they are not likely to feel compelled to engage in that behavior (Lerner, 1980; Lerner, Miller & Holmes, 1976; Miller, 1977). On the other hand, when engaging in non-vested behavior will not threaten their personal deservingness, they appear to be inclined toward helping others (Miller, 1977). Thus, the likely reason majority students will not want to spend four hours a day working to improve the lot of minority students on their campus is that they will feel this commitment would leave them less leisure time than they want or feel they deserve. However, the reason why majority students might not want to engage in less costly action, such as joining a committee committed to improve minority conditions on campus, may simply be that the myth of self-interest inhibits them.

We have claimed that scientific theories and collective representations both exaggerate the power of self-interest. Indeed, much of the power of self-interest in human affairs derives from the power accorded it by our cultural or collective representations. Homo Economicus is a social construction, not a biological entity. But myth or not, the image of humans as self-interested agents has powerful social and psychological consequences. Myths can create reality.

Acknowledgments

The research reported in this chapter was supported by National Institute of Mental Health grant MH44069 to Dale Miller and a National Science Foundation graduate fellowship to Rebecca Ratner. Thanks are due to Donald Green, Sally Lloyd-Bostock, Jane Mansbridge, Tali Mendelberg, Leo Montada, Deborah Prentice, and Eldar Shafir for comments on a previous draft.

References

Batson, C. D. (1991). The altruism question: Toward a social psychological answer. Hillsdale, NJ: Erlbaum.

Bem, D. J. (1972). Self-perception theory. In L. Berkowitz (Ed.), Advances in experimental social psychology. (Vol. 6, pp. 1–62). New York: Academic Press.

Brunk, G. G. (1980). The impact of rational participation models on voting attitudes. Public Choice, 35, 549–564.

Clark, R. D., & Maass, A. (1982). Social categorization in minority influence: The case of homosexuality. European Journal of Social Psychology, 18, 347–364.

Darley, J. M., & Fazio, R. H. (1980). Expectancy confirmation processes arising in the social interaction sequence. American Psychologist, 35, 867–881.

Dawes, R. M., van de Kragt, A. J. C. & Orbell, J. M. (1988). Not me or thee but we: The importance of group identity in eliciting cooperation in dilemma situations: Experimental manipulations. Acta Psychologica, 68, 83–97.

DeTocqueville, A. (1835/1969). Democracy in America. J. P. Mayer (Ed.), G. Lawrence, trans. Garden City, NY: Anchor Books.

Durkheim, E. (1982). The rules of sociological method, W.D. Halls, trans. New York: The Free Press.

Etzioni, A. (1988). The moral dimension: Toward a new economics. New York: The Free Press.

Fazio, R. H., Effrein, E. A. & Falender, V. J. (1981). Self-perceptions following social interaction. Journal of Personality and Social Psychology, 41, 232–242.

Feldman, S. (1984). Economic self-interest and the vote: Evidence and meaning. Political Behavior, 6, 229–252.

Festinger, L., & Carlsmith, J. M. (1959). Cognitive consequences of forced compliance. Journal of Abnormal and Social Psychology, 58, 203–210.

Frank, R. H., Gilovich, T. & Regan, D. T. (1993). Does studying economics inhibit cooperation? Journal of Economic Perspectives, 7, 159–171.

Goffman, E. (1956). Embarrassment and social organization. American Journal of Sociology, 62, 264–271.

Goffman, E. (1961). Asylums: Essays on the social situation of mental patients and other inmates. Garden City, NJ: Anchor Books.

Green, D. P., & Cowden, J. A. (1992). Who protests: Self-interest and white opposition to busing. Journal of Politics, 54, 471–496.

Holmes, J. G., Miller, D. T. & Lerner, M. J. (1995). Symbolic threat in helping situations: The "exchange fiction." Unpublished manuscript. University of Waterloo.

Kohn, A. (1990). The brighter side of human nature. New York: Basic Books.

Lasswell, H. D. (1948). Power and personality. New York: Norton.

Lau, R. R., Sears, D. O. & Jessor, T. (1990). Fact or artifact revisited: Survey instrument effects and pocketbook politics. Political Behavior, 12, 217–242.

Lerner, M. J. (1980). The belief in a just world. New York: Plenum Press.

Lerner, M. J., Miller, D. T. & Holmes, J. G. (1976). Deserving and the emergence of forms of justice. In L. Berkowitz (Ed.), Advances in experimental social psychology (Vol. 9, pp. 134–160). New York: Academic Press.

Lewin, K. (1951). Field theory in social science (Edited by D. Cartwright), New York: Harper.

Maass, A., Clark, R. D. III. & Haberkorn, G. (1982). The effects of differentially ascribed category membership and norms on minority influence. European Journal of Social Psvchology, 12, 89–104.

Mansbridge, J. J. (Ed.), (1990). Beyond self-interest. Chicago: University of Chicago Press.

Marks, G., & Miller, N. (1987). Ten years of research on the false consensus effect: An empirical and theoretical review. Psvchological Bulletin, 102, 72–90.

Miller, D. T. (1975). Personal deserving versus justice for others. Unpublished doctoral dissertation, University of Waterloo.

Miller, D. T. (1977). Personal deserving versus justice for others: An exploration of the justice motive. Journal of Experimental Social Psvchology, 13, 1–13.

Miller, D. T., & Prentice, D. A. (1994). Collective errors and errors about the collective. Personality and Social Psvchology Bulletin, 20, 541–550.

Miller, D. T., & Ratner, R. K. (1995). Unpublished data. Princeton University.

Miller, D. T., & Vidmar, N. (1981). The role of justice in punishment reactions: A social psychological analysis. In M. J. Lerner & S. Lerner (Eds.), The justice motive in social behavior (pp. 145–172). New York: Plenum Press.

Noelle-Neumann, E. (1986). The spiral of silence. Chicago: University of Chicago Press.

Perloff, R. (1987). Self-interest and personal responsibility redux. American Psychologist, 42, 3–11.

Regan, D. T., & Fazio, R. (1977). On the consistency between attitudes and behavior: Look to the method of attitude formation. Journal of Experimental Social Psvchology, 13, 28–45.

Schwartz, B. (1986). The battle for human nature. New York: W. W. Norton.

Sears, D. O., & Funk, C. L. (1990). Self-interest in Americans' political opinions. In J. J. Mansbridge (Ed.), Beyond self-interest (pp. 147–170). Chicago: University of Chicago Press.

Sears, D. O., & Funk, C. L. (1991). The role of self-interest in social and political attitudes. In M.P. Zanna (Ed.), Advances in experimental social psychology, (Vol. 24, pp. 2–91), New York: Academic Press.

Sears, D. O., & Lau, R. R. (1983). Indicating apparently self-interested political preferences. American Journal of Political Science, 27, 223–252.

Sen, A. K. (1977). Rational fools: A critique of the behavioral foundations of economic theory. Philosophy and Public Affairs, 6, 317–344.

Sierra Club v. Morton, No. 70–34. (9th Cir, 1972).

Sivacek, J., & Crano, W. D. (1982). Vested interest as a moderator of attitude-behavior consistency. Journal of Personality and Social Psvchology, 43, 210–221.

Snyder, M. (1993). Basic research and practical problems: The promise of a "functional" personality and social psychology. Personality and Social Psvchology Bulletin, 19, 251–264.

Snyder, M., & Omoto, A. M. (1990). Who helps and why? The psychology of AIDS volunteerism. In S. Spacapan & S. Oskamp (Eds.), Helping and being helped: Naturalistic studies (pp. 213–239). Newbury Park, CA: Sage Publications.

Stein, R. M. (1990). Economic voting for governor and U.S. Senator: The electoral consequences of federalism. Journal of Politics, 52, 29–53.

Tyler, T. R. (1990). Justice, self-interest, and the legitimacy of legal and political authority. In J. J. Mansbridge (Ed.), Beyond self-interest (pp. 171–179). Chicago: University of Chicago Press.

Tyler, T. R., & Dawes, R. M. (1993). Fairness in groups: Comparing the self-interest and social identity perspectives. In B. A. Mellers & J. Baron (Eds.), Psvchological perspectives on justice (pp. 87- 108). New York: Cambridge University Press.

Tyler, T. R., Huo, Y. J., & Lind, E. A. (1993) Preferring, choosing, and evaluating dispute resolution procedures: The psychological antecedents of feelings and choices. Unpublished manuscript.

Vidmar, N., & Miller, D. T. (1980). Social psychological processes underlying attitudes toward legal punishment. Law and Society Review, L (3), 401–439.

Wuthnow, R. (1991). Acts of compassion. Princeton, NJ: Princeton University Press.

4

Empathy, Altruism, and Justice: Another Perspective on Partiality

C. Daniel Batson

As children, our first encounter with the concept of justice was almost certainly secondhand. A sibling or friend was scolded for "not being fair," and we were given a turn with the toy (but too brief) or the candy was redivided so that we got more (but not enough). At times, we were the one chided and forced to give up part of our hoard. What did we learn from this primordial experience with fairness? Likely, we learned that appeals to justice can be a powerful lever for prying people and goodies apart. By the time we reached the playground, we knew that "Not fair!" was a potent accusation, one that almost always led to redress, justification (rationalization?), fight, or flight (Solomon, 1989).

Given these early experiences, it is no surprise that when as adults we feel victimized, as virtually all of us do at least some of the time, our cry is for justice. The cry may be quite impassioned, fueled by anger and frustration over relative deprivation (Crosby, 1982). Still, an appeal to justice is quite reasonable—and quite predictable. "Not fair!" demanded attention on the playground, so why not in adult society? Why not, indeed?

This question shifts our attention from talk of justice by victims, those treated unfairly, to talk of justice by nonvictims, either (a) those in a position of direct relative advantage (who are privileged at victims expense) or (b) bystanders (who do not directly benefit from the injustice

C. Daniel Batson • Department of Psychology, University of Kansas, 426 Fraser Hall, Lawrence, Kansas 66045-2160.

Current Societal Concerns about Justice, edited by Leo Montada and Melvin J. Lerner. Plenum Press, New York, 1996.

yet could do something to redress it). The importance of considering the role of justice in the lives of nonvictims should be obvious. Unless principles of justice can affect the behavior of nonvictims, victims might as well save their breath—except perhaps to employ justice as a rallying cry and call to arms within their own ranks. More civilly and optimistically, if nonvictims are motivated to uphold principles of justice, then they may work to right wrongs. Better yet, they may work to prevent injustice even before victims are forced to cry, "Not fair!"

1. Moral Philosophers' Love of Justice: A Universal and Impartial Moral Principle

Moral philosophers have long recognized the importance of justice. Since Kant (1785/1889), the goal of most has been to find one or more moral principles that are universal and impartial and can provide rationally defensible guides to the distribution of wealth and the adjudication of disputes. Justice seems to fill this tall order. Justice applies to everyone, and it is said to be blind. It offers a principle on which, advocates hope, we can all agree, whether we are victims or nonvictims.

It is a key assumption of many philosophers and psychologists interested in justice that once we accept a moral principle like justice, it will guide our actions. Convinced by reason of the rightness of the principle, we will be motivated to uphold it. In Kurt Lewin's (1951) terms, the principle of justice is a value (power field) capable of activating a motive (force field) whenever the principle is violated or threatened.

The logic I have outlined is apparent in the highly influential appeal to justice made by John Rawls (1971). Rawls argues for a principle of justice based on the allocation of goods and opportunities to the members of society from an Original Position behind the Veil of Ignorance, where no one knows his or her place in society—prince or pauper, laborer or lawyer, male or female, black or white. Why does Rawls require such a stance? Because it eliminates partiality and seduction by special interest. A universal, impartial principle of justice much like Rawls's is the basis for Lawrence Kohlberg's (1976) Post-Conventional or Principled moral reasoning, the highest level in his stage model of moral development.

2. Two Ways to Think about Partiality

Rawls's theory of justice is elegant and intriguing, but I believe the problem of partiality remains. When we step out from behind the hypothetical Veil of Ignorance and into the real world, we find that nonvictims are far more likely to allocate resources over which they have control to those they especially care about than to those they do not (Dovidio, 1984; Hornstein, 1982; Krebs, 1975).

2.1. Multiple Moralities, Multiple Justices

How is the advocate of a universal, impartial principle of justice to handle this partiality? Is showing preference for those you care about simply immoral? Rawls and Kohlberg would, I think, say yes—unless the partiality could be shown, on balance, to increase the welfare of the least well off in society (Rawls, 1971). But two other ways to think about partiality have received considerable attention in recent years.

First, a number of social and moral philosophers, including Blum (1980), Gilligan (1982), Nagel (1991), Noddings (1984), Tronto (1987), and Williams (1981), have argued for *multiple moralities*. In different ways, each calls for recognition of forms of morality that allow for special interest in the welfare of certain others or in the maintenance of certain relationships. In opposition to an ethic based on justice and fairness, these writers propose an ethic of care. Sometimes, care is proposed as an alternative principle to justice, either as a substitute for justice or in dynamic tension with it; at other times, care is proposed as an alternative to principled morality altogether. All three of these proposals about care are reflected at different points in Gilligan's (1982) well-known critique of Kohlberg's justice-based morality.

Typically, multiple-morality models treat morality as a personality variable, a trans-situational disposition. It is assumed that one person uses an ethic of justice; a second uses an ethic of care; a third may use both, neither, or some mix. Whatever ethic a person adopts will determine how he or she thinks and acts across a range of moral situations. Analysis is in terms of individual differences, often sex differences. It has been suggested that, whereas men are apt to adopt an ethic of universal, impartial justice, women are more likely to adopt an ethic of care (Gilligan, 1982; Noddings, 1984; but also see Tronto, 1987).

Several social psychologists interested in justice have addressed the problem of partiality in a second way. Indeed, solving this problem was, I believe, one of the major goals of the 1975 *Journal of Social Issues* symposium on justice edited by Mel Lerner. The way Lerner (1975) and Deutsch (1975) handled the problem was not by proposing multiple moralities but by proposing multiple justices: A justice based on equity guides our actions in casual or business relations (non-unit relations); a justice based equality guides our actions in friendships (unit relations); and a justice based on need guides our actions in close love and kin relations (identity relations). If one is choosing how to allocate resources among people with equal needs but to whom one has different relationships, then the justice of need applied to the person to whom one is close assures that this individual will receive special care over and above that given to others based on justices of equity or equality, which are not needsensitive. Key for the shift from one justice principle to another in these multiple-justice models is the nature of the nonvictim's relationship to those in need (Deutsch, 1975; Lerner, 1975).

It is, perhaps, not surprising that justice researchers would deal with the apparent violation of the principle of justice introduced by partiality by multiplying justices. Doing so allows them to continue to think of social interactions as rule (principle) governed and prosocial behavior as motivated by a desire to uphold justice, some justice. This is by no means the first time we psychologists have solved the problem of apparent exceptions by multiplication: We did it with instincts; we did it again with drives. It allows us to keep the required rethinking to a minimum.

2.2. Multiple Motives: Altruism and Justice as Two Distinct Prosocial Motives

Perhaps the multiple-moralities solution or the multiple-justices solution to the problem of partiality is correct. Personally, I have doubts. My doubts lead me to propose a far messier way to handle the problem of partiality. Rather than adding new moralities or new forms of justice, I wish to suggest that often partiality reflects a qualitatively different form of motivation, a form quite distinct from a motive to uphold justice or, indeed, any other moral principle. This motivation is *altruism*. (Tarring myself with the same brush just used on justice researchers, it is not surprising that I would see altruism where they saw new forms of justice. It keeps my rethinking to a minimum.)

Following Lewin (1951), I am thinking of motives as goal-directed forces. Thinking of motives in this way, it is important to distinguish among instrumental goals, ultimate goals, and unintended consequences. An *instrumental goal* is sought as means to reach some other goal; an *ultimate goal* is sought as an end in itself; an *unintended consequence* is a result of acting to reach a goal but is not itself sought as a goal. It is the ultimate goal that defines a motive; each different motive has a unique ultimate goal. A person can have more than one motive—ultimate goal—at a time. If pursuit of one ultimate goal prevents pursuit of another, then the person will experience motivational conflict.

I wish to suggest that altruism and justice are two distinct prosocial motives, each with its unique ultimate goal. Altruism is motivation with the ultimate goal of increasing the welfare of one or more individuals other than oneself. It is typically contrasted with *egoism*, which is motivation with the ultimate goal of increasing one's own welfare (see Batson, 1991).

Let me emphasize that, as I am using the term, altruism is a form of motivation. As such, it should not be confused with *helping behavior*. Helping may or may not be altruistically motivated; often helping is egoistically motivated. Nor should altruism be confused with self-sacrifice; self-sacrifice concerns cost to self not benefit to other.

The most commonly proposed source of altruistic motivation is empathic emotion. By *empathy* I mean other-oriented feelings congruent with the perceived welfare of another person (Batson, 1987, 1991). If the other is perceived to be in need, empathy includes feelings of sympathy, compassion, tenderness, and the like. Empathy is usually considered to be a product not only of perceiving the other as in need but also of adopting the other's perspective, which means imagining how the other is personally affected by his or her situation (Stotland, 1969). It is for this reason that empathic feelings are called other-oriented. Such feelings have been named as a source—if not *the* source—of altruism by Thomas Aquinas, David Hume, Adam Smith, Charles Darwin, Herbert Spencer, William McDougall, and in contemporary psychology by Martin Hoffman (1976), Dennis Krebs (1975), and myself (Batson, 1987, 1991). I have called the proposal that feeling empathy for a person in need evokes altruistic motivation the *empathyaltruism hypothesis*. In recent years, over 25 experiments have been conducted to test this hypothesis, providing remarkably strong support (see Batson, 1991, for a review; but also see Cialdini, Schaller, Houlihan, Arps, Fultz, & Beaman, 1987; Schaller & Cialdini, 1988; Smith, Keating, & Stotland, 1989).

Contrast empathy-induced altruistic motivation with *justice motivation*. Justice motivation has as its ultimate goal upholding a principle of justice; it is instigated by (a) valuing some principle of justice and (b) perceiving a situation that violates or threatens that principle. As equity researchers have pointed out (e.g., Walster, Berscheid, & Walster, 1973), there are two major ways to uphold a principle of justice. One is to change the situation in a way that redresses the perceived unfairness; the other is to revise one' perception of the fairness of the situation or one's threshold for unfairness. Either revision can transform the situation into one that no longer seems unfair and so no longer threatens the valued principle.

The abstractness of general, universal principles of justice facilitates revision of one's perceptions. Most of us are adept at rationalization, at justifying to ourselves—if not to others—why a situation that benefits us or those we care about is not really unfair. Why, for example, in Jonathan Kozol's (1991) apt phrase, the "savage inequalities" between the public school systems of rich and poor communities in the U.S. are not really unjust. Why storing our nuclear waste in someone else's back yard or using a disproportionate amount of the earth's natural resources is fair. As Mel Lerner (1980) and his colleagues have so dramatically demonstrated, justice is satisfied if, by derogating the victims of injustice, we can realign our perceptions of them so that they seem to get what they deserve and deserve what they get.

2.3. The Problem of Partiality as a Conflict between Altruism and Justice

With this brief sketch of the difference between altruism and justice motivation in mind, let me return to the problem of partiality. At least as envisioned by Rawls and Kohlberg, principles of justice are universal and impartial. Empathy—induced altruism is neither. Feelings of empathy are directed toward other people as individuals; it seems unlikely that we can feel empathy for an abstract social category like *humanity, the disadvantaged, the poor,* or *the homeless,* although empathic feelings may be generalized from specific individuals to groups of similar others (Dovidio, Schroeder, Allen & Matthews, 1986). To paraphrase Stalin, one person suffering is a tragedy; a million suffering is a statistic. Further, the likelihood that needs of different individuals will evoke empathic feelings is not equal; empathy is more likely to be felt for those (a) who are friends, kin, or similar to us, (b) to whom we are emotionally attached, (c) for whom we feel responsible, or (d) whose perspective we adopt (Batson, 1991; Krebs, 1975; Stotland, 1969). As Leo Montada and Angela Schneider (1989) nicely demonstrated, sympathy reported by nonvictims for remote victims of social injustice is apt to be cool and abstract, more a reflection of one's principles than an expression of emotion.

At least as important as the partiality of our empathic feelings is the partiality of the altruistic motivation evoked. Once empathic feelings are aroused (whether easily or with some effort), the ensuing altruistic motivation is directed only toward the individual or individuals for whom empathy is felt.

These observations about the partiality of empathy-induced altruism lead me to suggest that the problem of partiality in resource allocation often involves a conflict not of multiple moralities or of multiple justices but of multiple motives. The allocator experiences a conflict between altruism and justice. A person may well accept one or more of the universal and impartial principles of justice espoused by Rawls, Kohlberg, and various social psychologists studying justice. That person may be motivated to uphold justice as an ultimate goal. But if, because of a special relationship or other circumstance, that person is led to feel empathy for one or more of the individuals involved, then altruistic motivation will be aroused. The ultimate goal of this motive is to increase the welfare of the target of empathy. If pursuit of this goal increases justice, fine; if not, the person is likely to experience motivational conflict, and justice may suffer.

From the perspective of justice, then, empathy-induced altruism is a potential threat. Far from always being a source of moral behavior, as has often been assumed (cf., Eisenberg, 1991; Hoffman, 1989; and Mook, 1991), in a resource-allocation situation altruism may be a source of immoral injustice.

3. Some Empirical Evidence

I have built a rather elaborate conceptual castle in the clouds. It is time (perhaps way past time) to ask about empirical support. Is it true that inducing empathy for one of the individuals in an allocation situation can lead the empathizer to act unfairly, showing partiality to that individual at the expense of justice? Colleagues and I have recently conducted three experiments in an effort to answer this question.

3.1. Experiment 1: Empathy in a Social Dilemma

In the first, we (Batson, Batson, Todd, Brummett, Shaw & Aldeguer, 1994, Study 1) put 120 undergraduate men and women in a social dilemma. Each was given 2 blocks of raffle tickets (8 tickets per block); tickets were good for chances at winning a $30.00 gift certificate at the store of the winner's choice. Participants could keep each ticket block for themselves, give it to one of the other three participants in the session (actually fictitious), or give it to the group as a whole. If a block was given to the group, it was enhanced in value, becoming worth 12 instead of 8 tickets, and these 12 tickets were divided equally among the four participants, 3 tickets each. The two blocks could be allocated in the same way or differently.

Characteristically for a social dilemma, then, allocation that was best for the group as whole and fairest to all was not best for any single participant; allocation best for any single participant was not best for the group as a whole or fairest (Dawes, 1980). Uncharacteristically, it was possible to allocate resources to another person in the group as an individual. Insofar as I know, this option has not been provided in previous social dilemma research. Previous research has pitted egoistic self-interest against justice and the collective good; the possibility of altruism has not been addressed. We wished to give altruistic motives a chance to conflict with justice motives.

To arouse altruistic motivation, we induced empathy for one of the other participants. One-third of the subjects were in a no-communication condition; the rest were in a communication condition and received a note from one of the other participants in the session—sometimes a woman (Jennifer), sometimes a man (Mike)—prior to making their allo-cation decision. (Sex of subject and of note-writer made no difference, so I shall only refer to Jennifer.) This note, ostensibly written before Jennifer knew what the study was about, told of her being recently dumped by her boyfriend, feeling depressed as a result, and needing something good to happen to cheer her up. Communication/low-empa-thy subjects read this note from an objective perspective; they were instructed not to get caught up in the writer's feelings, just remain objective and detached. Communication/ high-empathy subjects were instructed to try to imagine how the writer felt about the events de-scribed. Only communication/high-empathy subjects were expected to feel much empathy for Jennifer and, hence, much altruistic motivation to cheer her up.

Ticket blocks allocated to self, Jennifer (Mike), and the group as whole by subjects in the three experimental conditions are presented in Table 1. As you can see, in the no-communication condition, when subjects knew nothing about Jennifer (Mike), they allocated either to themselves or to the group, suggesting a conflict between egoistic self-interest and motivation to uphold justice or enhance the collective good. In the communication/low-empathy condition, in which subjects knew about Jennifer's (Mike's) need but felt little empathy, they did much the same. In the communication/high-empathy condition, however, in which subjects knew about the need and felt empathy, they significantly increased the resources allocated to Jennifer (Mike). Note that this

Table 1. Ticket Blocks Allocated to Each Target: Experiment 1

	Experimental condition		
	Communication		
Allocation target	No communication	Low empathy	High empathy
Self	33	36	36
Jennifer (Mike)	0	2	15
Group as a whole	46	42	29

Note. N = 40 in each condition.
Adapted from Batson, Batson et al. (1994).

increase was not at their own expense; it was at the expense of overall fairness and the welfare of the group as a whole.

After making their allocation decision, subjects completed a questionnaire on which they were asked how much they wanted to maximize the number of tickets received by themselves, by each of the other participants, and by the group as a whole. In all three conditions, subjects reported a strong desire to maximize the number of tickets they received. In the no-communication and communication/low-empathy condition, the desire to maximize the number of tickets received by the group as a whole ran a close second. In the communication/high-empathy condition, however, the desire to maximize the number of tickets received by Jennifer (Mike) was stronger than the desire to maximize the number of tickets received by the group as whole; specifically, this was true for those subjects who allocated at least one of their blocks to Jennifer (Mike).

Although results of this experiment are consistent with the idea that empathy-induced altruism introduces partiality that can undercut justice, the experiment was not designed explicitly to test this idea. As a result, there are several ambiguities. First, justice motivation and group welfare were confounded. Second, subjects could benefit themselves directly by their allocation, so egoistic motives were involved along with justice and altruism, complicating matters. Experiments 2 and 3 focus more specifically on the conflict between empathy-induced altruism and justice, providing less ambiguous tests.

3.2. Experiment 2: Assigning Workers to Tasks

In Experiment 2, we (Batson, Klein, Highberger & Shaw, 1993, Experiment 1) placed 60 undergraduate women in the role of a supervisor, responsible for assigning the two other female participants in the session, the workers, to tasks. One task had positive consequences; for each correct response the participant assigned to this task would receive a raffle ticket for a $30.00 gift certificate at the store of her choice. The other task had negative consequences; for each incorrect response the participant assigned to this task would receive a mild but uncomfortable electric shock (2–3 times the strength of static electricity). Subjects knew that they would never meet the other participants; participants were identified only by letter—A, B, and C—with subjects always Participant B. Instructions explained subjects' supervisor role:

As the supervisor, it is your responsibility to decide which worker does which task. One worker must be assigned to do the positive consequences task; the other to do the negative consequences task.

Most supervisors feel that flipping a coin is the fairest way to assign workers to the tasks, but the decision is entirely up to you. You can assign the workers however you wish. They will not know how they were assigned, only to which task they are assigned. And, of course, your anonymity as supervisor is assured.

A coin (a quarter) was provided in the research cubicle for subjects to flip if they wished.

To arouse altruistic motivation, we induced empathy for one of the other participants as in the previous experiment. One-third of the subjects received no communication from either participant; the rest received a communication from Participant C. The communication, ostensibly written before Participant C knew what the study was about, was the same note about being dumped, feeling depressed, and needing something good to happen used in Experiment 1. As before, communication/low-empathy subjects read this note from an objective perspective; they were instructed not to get caught up in the writer's feelings, just remain objective and detached. Communication/high-empathy subjects were instructed to try to imagine how the writer felt about the events described. Only communication/high-empathy subjects were expected to feel much empathy for Participant C and, hence, much altruistic motivation to cheer her up.

The frequency with which Participant C was assigned to each task by subjects in the three experimental conditions is presented in Table 2. As you can see, in the no-communication condition, Participant C was assigned to the positive-consequences task 50% of the time and to the negative-consequences task 50% of the time. No partiality there; only even-handed justice. In the communication/low-empathy condition, in which subjects knew about Participant C's need but felt little empathy, assignment was also 5050. Again, no partiality. But in the communica-

Table 2. Assignment of Participant C to Task Consequences:
Experiment 2

| | Experimental condition | | |
| | Communication | | |
Consequences for C	No Communication	Low empathy	High empathy
Positive	10	10	15
Negative	10	10	5

From Batson, Klein et al. (1993).

tion/high-empathy condition, in which subjects knew about the need and felt considerable empathy, Participant C was assigned to the postive-consequences condition 75% of the time; clear partiality ($p < .015$).

After making the assignment, subjects were asked to "briefly explain why you assigned the workers as you did." In the no-communication condition, all 20 subjects said they flipped the coin or used some other random method (e.g., "eenie, meenie, miney, moe" or "A to positive because A comes first"). In the communication/low-empathy condition, 17 said they flipped the coin or used some other random method; 3 said they chose to put C in positive. In the communication/high-empathy condition, 10 said they flipped the coin or used some other random method; 10 said they chose to put C in positive. Of the 10 in this last condition who used a random method, 5 assigned C to positive and 5 assigned C to negative.

Subjects were also asked, "In your opinion, what was the most fair way to assign the workers?" In each condition, 18 of 20 subjects (90%) said the most fair was to flip the coin or use some other random method. Only 2 subjects (1 communication/low-empathy, 1 communication/high-empathy) said choosing to put C in the positive condition was most fair. The remaining 4 subjects either said there was no fair way (2) or gave no response (2).

Subjects were also asked: "Do you think the way you assigned the workers to condition was morally right?" (1—*Not at all*, 9—*Yes, totally*). There were no reliable differences across the three experimental conditions on this item (overall $M = 6.51$), but in the communication/high-empathy condition, those subjects who chose to put C in the positive condition reported feeling that the way they assigned the workers was less morally right (M—5.10) than did subjects who used some random method (M 7.90, $p < .01$) .

Results of this experiment indicate, then, that inducing empathy for one of the two workers led a number of subjects (10 of 20) to turn their back on fairness and show partiality, acting to increase the welfare of the person for whom they felt empathy. Results were entirely consistent with the suggestion that empathy evokes altruistic motivation that can conflict with justice motivation. Presumably, among subjects faced with this conflict the stronger motive won out. For half of the high-empathy subjects, the stronger motive was justice; they used some random method. For the other half, the stronger motive was altruism; they chose to assign Participant C the positive-consequences task, even though they did not feel this was fair or very morally right.

Experiment 2, once again, provides evidence entirely consistent with the suggestion that empathy-induced altruism can lead people to act partially, sacrificing justice. It is also worth noting, however, that the allocation situation in Experiment 2 was tied to a work setting. Perhaps justice is more fragile in such settings than in allocation of resources to the needy of society. Second, it is worth noting that in Experiment 2 the fairness of treating the two workers equally was explicitly stated. Perhaps this made justice motivation stronger than it might have otherwise been. Third, it is worth noting that the form of justice at issue in Experiment 2 was procedural justice; distributive justice could not be achieved. Although the results of Experiment 1 suggest otherwise, perhaps people are less likely to show empathy-induced partiality when doing so conflicts with distributive as well as procedural justice. In Experiment 3, we attempted to create a situation that would address each of these concerns.

Finally, it is worth noting that all subjects in Experiment 2 were women, who Gilligan (1982) and others have suggested are especially likely to display an ethic of care. Perhaps there is a sex difference when empathy-induced altruism is pitted against fairness or justice. To explore this possibility, we ran both women and men in Experiment 3.

3.3. Experiment 3: Playing God

In Experiment 3, we (Batson, Klein et al., 1993, Experiment 2) had 30 undergraduate women and 30 undergraduate men listen and react to a pilot radio broadcast. Ostensibly, there were a number of pilots, each an interview with a different child with a terminal illness who was on the Waiting List for help from an organization called the Quality Life Foundation. All subjects were "randomly" assigned to hear the interview with Sherri Summers, a 10-year-old girl with a muscle-paralyzing disease, myasthenia gravis. If Sherri could get off the Waiting List and into the Immediate Help Group, the Foundation would provide her with an extremely expensive medication that would improve the quality (not the length) of her life. There were, however, a number of other children ahead of Sherri on the Waiting List. Placement on the list was determined by length of wait, seriousness of need, and time left to live.

To manipulate empathy, half of the subjects were instructed to try to remain objective while listening to the interview (low-empathy condition); the other half were instructed to try to imagine how the child being interviewed feels (high-empathy condition). After listening, subjects were given an unexpected opportunity to move Sherri off the Waiting List into the Immediate Help Group.

A letter from the professor in charge of the research explained that it had occurred to him that some participants might want to assist the child they heard, and so he had gotten the Quality Life Foundation to agree to let research participants move the child they heard into the Immediate Help Group, if they wished. The letter emphasized the consequences of this decision:

Moving your child up into the Immediate Help Group means that children who are currently higher on the Waiting List than your child, due to earlier application, greater need, or shorter life expectancy, will have to wait longer. On the other hand, moving your child up would make a very significant difference in the quality of life for the time this child has left.

Obviously, the decision of whether to move the child you heard into the Immediate Help Group is a very important one, but one we feel you should be given the opportunity to make. Neither the child nor his or her family knows that this opportunity is being provided; they will be informed *only* if you decide to move the child.

Subjects were given a form on which to indicate their decision, and an envelope to keep the decision confidential.

Subjects in the high-empathy condition were more likely to show partiality, moving Sherri into the Immediate Help Group at the expense of others more needy (.73), than were subjects in the low-empathy condition (.33, $p < .001$). It did not appear that men were any less vulnerable to empathy-induced partiality than were women; there were no reliable effects for sex ($zs < 1.0$). Moreover, empathy did not lead subjects to adopt a Empathy, altruism, and justice 20 general principle of justice based on need, as Hoffman (1989) had predicted; it led to partiality in spite of relative need.

3.4. Summary

Results of these three experiments are, I believe, entirely consistent with my proposal that the problem of partiality is often not a matter of different forms of justice or fairness—even a justice of need—but a conflict between two different motives: justice and empathy-induced altruism. Feeling empathy for a person in need led many subjects to forsake fairness and justice in the interest of benefiting the person for whom they felt empathy. Partiality occurred even when they knew this person's need was not as great as the need of others. Empathy-induced altruism can, it seems, conflict with and, at times, overpower justice.

It is worth remembering that in these experiments we used a relatively weak empathy induction. The person in need was not kin or a close friend (the assumed condition producing a shift from equity or equality to a justice of need—Deutsch, 1975; Lerner, 1975), not even someone subjects had met—or seen; subjects simply read a note or heard an interview while trying to imagine how the other felt. Presumably, a more potent empathy induction would produce even more partiality and injustice.

Lerner ended his essay in the *Journal of Social Issues* with a question: "Is there anything as powerful in the social dialogue as the appeal to justice?" (1975, p. 19). I would answer: If the social dialogue means *talk*, perhaps not; if it means *behavior*, perhaps so. Empathy-induced altruism appears, at times, to be as powerful a motive as justice. And we should not forget egoistic self-interest in its various forms. The justice motive is indeed powerful, but it can at times be overpowered by other motives, including altruism.

4. Implications: Problems and Promise for Justice of Empathy-Induced Altruism

In Order to test the independence of altruistic and justice motives, the three experiments described focus on situations in which these two motives conflict, in which compassion creates problems for justice. That such situations exist outside the lab was underscored by a *Time* magazine essay I read following the landing of U.N. troops In Somalia. Walter Isaacson suggested that empathy was a potent factor in the decision, so potent as to pose a problem:

In a democracy, policy (unless pursued in secret) must reflect public sentiment. But sentiment can ooze sentimentality, especially in the age of global information, when networks and newsmagazines can sear the vision of a suffering Somalian child or Bosnian orphan into the soft hearts of millions. Random bursts of compassion provoked by compelling pictures may be a suitable basis for christmas charity drives, but are they the proper foundation for a foreign policy? Will the world end up rescuing Somalia while ignoring the Sudan mainly because the former proves more photogenic? (*Time* essay, December 21, 1992).

The answer is, I fear, "yes." Empathy, sympathy, compassion can evoke altruistic partiality that impedes justice.

At the same time, the power of empathy-induced altruism to override justice is only half the story. A more positive implication of recognizing the independence of these two motives is that one can think about using them in concert. Justice is a powerful motive but vulnerable to rationalization; it is easily co-opted. Empathy-induced altruism also is a powerful motive but limited in scope; it produces partiality. Perhaps if we can engender in nonvictims empathy for the victims of injustice, then we can get these two motives working together rather than at odds. Desire for justice may provide perspective and reason; empathy-induced altruism may provide emotional fire and a push toward seeing the victims' suffering end, preventing rationalization. Said another way, empathy may enable us to bridge the gulf between nonvictim and victim (Hoffman, 1989; Solomon, 1989, 1990), not because we identify or see ourselves as one with the victims but because, adopting their perspective, we come to care for them, and that care prevents derogation and other forms of rationalization of their plight (Aderman, Brehm & Katz, 1974).

Something of this sort occurred, I believe, in a number of rescuers of Jews in Nazi Europe. A careful look at data collected by Oliner and Oliner (1988) and their colleagues suggests that involvement in rescue activity frequently began with concern for a specific individual or individuals for whom compassion was felt—often an individual known previously. This initial involvement subsequently led to further contacts and rescue activity and to a concern for justice that extended well beyond the bounds of the initial empathic concern.

Admittedly, combining empathy-induced altruism and justice motives is risky. For the reasons already noted, it is like playing with fire. But where would we be without fire? If done wisely and carefully, the result might be a joining of head and heart into what philosopher Robert Solomon (1990) has called "a passion for justice," a passion that can lead us to change the social order, not just our minds. And what is the alternative? It is, I fear, a Hobbesian war of all against all in which justice is reduced to the "Not fair!" each of us shouts in our role as victim (whether we are Bosnian or Serb, black or white, man or woman), vainly hoping some parent will intervene and uphold our special interest, while we reach for the sticks and stones.

References

Aderman, D., Brehm, S. S. & Katz, L. B. (1974). Empathic observation of an innocent victim: The just world revisited. Journal of Personality and Social Psychology, 29, 342–347.

Batson, C. D. (1987). Prosocial motivation: Is it ever truly altruistic? In L. Berkowitz (Ed.), Advances in experimental social psvchology (Vol. 20, pp. 65–122). New York, NY: Academic Press.

Batson, C. D. (1991). The altruism question: Toward a social-psychological answer. Hillsdale, NJ: Erlbaum Associates.

Batson, C. D., Batson, J. G., Todd, R. M., Brummett, B. H., Shaw, L. L. & Aldeguer, C. M. R. (1994). Empathy and the collective good: Caring for one of the others in a social dilemma. Unpublished manuscript, University of Kansas.

Batson, C. D., Klein, T. R., Highberger, L. & Shaw, L. L. (1993). Empathy-induced altruism as a source of injustice: Evidence for competing prosocial motives. Unpublished manuscript, University of Kansas.

Blum, L. A. (1980). Friendship, altruism, and morality. London: Routledge.

Cialdini, R. B., Schaller, M., Houlihan, D., Arps, K., Fultz, J. & Beaman, A. L. (1987). Empathy-based helping: Is it selflessly or selfishly motivated? Journal of Personality and Social Psychology, 52, 749–758.

Crosby, F. J. (1982). Relative deprivation and working women. New York: Oxford University Press.

Dawes, R. M. (1980). Social dilemmas. Annual Review of Psychology, 31, 169–193.

Deutsch, M. (1975). Equity, equality, and need: What determines which value will be used as the basis of distributive justice? Journal of Social Issues, 31(3), 137–149.

Dovidio, J. F. (1984). Helping behavior and altruism: An empirical and conceptual overview. In L. Berkowitz (Ed.), Advances in Experimental social psychology (Vol. 17, pp. 361–427). New York: Academic Press.

Dovidio, J. F., Schroeder. D. A., Allen, J. L. & Matthews. L. L. (1986, March). Altruistic versus egoistic motivations for helping (L. A. Penner, Chair). Current theoretical issues in helping. Symposium conducted at the Annual Meeting of the Southeastern Psychological Association, Orlando, Florida.

Eisenberg, N. (1991). Values, sympathy, and individual differences: Toward a pluralism of factors influencing altruism and empathy. Psychological Inquiry, 2, 128–131.

Gilligan, C. (1982). In a different voice: Psychological theory and women's development. Cambridge, MA: Harvard University Press.

Hoffman, M. L. (1976). Empathy, role-taking, guilt, and development of altruistic motives. In T. Lickona (Ed.), Moral development and behavior: Theory research, and social issues (pp. 124–143). New York: Holt, Rinehart & Winston.

Hoffman, M. L. (1989). Empathic emotions and justice in society. Social Justice Research, 3, 283–311.

Hornstein, H. A. (1982). Promotive tension: Theory and research. In V. J. Derlega & J. Grzelak (Eds.), Cooperation and helping behavior: Theories and research (pp. 229–248). New York: Academic Press.

Kant, I. (1889). Kant's critique of practical reason and other works on the theory of ethics (4th ed.) (T. K. Abbott, Trans.). New York: Longmans, Green & Co. (Original work published 1785).

Kohlberg, L. (1976). Moral stages and moralization: The cognitive-developmental approach. In T. Lickona (Ed.), Moral development and behavior: Theory, research, and social issues (pp. 31–53). New York: Holt, Rinehart, & Winston.

Kozol, J. (1991). Savage inequalities: Children in America's schools. New York: Crown.

Krebs, D. L. (1975). Empathy and altruism. Journal of Personality and Social Psychology, 32, 1134–1146.

Lerner, M. J. (1975). The justice motive in social behavior: Introduction. Journal of Social Issues. 31(3), 1–19.

Lerner, M. J. (1980). The belief in a just world: A fundamental delusion. New York: Plenum.

Lewin, K. (1951). Field theory in social science. New York: Harper.

Montada, L. & Schneider, A. (1989). Justice and emotional reactions to the disadvantaged. Social Justice Research, 3, 313–344.

Mook, D. G. (1991). Why can't altruism be selfish? Psychological Inquiry, 2, 139–141.

Nagel, T. (1991). Equality and partiality. New York: Oxford University Press.

Noddings, N. (1984). Caring: A feminine approach to ethics and moral education. Berkeley: University of California Press.

Oliner, S. P. & Oliner, P. M. (1988). The altruistic personality: Rescuers of Jews in Nazi Europe. New York: The Free Press.

Rawls, J. (1971). A theory of iustice. Cambridge, MA: Harvard University Press.

Schaller, M. & Cialdini, R. B. (1988). The economics of empathic helping: Support for a mood management motive. Journal of Experimental Social Psychology, 24, 163–181.

Smith, K. D., Keating, J. P. & Stotland, E. (1989). Altruism revisited: The effect of denying feedback on a victim's status to empathic witnesses. Journal of Personality and Social Psychology, 57, 641–650.

Solomon, R. C. (1989). The emotions of justice. Social Justice Research, 3, 345–374.

Solomon, R. C. (1990). A passion for justice: Emotions and the origins of the social contract. Reading, MA: Addison-Wesley.

Stotland, E. (1969). Exploratory studies of empathy. In L. Berkowitz (Ed.), Advances in experimental social psychology (Vol. 4, pp. 271313). New York: Academic Press.

Tronto, J. (1987). Beyond gender differences to a theory of care. Signs, 12, 644–663.

Walster, E., Berscheid, E. & Walster, W. G. (1973). New directions in equity research. Journal of Personality and Social Psychology, 25, 151–176.

Williams, B. (1981). Persons, character, and morality. In B. Williams (Ed.), Moral luck: Philosophical papers 1973–1980 (pp. 1–19). Cambridge: Cambridge University Press.

5

Intergenerational Relations, Inequality, and Social Justice

Karen S. Cook and Shawn Donnelly

1. Introduction

Various authors have recently begun to connect the literatures on intergenerational relations and gerontology with the work on social justice (e.g., Norris, 1987). This chapter attempts to relate two specific literatures within this broader field of current research. We take one of the dominant theoretical perspectives in Sociology, social exchange theory, and extend it to apply to intergenerational relations.

Whether or not intergenerational justice exists, and if so, what principles of justice would obtain across generations is a matter of philosophical debate. Rawls (1972), for example, defines justice as "mutual advantage." Commenting on Rawls notion of justice, Barry (1989, p.189) argues that "if justice equals mutual advantage, there can be no justice between generations." That is, "whether or not they (Rawls' circumstances of justice) obtain between the generations alive at one time and their successors is a logical matter. They cannot. The directionality of time guarantees that while those now alive can make their successors better or worse off, those successors cannot do anything to help or harm the current generation" (Barry, 1989, p. 189).

Barry identifies some of the problems inherent in the application of Rawls' theory of justice to intergenerational relations (both with the

Karen S. Cook and Shawn Donnelly • Department of Sociology, Duke University, Durham, North Carolina 27708.

Current Societal Concerns about Justice, edited by Leo Montada and Melvin J. Lerner. Plenum Press, New York, 1996.

principle itself and with the motivational assumption underlying it). First, the circumstances of justice, as articulated by Rawls, do not apply among noncontemporaries. Second, it is quite problematic to assume that the obligations of current generations toward future generations will depend "purely upon the goodwill of contemporaries toward their descendants" (Barry, 1989, p. 192). These issues must be addressed in any attempt to specify the principles of justice that apply to intergenerational relations.

As Barry (1989, p. 192) puts it, "It is not a matter of justice between generations (other generations are not, after all parties to the agreement). It is, rather, a matter of justice with respect to future generations." How this type of justice is worked out in reality and what constitutes the form of justice such relations take in any society are open questions. Various justice evaluation schemes exist in the philosophical and social science literatures which specify the nature of individual rights, entitlements and duties as well as explicate the basic rules of justice that apply to the distribution of valued goods and services among contemporaries in any society or social system. However, this literature rarely addresses intergenerational justice. (Barry and Rawls are exceptions.) Many issues related to aging, intergenerational relations, and social welfare policies revolve around social justice concerns, but for the most part justice issues have only recently begun to penetrate the gerontology literature (e.g., Norris, 1987). At the same time concerns over generational equity (or intergenerational inequity) are being voiced more frequently in policy discussions especially as the aging population in the United States and Canada is increasing (cf. Tindale and Neysmith, 1987; Brubaker, 1990). As the "baby boom" population ages in these countries, the size of the elderly population will exceed that of the younger generations. Since social security systems are set up such that the younger generations provide the wage support for the system, this demographic shift has serious implications regarding justice for future generations (Longman, 1987), unless changes in the system are made such as current modifications in the U.S. which raise the age of entitlement to social security and increase the wage limits for taxation to generate more revenue.

In American society, the elderly and the very young are likely to compete increasingly for limited societal resources. As a result, issues concerning eldercare and the ramifications of this competition for resources in terms of intergenerational conflict and justice will demand attention in the future from both social scientists and policymakers. The overall limitations in the available economic resources are already causing a reevaluation of what constitutes a fair distribution of societal resources. For instance, current debates in the United States focus on whether social security benefits should be based on entitlement or on need. (Means testing for benefits is again under serious consideration in Congress.) Research on the application of various conceptions of justice or equity in the arena of intergenerational relations will thus be increasingly needed.

Analysis of social justice in intergenerational relations is important in part because of the widespread policy implications of the nature of the relations between the generations in any society and, more specifically, of the levels of investment of current generations in subsequent generations. Social welfare, child welfare, educational and family policy, environmental policy, aspects of health policy, aging and long-term care issues are all affected by the fundamental nature of the intergenerational relations in a society. While economic considerations are often paramount, there are also significant social and political dimensions to these social problems.

In this chapter we explore the utility of social exchange theory for modeling intergenerational relations and examine the topic of intergenerational justice from this perspective. Some of the previous work in the area of aging has applied an exchange framework to the analysis of the interactions of the elderly (e.g., Dowd, 1975, 1980); however, this work has received strong criticism from Kahana (1987). One problem with much of this earlier work is that it used a narrow version of exchange theory, focusing primarily on a dyadic conception of exchange. We discuss more recent developments in exchange theory which have not been previously incorporated into the aging and intergenerational justice literatures and investigate their implications for modeling intergenerational relations in new ways. Specifically, we argue that intergenerational relations may best be conceptualized as a chain generalized form of exchange rather than as a dyadic, "restricted" form of exchange (see Ekeh, 1974; Yamagishi & Cook, 1993). Before discussing extensions of the social exchange model we will first provide a short overview of exchange theory and review briefly previous applications of the theory to issues of aging and eldercare.

2. The Exchange Model and Intergenerational Relations

2.1. The Basic Model

Exchange theory has been one of the dominant approaches to the analysis of social relations for almost four decades and it continues to provide a useful way of framing questions concerning the nature of social relationships ranging in content from economic, short-term transactions or bargains to social, often longterm relations like those involved in friendships, marriages and other types of close relationships. The most basic assumption of the theory is that relations between actors (either individuals or corporate actors) are generally governed by the rewards and costs involved in the relationship. Exchange relations typically persist when they are mutually beneficial to the actors involved; that is, at some level the actors find the relationship "profitable" in the sense that the rewards exceed the costs. It is argued in theory that relations which are not beneficial to the actors will eventually terminate (though this depends upon the availability of other exchange partners and the existence of normative and structural constraints on relationship dissolution). It is an empirical fact that some relationships persist (especially those that are only quasi-voluntary) under conditions in which the costs exceed the rewards for at least one party to the exchange relation. Often in such situations the more dependent actor has few, if any, perceived or actual alternatives to the relationship (see Burgess & Nielsen, 1974).

Two of the key concepts within the exchange framework developed by Emerson (1972a,b; 1976; 1981) are power and dependence. Power differences in exchange relations emerge as a result of the differential dependencies of the parties in the relation. Dependence is a function of (a) the value of the resource(s) provided by a specific actor and (b) the availability of the resource(s) from alternative sources (i.e. other actors). Dependence upon a specific actor increases as the value of the resource(s) provided by that actor increases and it decreases to the extent that access to alternative sources of these resources increases. According to Emerson (1972a,b) power is a direct function of dependence: the power of actor A over actor B (or Pab) is equal to the dependence of actor B upon A (or Dba). This theorem is represented as: Pab = Dba. In this formulation dependence is thus the source of power within an exchange relationship.

These notions have been extended in the past decade to networks consisting of connected exchange relations, thus clarifying the structural bases of power and dependence (e.g., Cook & Emerson, 1978; Cook, Emerson, Gillmore & Yamagishi, 1983). Exchange relations between two or more actors are viewed in this work as building blocks for larger networks of social relations. Power within these networks is determined by the structure of the network (Cook et al., 1983, Yamagishi et al., 1988) which determines the accessibility of particular resources (i.e. network ties deny or grant direct and indirect access to sources of valued resources) and the nature of the exchange connections (i.e. to substitutable or complementary sources). An important contribution of this work in Sociology is that social structure can thus be conceptualized in network terms (Cook & Whitmeyer, 1992). Exchange networks represent the "structured" access of actors to valued resources.

Another set of key concepts and propositions central to exchange theory are the power-balancing mechanisms discussed by Emerson (1962; 1972a,b; 1976; 1981). These operations represent mechanisms by which actors in power-imbalanced exchange relations (i.e. relations in which there is a power inequality such that one actor is more dependent in the relationship) can gain power. The four operations discussed by Emerson (1972a,b) include:

1. withdrawal from the relation or network,
2. network extension or the addition of alternative sources,
3. "status-giving" or altering the value of the resource(s) obtained, and
4. coalition formation (which in a network implies a reduction in the number of alternative sources).

These processes have various determinants and consequences that are just now being worked out empirically (see Cook, 1987).

Analytically, these power-balancing mechanisms can be used to provide some insight into the nature of intergenerational relations and the potential for intergenerational conflict. In the mid-seventies Dowd (1975), for example, explored what he called the "withdrawal" of the aged in American society, referred to in the aging literature at that time as "disengagement," considered then to be a natural part of the aging process. Using an exchange framework Dowd defined withdrawal as a result of the loss of power resources. In his framework it was also viewed as a mechanism for maintaining power by withdrawing from those social relations characterized by power-imbalance. This process, Dowd argued, explained the documented preference for "same-age" interaction among the aged. According to Dowd (1980), same-age interactions are more likely to be power-balanced than interactions which "cross boundaries," defined by age groupings. More powerful actors in power-imbalanced relations and networks are able to dictate the terms of exchange. Maintaining power-balanced relations allows for greater control over the going rates of exchange. The end result of this process, however, is age segregation in the society at large which may have other less positive consequences for society and particularly for intergenerational relations since it leads to the relative isolation of the old from the young.

Dowd's (1975; 1980) application of exchange notions emphasizes only the dependency side of the equation and assumes that aging inevitably results in the loss of power resources. The loss of power is viewed by him as a function of two factors: a reduction in access to instrumental resources (i.e. those resources provided by active employ- ment) and a reduction in the size and density of the social networks of the aged (i.e. more limited access to alternative sources). This particular view of aging, however, has been heavily disputed and is inconsistent with other empirical evidence indicating that withdrawal is not an inevitable consequence of aging. It should be noted that Dowd (1980) focused his attention on the societal level; in his analyses he generally treated the aged as a distinct social group. He also focused on intergen- erational relations involving non-familial relationships. He focused on the aggregate level treating intergenerational relationships as relations across categories of individuals in different age cohorts (not within families or kinship networks). Changing the focus to intergenerational relations within families or kinship groups adds complexity to the analysis. Looking at intergenerational relations within families brings in mutual interdependency and past history of the relations to a much greater degree. Furthermore, levels of trust and commitment become important factors in the analysis of longitudinal exchange relations (see Yamagishi & Cook, 1983). Withdrawal is less likely to occur in familial relations in which there is a greater degree of mutual interdependence.

There is no clear theoretical reason to believe that withdrawal would, however, be the preferred response to loss of power. According to Emerson's (1962; 1972a,b) version of exchange theory there are other power-balancing mechanisms available to actors who find themselves in power-imbalanced situations. For instance, coalition formation is one alternative power-balancing mechanism. Power disadvantaged actors can gain power through coalescing to obtain greater control over the rates of exchange. Dowd (1980) mentions the possibility of coalition forma- tion, but argues that it requires age consciousness and the recognition of common political interests among the aged which can be problematic. But the recognition of common political interests among the aged has occurred in the United States. Examples of the most visible attempts by the aged to engage in highly successful collective actions include the rise of "gray power" in the form of the Grey Panthers and the tremondous growth of other interest group organizations like the AARP (American Association of Retired Persons) and the GAS (Gerontological Society of America). While these organizations share some goals and political interests in common, there are also differences in goals and charac- teristics of their constituencies that, under some circumstances, make collective action more difficult as Dowd recognized.

The potential for intergenerational conflict actually rises as a result of coalition formation and collective action among the aged to the extent that a constant-sum "game" is assumed to represent the relations between the generations (e.g., scarcity of resources in the form of welfare and other social and economic benefits). Programs like aid to families with dependent children (AFDC), for instance, are sometimes viewed as competing for resources that might be used for better long-term care facilities or health care for the elderly.

2.2. The Basic Model and Intergenerational Relations

The power-dependence reasoning of the basic exchange model has a number of implications for intergenerational relations as well as intergenerational justice. As we have indicated some theoretical and empirical work on aging and eldercare has explicitly used social exchange theory in the analysis of aging issues (e.g., Dowd, 1975; 1980). Other work has been influenced by powerdependence reasoning even though it has not explicitly used social exchange theory. Various studies indicate that middle aged children of elderly parents often take steps to preserve the independence of their parents. Matthews and Rosner (1988), for example, in their study of filial responsibility regarding the care of elderly parent, found that an implicit "principle of least involvement" tended to guide the siblings' behavior toward their elderly parents in terms of the provision of care. They found that siblings wanted to avoid making their parents any more dependent than necessary.

The consequences of aging can impinge on the nature of the parent-child relationship, altering the power balance. An imbalance created by parents becoming dependent on their children can be uncomfortable for both the children and the parents. Not only is there a power imbalance, but there is also a reversal of the direction of the power imbalance and concomittantly a reversal of roles. A high level of dependency of elderly parents on their adult children not only causes an uncomfortable emotional state, but, if severe enough, causes a high degree of stress in the children which may result in a deterioration of their emotional and physical health (see Cicirelli, 1990, for a review of the literature on this topic). The dependency of the elderly family members on younger members can create stress in both the care giver and the care receiver (Brubaker et al., 1990). For these reasons, the children often try to maintain some sort of power balance in the parent-child relationship as long as possible. These findings provide support for the underlying power-balancing dynamics which are assumed in social exchange theory

(Emerson, 1972a,b) to be important factors in longitudinal exchange relationships, such as those typically found in families.

Most explicit applications of the social exchange model to issues concerning the elderly, like Dowd's work discussed above, have focused on the relative power or lack of power that the elderly possess because of their decreasing ability to directly access resources in society (e.g., Dowd, 1980). As Dowd (1980) puts it, the elderly generally possess fewer valued resources, yet at the same time possess a devalued status in society. As a result, they are likely to engage in fewer exchanges or interactions than other groups in society. He further argues that this process results in the elderly associating mainly with age peers because this is where they are likely to find power balanced relationships.

Kahana et al. (1987), responding in part to Dowd's arguments, argue that an exchange orientation is limited in its ability to explain many of the interactions involving the elderly. Specifically, they argue that an exchange framework is not satisfactory as an explanation of the helping behavior exhibited by the elderly. These authors propose that this helping behavior is not motivated by self-interest, but rather by non-egoistic motives not considered within the exchange framework. According to Kahana et al. (1987), the elderly exhibit patterns of giving or helping in relationships that exceed their degree of receiving in such relationships. This evidence of altruistic behavior, they argue can't be explained in exchange theory terms, but may be better understood from a life-span developmental perspective. It is proposed that "successful helping in later years leads to the sense of competence, to high self-esteem, and to positive morale, and that these, in turn, lead to a sense of life-satisfaction, including the achievement of meaningfulness and worthwhileness" (Kahana et al., 1987, p. 455). While not rejecting exchange theory as a tool for conceptualizing social interaction, they argue that a "contributory" model based on altruistic motives may be a better model for explaining the helping behavior of the elderly. They further argue that the reliance of exchange theory on economic and learning theory principles "yields not only a pessimistic view of personal and social options for late life, but it renders the elderly dependent respondents to stimuli which they cannot control" (Kahana et al., 1987, p. 456). Such criticisms fail to take into account the full development of social exchange theory in the past decade (see Molm & Cook, 1994). As noted earlier power-dependence principles within exchange theory make various predictions about the behavior of the more dependent actors. The theory does not assume that power-dependent actors are necessarily passive respondents to their situations.

In fact the contributory framework articulated by Kahana et al. (1987) is not fundamentally inconsistent with exchange theory. Contributing in the context of long-term relationships helps people to become less dependent and as a result they retain a sense of independence which is important in all stages of life, but may have particular significance in later life. Exchange theory focuses on longitudinal exchange relations and thus applies quite naturally to the analysis of the relationships of the elderly with those with whom they are interdependent. The elderly may not have the same access to strategic resources which can be used in exchange relations as they once did, and thus may find themselves in more dependent situations; but by helping others (friends, family members, etc.) they are making contributions to the various relationships in their lives and thus helping to maintain power balance in their exchange relations. Maintaining a sense of independence and fostering relationships in which one is not overly dependent is likely to enhance self-esteem and feelings of selfworth. Kahana's criticism of the utility of exchange theory for the analysis of helping behavior among the elderly is based on a narrow conception of exchange theory. Putting this behavior into the context of longitudinal relationships and exchanges over time among friends and family members focuses attention on reciprocity, power-balancing mechanisms and the maintenance of exchange relations (which often involves periods of asymmetric giving and receiving). In this context helping behavior among the elderly is viewed as one mechanism for maintaining significant exchange relations with important others in their social environment, as well as a way in which they can contribute to such relations even with limited access to other types of resources.

In using an exchange perspective in the analysis of intergenerational relations, in particular, we thus need to extend the analysis beyond the dyadic level to networks of relations and to focus more on the longitudinal aspect of exchange relations. Many previous applications of exchange theory in this research area (e.g., Dowd, 1980) have not considered the significance of the longitudinal dimension or the embeddedness of specific relations in a larger social network. Power is, in part, a function of the availability of alternative sources from which to obtain desired resources. In this respect, focusing purely on dyads gives an inadequate picture of the power dynamics in various relationships. Viewing family relationships in network terms may advance our understanding of the intergenerational relations within families. Looking at specific exchanges at one particular time and place in an attempt to ascertain the respective power differences among the individuals involved may provide an inaccurate assessment unless one takes into account the past history of the relationships involved, the levels of trust and commitment between the exchange partners, and the nature of the reciprocity in the flow of resources in the relations. In the next section we begin to extend the analysis of intergenerational relations by conceptualizing them as a form of exchange different from the dyadic model traditionally associated with the basic exchange model.

3. Extensions of the Social Exchange Model

3.1. Forms of Exchange

Social exchange relations may take different forms under different social circumstances. The model most familiar to sociologists is the basic exchange model derived in part from economics and behavioral analysis in which the exchange relations are conceived as dyadic transactions or interactions involving the contingent flow of benefits within the exchange relation over time. Emerson (1976) referred to these transactions or mutually reinforcing interactions as elementary exchange relations which could take the form of either a direct exchange (e.g., negotiation between two parties) or an indirect exchange in which the terms of trade are negotiated through some third party (e.g., involving an agent or broker). Ekeh (1974) refers to elementary exchange as "restricted exchange." In restricted, typically dyadic exchange, the partners reciprocate to one another directly. What one partner receives is contingent upon what s/he has given to the other person. This is the form of direct, dyadic exchange that has been considered most often in the aging literature.

A different class of exchanges take the form of "generalized exchange." In these exchanges the distinguishing feature is that there is no direct reciprocity between the actors involved in the exchange. In addition, there is no direct negotiation or bartering over the terms of trade. Instead the exchange is indirect involving what Ekeh (1974) calls "univocal reciprocity." What a person receives from another is not directly contingent upon what he/she has given to that person. There is no "direct" give and take between two individuals. A typical example is the tradition in some cultures of barn raising or house building in which the parties to the exchange each contribute to the collective effort without the immediate expectation of a return, but with the expectation of reciprocated labor in the event that any other actor involved in the event would require a barn or a house to be built. This type of generalized exchange is referred to by Ekeh (1974) as "group-generalized" exchange.

Often in group-generalized exchange individuals contribute to some collective good and share in the collective benefits. Such situations often involve the classic problems (e.g., free-riding) identified with the logic of collective action (see Olson, 1965; Yamagishi & Cook, 1993; etc.).

A different type of generalized exchange is what Yamagishi and Cook (1993) refer to as "network generalized" exchange. (Ekeh, 1974, refers to this as a "chain-generalized" exchange.)

In this case each actor in the chain provides a service or a resource of value to another actor in the network, but the receiving actor never reciprocates directly to the actor who provided the resource or service. The actor who provided the resource or service receives benefits from another actor in the resources is unidirectional. The Kula Ring (Malinowski 1922) is often used as an example of this type of generalized exchange. The key distinction between group generalized and network (or chain) generalized exchange is that in network generalized exchange people give and receive services and resources from specific individuals in the network (chain), while in the group generalized form of exchange people give and receive services and resources from a group, not particular individuals (Yamagishi & Cook, 1993). Yamagishi and Cook argue that because individuals within the networkgeneralized structure are dependent upon specific others for benefit, coopration will be higher than in a group generalized exchange structure where the actions or inactions of specific individuals are not likely to have as great an effect.

3.1.1. Forms of Exchange and Intergenerational Relations.

We argue that the model of generalized exchange advanced by Ekeh (1974) and others (Yamagishi & Cook, 1993) is a useful way of conceptualizing intergenerational relations, particularly intergenerational relations within families. It is our contention that intergenerational relations can be viewed fruitfully as a form of longitudinal generalized exchange, specifically an open-ended generalized chain. It was pointed out earlier that many of the empirical analyses of exchange theory regarding the elderly have focused on non-familial relations. By viewing intergenerational relations among kin as an open-ended generalized chain, the family is considered in network terms instead of dyadic terms and the focus is on generalized exchange instead of restricted dyadic exchange. By recognizing that intergenerational relations take the form of generalized exchange rather than direct or "restricted" exchange relations, much of the debate concerning the applicability of basic exchange notions to intergenerational relations (e.g., Kahana, Midlarsky & Kahana,

1987) is significantly altered. Kahana et al. (1987) argue that much of the helping behavior exhibited by the elderly is not reciprocated and hence not egoistically motivated, thus exchange theory is inadequate to explain it. If we shift the focus to generalized exchange networks such criticism loses its force. To understand what constitutes a fair or just exchange particularly within families, we cannot just look at isolated dyadic exchange relations. Exchanges in an intergenerational context occur over an extended time frame between various family members. Specific relations may appear unbalanced or unfair if we look at a particular point in time or at a particular relation within the structure, but by looking at the network as a whole we may discover greater balance and justice.

Viewing intergenerational exchange, not as isolated interactions among exchange partners, but as exchanges that occur among actors linked in a network or "chain" of connected exchange relations alters the basic conceptualization of intergenerational relations and raises issues of maintenance of the network or "chain of concern," trust, solidarity and ultimately justice (beyond the notion advanced by Rawls' of a "just savings rate"). What is described in the gerontology literature as an alternative perspective to that of intergenerational conflict (based on the zero-sum notion across generations) is referred to as the model of "interdependence of generations" (e.g., Kingson et al. 1986). This model, according to Dowd (1987) is more "an ideology than a fact," implying that the existence of familial and other ties across generations is sufficient to yield "just" interactions which is inconsistent with elder abuse and other problems facing the aged in our society. Such problems are symptoms of the failure of justice in these relations. (Note that elder abuse, however, is consistent with the theoretical notion of extreme dependence and the loss of power resources.) These perspectives—that of intergenerational conflict and of integenerational interdependence—need not be viewed as alternatives. It is, in fact, the presence of interdependence across generations that results in intergenerational conflict under conditions of scarcity. Justice rules that emerge under conditions of scarcity tend to differ substantially from those that emerge under conditions of plenty (cf. Lerner & Lerner, 1980).

Our discussion has focused primarily upon intergenerational relations within the context of kinship ties and family obligations. We have pictured intergenerational relations as a form of chain-generalized exchange (where the chain is open-ended and not closed as a circle would be, like the Kula ring). The issues surrounding this form of exchange, as discussed in the literature (e.g., Ekeh, 1974), focus on trust and the credit mentality that are essential for the maintenance of such an exchange system. Kinship ties, especially close family relations, often serve to provide the trust and long-term credit required to maintain the flow of resources from one generation of kin to the next, based on what Ekeh (1974) calls "univocal reciprocity." A breakdown in kinship ties might jeopardize the generalized exchange of resources across generations. In Western, post-industrial societies geographic mobility of the more recent generations and the trend toward smaller families (living in separate households) has weakened ties of kinship and family.

One of the difficulties in establishing and maintaining this particular form of open-ended chain generalized exchange is the well-known "free rider" problem in the rational choice literature (e.g., Yamagishi & Cook, 1989). That is members of one generation in the chain may renege on their obligation to provide certain resources (e.g., invest in their education and provide for their welfare) for subsequent generations thus "breaking the chain of concern." The accompanying belief might then emerge that other institutions rather than the family are responsible for providing such resources (a common theme that has emerged in debates in Western societies over the extensive growth of government and its role in society).

4. Conclusion

It is not at all clear that any society, especially modern societies, can take it for granted that matters of intergenerational tendency to invest in offspring. According to Barry (1989, p. 192),

"Rawls has the comforting belief that the lnterests of more remote generations will be taken car of so lang as there are 'ties of sentiment between successive qenerations.' "Such a mechanism has been referred to as resulting in a "chain of concern" (or what exchange theorists, as noted above, have called chain-generalized exchange involving "univocal" reciprocity). A different version of this argument has been proposed by various authors who argue that intergenerational justice is not especially problematic because "representatives from periods adjacent in time have overlapping interests" (see Barry, 1989, p. 193–194 for discussion). Given this general orientation, Rawls' focuses most of his attention on the question of the "just savings rate" or "just rate of capital accumulation," as constituting the most important issue with respect to intergenerational relations (see Barry 1989, p. 193).

What Barry argues is left out is any discussion of the "just rate of air and water pollution," or of the depletion of natural resources. For environmental issues generally, it is almost certainly not sufficient to rely on the investment of parents in their offspring or the overlapping interests of immediately successive generations, since the effects of the ill-use of natural resources or of pollution may extend well into the future, far beyond generations even three or four steps removed. Relying on a "chain of concern" may be insufficient in these matters because the potential ill-effects are too extensive and of such a magnitude that this form of intergenerational justice will be wholly inadequate to meliorate such consequences. Not even the appropriate "just savings rate" (cf. Rawls, 1972) will help since the problems are, in some cases, cumulative and incapable of being remediated by appropriate levels of capital accumulations (such as could be created by simple alterations in the savings rate over time).

We have obviously not addressed the implications of the theoretical treatment of intergenerational justice relations based on an exchange perspective for many of the classes of situations which involve such concerns, especially for environmental issues (very likely to be dominant worldwide in the next few decades). We have attempted to flesh out an exchange model of intergenerational relations, extending it beyond existing theoretical treatments (e.g., those of Dowd, 1975, 1980, 1987 and others). What remains to be done is a more detailed theoretical extension including more clearly stated testable propositions and a thorough treatment of the existing empirical literature on intergenerational relations. To use Dowd's (1975) terms this effort can be considered a "preface to theory."

Barry (1989, p. 201) argues that "it is best not to think of (justice in terms of) a choice made by a particular generation at a single point in time but of a pattern of collaboration across many generations in a scheme of justice," a notion compatible with the idea of longitudinal generalized exchange relations. While successive generations cannot take part in a system of "mutual benefit," Barry continues, they can, however, "play their accepted by all as just." This principle of fair play (or justice as impartiality) dictates that each person has an obligation to "do one's bit" to sustain just institutions. In this case justice operates in the absence of any possibility of direct reciprocity or mutual benefit. Instead the quid pro quo notion of exchange is replaced by an obligation embedded in a "just" system of institutionalized generalized exchange relations between the generations involving univocal reciprocity (e.g., Ekeh, 1974).

References

Barry, B. (1989). Theories of justice. Berkeley: University of California Press.

Brickman, P. Foler, R. Goode, E. & Schul,Y. (1981). Microjustice and macrojustice. In M. J. Lerner & S. C. Lerner (eds.),The justice in social behavior (pp. 173–202). New York: Plenum Press.

Brubaker, T. H. (1990). An overview of family relationships in later life. In T. H. Brubaker (ed.), Family relationships in later life. (2nd Ed., pp. 13–26) Newbury Park CA: Sage.

Brubaker, E., Gorman, M. A. & Hiestand, M. (1990). Stress perceived by elderly recipients of family care. In T. H. Brubaker (ed.), Family relationships in later life (2nd Ed., pp. 267–281) Newbury Park, CA: Sage.

Burgess, R. L. & Nielsen, J. M. (1974). An experimental analysis of some structural determinants of equitable and inequitable exchange relations. American Sociological Review, 39, 427–443.

Cicirelli, V. G. (1990). Family support in relation to health problems of the elderly. In T. H. Brubaker (ed.) Family relationships in later life. (2nd ed., pp. 212–228) Newbury Park, CA: Sage.

Cook, K. S. (ed.). (1987). Social exchange theory. Newbury Park, CA: Sage.

Cook, K. S. & Emerson, R.M. (1978). Power, equity, and commitment in exchange networks. American Sociological Review, 43, 721–739.

Cook, K. S., Emerson, R. M., Gillmore, M. R. & Yamagishi, T. (1983). The distribution of power in exchange networks: Theory and experimental results." American Journal of Sociology, 9, 275–305.

Cook, K. S., Molm, L. D. & Yamagishi, T. (1993). Exchange relations and exchange networks: Recent developments in social exchange theory. In J. Berger & M. Zelditch (eds.). Theoretical research programs: Studies in the growth of theory (pp. 296.322).

Cook, K. S. and J. Whitmeyer. 1992. "Two approaches to social structure: exchange theory and network analysis. Annual Review of Sociology, 18, 109–127.

Daniels, N. (1988). Arn I my parents keeper? New York: Oxford University Press.

Dowd, J. J. (1975). Aging as exchange: A preface to theory." Journal of Gerontology, 30, 584–594.

Dowed, J. J. (1978). Aging as exchange: A test of the distributive justice proposition. Pacific Sociological Review, 21, 351–375.

Dowed, J. J. (1980). Exchange rates and old people. Journal of Gerontology, 35, 596–602.

Dowed, J. J. (1987). Justice in old age: An analysis of corporatist social theory. Social Justice Research, 1, :477–499.

Ekeh, P. P. (1974). Social exchange theory: The two traditions. Carnbridge, MA: Harvard University Press.

Emerson, R. M. (1962). Power-dependence relations." American Sociological Review, 27, 31–40.

Emerson, R. M. (1972a). Exchange theory, Part I: A psychological basis for social exchange. In J. Berger, M. Zelditch & B. Anderson (eds.), Sociological theories in progress (Vol. 2, pp. 38–57). Boston: Houghton Mifflin.

Emerson, R. M. (1972b). Exchange theory, Part II: Exchange relations and networks." in J. Berger, M. Zelditch & B. Anderson (eds.), Sociological theories
in progress (Vol. 2, pp. 58–7). Boston: Houghton Mifflin.
Emerson, R. M. (1976). Social exchange theory. Annual Review of Sociology, 2,
335–362.
Emerson, R. M. (1981). Social exchange theory. In M. Rosenberg & R. Turner
(eds.) Social psychology: Sociological perspectives (pp. 30–5).ew York:
Academic Press.
Gouldner, A. (1960). The norm of reciprocity." American Sociological Review,
25, 161–178.
Hesse-Biber, S., & Williamson, J. (1984). Resource theory and power in families:
Life cycle considerations. Family Process, 23,261–278.
Kendig, H. (1986). Aging families and social change. In H. L. Kendig (ed.),
Aging and families: A support networks perspective (pp. 169–185). Sidney:
Allen and Unwin.
Kahana, E., Midlarsky, E. & Kahana,B. (1987). Beyond dependency, autonomy,
and exchange: Prosocial behavior in late-life adaptation." Social Justice
Research, 1,439–459.
Kingson E. R., Hirshorn, B. A. & Cornman, J. M. (1986). Ties that bind: The
interdependence of generations. Washington D.C.: Seven Locks.
Lerner, M. J. & Lemer, S. C. (eds.). (1981). The justice motive in social behavior.
New York: Plenum Press.
Levi-Strauss, C. (1969). The elementary structures of kinship. Boston: Beacon
Press.
Lewis. R. A.. (1990). The adult child and older parents. In T. H. Brubaker (ed.),
Family relationships in later life. (2nd Ed., pp. 68–85) Newbury Park, CA:
Sage.
Longman, P. (1987). Born to pay: The new politics of aging in America. Boston:
Houghton Mifflin Company.
Malinowski. B. (1922). Argonauts of the Western Pacific. London: Routledge
and Kegan Paul.
Matthews, S. H. & T. T. Rosner (1988). Shared filial responsibility: the family as
the primary caregiver." Journal of Marriage and the Family, 50, 185–195.
Molm, L. D. (1987). Power-dependence theory: Power processes and negative
outcomes. In E. J. Lawler & B. Markovsky (eds.), Advances in group proc-
esses (Vol. 4, pp. 171–198) Greenwich. CT: JAI Press.
Molm, L. D. (1988). The Structure and use of power: A comparison of reward
and punishment power." Social Psychology Quarterly, 51, 108–122.
Molm, L. D. (1989). Punishment power. A balancing process in power-depend-
ence relations." American Journal of Sociology, 94, 1392–1418.
Norris, J. E. (1987). Justice and intergenerational relations: An introduction.
Social Justice Research, 1, 393–403.
Olson, M. (1965). The logic of collective action. Cambridge: Harvard University
Press.
Rawls, J. (1972). A theory of justice. Cambridge, MA: Belknap Press.
Sahlins, M. (1972). Stone age economics. London: Tavistock.

Tindale, J. A. & Neysmith, S. M. (1987). Economic justice in later life: A Canadian perspective." Social Justice Research, 1, 461–475.

Walster, E., Walster, W. & Bersheid, E. (1978). Equity: Theory and research. Boston: Allyn and Bacon.

Yamagishi, T., Gillmore, M. R. & Cook, K.S. (1988). Network connections and the distribution of power in exchange networks. American Journal of Sociology, 93, 833–851.

Yamagishi, T. & Cook, K. S. (1993). Generalized exchange and social dilemrnas. Social Psychology Quarterly. 56, 235–248.

6

Have Feminists Abandoned Social Activism? Voices from the Academy

Faye J. Crosby, Janet Todd, and Judith Worell

Social movements come into being and persist when individuals and groups perceive contradictions and inequalities in the larger social order. As a broad social movement that evolved to address gender and other social inequalities, feminism has persisted in many forms throughout modern history (Taylor, 1989). As American feminists struggle collectively to reform and transform the social institutions through which their lives are encoded, questions have been raised about the continuing vitality and commitment of this movement. Has feminist activism become diluted and ineffectual, or are we witnessing a gradual transformation of the movement into multiple channels that defy simplistic conceptions of advocacy? We explore these issues of social activism in the narratives of a sample of 77 feminist psychologists who teach in three academic contexts: women's colleges, co-educational colleges, and universities. Their responses to a lengthy interview and questionnaire illuminate the questions we asked and extend our understanding of feminist advocacy well beyond the simple statement of one respondent that "I don't march..."

What is a feminist? A few years ago, Eleanor Smeal sent out a flyer to all members of the National Organization of Women in which bold black letters against a lavender background asked the same question: "What is a feminist?" The black-on-purple answer came directly from

Faye J. Crosby, Janet Todd, and Judith Worell • Department of Psychology, Smith College, Northampton, Massachusetts 01063.

Current Societal Concerns about Justice, edited by Leo Montada and Melvin J. Lerner. Plenum Press, New York, 1996.

the New Lexicon Webster's Dictionary of the English Language (1989) defining feminism as "the policy, practice or advocacy of political, economic, and social equality for women." A feminist was defined as "an advocate of feminism." Clearly, feminists, inside and outside of academia, have long been invested in issues of social justice. They have thought about and worked toward the creation of a world in which there is gender fairness.

Yet, as the contemporary women's movement matures, many speculate about diminished energies. Recently, there has been an extended public debate about whether or not the dedication to social change has declined among feminists and other liberal thinkers (Faludi, 1991). Echoing the public debate is a similar concern among social scientists (Daniels, 1991). While some (Eagly, 1993; Hyde, 1994; Worell, 1991; Worell & Robinson, 1993) characterize today's academic feminists as people who are highly committed to advocacy, others claim that academic feminists have turned away from activism (Kahn & Yoder, 1989).

Kahn and Yoder, in a 1989 article, discuss the conservative impact of psychology as a whole on developments in current theory and research in the psychology of women. They emphasize that the feminist movement is a civil rights movement that demands change at all levels of society, from the individual and interpersonal to the organizational and societal/cultural. These authors lament, however, that the psychology of women has become increasingly conservative with its primary, if not sole, focus on gender differences and individualistic theories of the personality of women.

Which view more accurately describes the current situation of feminism in psychology? To what extent do feminist psychologists today envision advocacy as an integral part of feminism and how much do they work for social justice and social change? The primary purpose of our chapter is to shed light on this set of questions. We do so by assessing the extent to which women professors of psychology who are self-identified feminists include activism as part of their definition of feminism, and link what they do in the classroom to what they do outside it.

A secondary goal of our study is to investigate the correlates of activism among the feminists in our sample. For the demographic characteristics we measure, are there any that predict whether a feminist will be more activist or less activist? Activism may sometimes be born of hardship, or at least of being somewhat at odds with the established order (Lalonde & Cameron, 1994). Among our respondents, is a working class background or a statistically unusual sexual orientation especially associated with activism? Are feminists who were educated at or who teach at women's colleges especially likely—as some (Lormier, 1991) assert—to be leaders in the fight for social justice?

For the attitudinal characteristics we measure, are there any that are linked with the extent of activist behaviors? The nature of the link between feminist attitudes and feminist behavior is addressed by Branscombe and Deaux (1991) in terms of what moderates the relationship between feminist attitudes and behavior and when do feminist attitudes guide behavior. These authors suggest that an individual's feminist attitudes do not differ across situations, but a person's behavior may vary depending on the accessibility of the feminist attitude at the time a behavior is chosen and performed. The findings of their study support their assertions; when feminist beliefs were activated, or primed, by first asking individuals about their feminist beliefs and second asking about their intended behaviors, the feminist beliefs did guide behavioral intentions in a direction consistent with the individual's expressed attitude. They concluded that the accessibility of feminist attitudes is "a powerful determinant" of whether the person describes an intention to behave in accordance with those feminist attitudes. We apply their conclusions to the question of whether consistent self-presentation as "feminist" may prime the individual's attitude structure, resulting in a greater commitment to advocacy and increased social activism.

Given that all of our respondents are professors, it is relevant to ask about teaching attitudes and experiences. Do activists experience the classroom differently than non-activists? Studies of adult female development suggest that activists connect their personal identity to a wider social identity (Stake & Gerner, 1987) and that an embedded social identity and a strong personal commitment to social justice help to sustain a sense of vitality (Astin & Leland, 1991; Worell & Remer, 1992). It seems likely, therefore, that activist professors might enjoy their teaching more than (or differently than) non-activist professors.

1. Method

1.1. Overview

The research reported here is from a project on female professors of psychology who describe themselves as feminists and who teach in women's colleges, coeducational colleges, and universities in the United States. The main purpose of the project was to understand how the scholars define feminism, how they came to be feminists and how they sustain their commitment to feminism. The data were collected in 1992 and 1993.

1.2. Sample

There are no published lists of self-identified feminists, but there are lists of women who are likely to self-identify as feminists. One such list exists for members of Division 35 (The Psychology of Women Division) of the American Psychological Association (APA). In September, 1992, we obtained the names and institutional affiliations of the members of Division 35 who specified that their primary form of employment was education, rather than therapy. We separated the names into four categories: 29 women who taught at women's colleges; 88 who taught at co-educational colleges; 383 who taught at universities; and the remainder who were ineligible for inclusion because their information was incomplete. A woman was also deemed ineligible for inclusion in the sample if she listed a law firm, a consulting firm, or a professional school rather than a graduate school, university, or college as her place of employment; if she had been part of our pilot work; or if she was in any way affiliated with the funding agency.

We drew up to 35 names at random from each of the three sampling categories with the intention of including 25 women from each category in our study. Due to the timing of acceptances, the final sample included 77 individuals, of whom 4 were African American. The majority of respondents were middle age, ranging in age from 36 to 70.

1.3. Data Collection

Data collection proceeded in three steps. First, we contacted the prospective participants by letter. All individuals who responded with a signed informed consent form were then contacted by telephone, and appointments were made for telephone interviews. Ninety-two percent of the women contacted agreed to participate in the study; and the high participation rate was true for women in each teaching environment. In the second step, scripted interviews were conducted and tape-recorded over the telephone. Most of the interviews were conducted by one of two advanced graduate students whom we had trained. Each interview lasted between 45 minutes and 2 hours and each was later transcribed. Following the interview, which had mostly open-ended questions, each respondent was mailed a questionnaire including mainly close-ended questions. All but one of the respondents returned the completed questionnaire.

1.4. Instruments: Measures and Coding

1.4.1. Developing the Protocol

As a first step in developing the measures, we worked with a student who prepared an exhaustive guide to writings on the topic of feminism in the academy (Reinhardy, 1992). We then developed a preliminary survey instrument, incorporating as many of the issues as we could from the literature covered in the guide. Some of the items concerned the role of advocacy and activism in feminist pedagogy. We conducted interviews with experts and revised the instruments according to their suggestions. We then tested the nearly-final product with two additional experts, each of whom was interviewed by one of the graduate students.

1.4.2. Extent of Activism

Four questions, three from the interview and one from the questionnaire, provided measures of the extent of activism. Toward the beginning of the interview, respondents were asked; "In your own words, what does it mean to be a feminist. When you say 'I am a feminist,' what do you mean?" Verbatim answers to this question were sorted into two categories: those that made an explicit reference to advocacy for social change and those that did not. * Respondents who referred to social change emphasized doing, or action, as part of their definition. For example, one woman responded: "I think it means having at the forefront of one's work and personal life the idea that women as a group have been discriminated against, have been oppressed, have been made invisible, and to do what one can, in terms of one's work, intellectual work, one's personal life, one's social life, to undermine that oppression. To do something about it."

Midway through the interview, in the context of tracking their development relevant to feminism, respondents were asked if they had ever gone through a stage of "action toward social change." Responses were sorted into two categories: those who characterized themselves as involved in social change currently and/or previously; and those who did not see themselves as activists. Toward the end of the interview came

* Inter-rater reliability for interview question 3 = 94%

this question: "If activism is part of your definition of feminism, what are the links between what you do in the classroom and what you do outside it—on the campus or in the community?" Answers were coded and put into two groups: the high-activists, who mentioned three or more activities and the low-activists, who mentioned fewer than three activities.

The final measure of activism was scored from the questionnaire. The first entry on the questionnaire presented respondents with "a list of items that some authors have identified as part of feminism" and requested that they "indicate which items are part of your personal definition of feminism." Among the thirteen items listed was one stating "works actively to change social structures." Respondents could either endorse the item or not.

1.4.3. Nature of Activities

We analyzed the interview question linking the classroom to activities outside it. Answers included a wide variety of activities both on and off campus. We divided these activities into six dimensions of activism: a) On campus—with groups and committees; b) Off campus—speaks, participates, promotes; c) Donates money; d) Demonstrates; e) With students—promotes change in ideas and behaviors; and f) Challenges and confronts sexism and injustice. *

1.4.4. Correlates of Activism

We looked at the demographic and attitudinal information about each respondent that might covary with activism. Most of the demographic information came from the questionnaire. The questionnaire closed by asking respondents their educational history, age, ethnicity, and sexual orientation. We divided the sample into those who had or had not attended a women's college; were White or other; did or did not come from a working class background; were heterosexual or other; and taught at either a women's college (n = 25), a coeducational college (n = 25), or a university (n = 26). One woman taught at an institution that was changing from being single-sex to co-education, and her data were therefore omitted on some items.

The questionnaire and interview contained some attitudinal measures that seemed potentially related to activism. The first question in

---

* Inter-rater reliability for interview question 24 = 100%

the interview asked: "Do you label yourself as a feminist?" and provided five response options: always, usually, sometimes, seldom, never. The second item posed the question, "Do your colleagues consider you to be a feminist?" and included the same response options. For both questions, we divided the sample into those who said "always" and all others.

Both the interview and the questionnaire assessed pedagogical practices which might be closely linked to activism. Two-thirds of the way through the interview, the respondents were asked: "Would you say that you make a conscious effort to employ any of your feminist values in your teaching?" and "Would you say that your goals in any of your classes have been influenced by your feminist values or feminist episte-mology?" Coders examined the answers to each of these questions and, following a procedure that is described in detail elsewhere (Kmeic, Crosby, & Worell, in press), derived three scores. One binary score divided the sample into those who made a considerable effort and all others; another into those whose goals were much influenced and all others; and a third measure looked at a composite coding produced when coders examined the two questions together and scored them on a one to five scale, from little to much involvement. In the questionnaire, we asked respondents to identify and then rank order their goals as a feminist teacher. Among the list of six goals was this one: "training women who will make a difference in the world."

Finally, to see if high-activists derive more pleasure from their work than do low-activists, we examined answers to an item that asked respondents "if you could assign numbers to the pleasure and the difficulties of feminist teaching, from 1 to 10, what number would you assign to the pleasures? To the difficulties?" For each respondent, we obtained three scores: pleasures, difficulties, and balance (pleasure minus difficulties).

2. Results

2.1. Preliminary

We first examined the data according to the interviewer. We found that the scores of respondents interviewed by Interviewer One did not differ from the scores of respondents interviewed by Interviewer Two.

2.2. Extent of Activism

The percentage of feminist professors to embrace activism varies across the different measures. Only 41% of the sample spontaneously mentioned social action or activism when asked what they mean by the terms "feminism" and "feminist." In contrast, 87% mentioned gender equality; 33% mentioned an understanding of gender and gender issues; and 19% mentioned pro-woman. If this were our only measure of how much feminists today advocate for social justice, we would be forced to conclude, along with Kahn and Yoder (1989), that contemporary feminism is somewhat sedentary.

A different picture emerges from the other measures. Eighty-two percent of the sample say that they did go through or are currently going through a stage of social activism in their development as feminists. When asked to link what they do in the classroom with what they do outside of it, 61% of the sample list three or more activities that reflect feminist principles or values and are aimed at social change. Finally, when provided with a list of items and asked which ones are part of the respondent's personal definition of feminism, 92% of the participants endorse activism as a part of their definition.

2.3. Nature of Activism

Table 1 presents the kinds of activities that our participants report. As is evident from the table, feminist professors do not confine themselves to the campus. As Eagly (1993) contends, feminist in the academy today are concerned with what might be called a "political agenda." The 77 women gave a total of 246 examples of activities in which they have participated that promote political, economic, or social equality for women. The responses were rich with the ways in which feminist professors translate their beliefs into actions that go well beyond marches and demonstrations. Ways in which women were active on campus included, among many others, organizing to develop a women's center, serving on committees that specifically deal with women's issues, writing a model sexual harassment policy, or setting up day care on campus. Off campus, examples of ways women promote social change include, again among many others, such activities as raising feminist issues while serving on various boards or committees, speaking with the media regarding women's issues and from a feminist perspective, testifying in court as an expert witness, or working with school systems to introduce non-sexist curricula. Women mentioned donating money to

Table 1. Dimensions of Feminist Activism

	N	%	# Reported
On-Campus—With goups and committees	29	38	64
Off-Campus—Speaks, participates, promotes	41	53	84
Donates Money	12	16	15
Demonstrates	16	21	18
Writes, does research	15	19	15
With students - Promotes change in ideas and behavior	33	43	44
Challenges & confronts sexism and injustice	6	8	6
Total			246

Note. N = total number of respondents who report at least one of this activity. #Reported = total number of times this activity was reported by respondents. %=percentage of total respondents who report at least one of this activity.

political organizations that work on behalf of women's rights. Women participated in pro-choice and Take Back the Night rallies. Women were activist in their writings and choice and method of research. Feminist professors promoted change in ideas and behaviors by encouraging their students to be active through specific assignments and by redefining activism in such a way that students could recognize the many things they can do. Finally, women were activist by confronting, and not ignoring, sexism and injustice as it occurs in their day-to-day lives. (See appendix A for an expanded, although not complete, list of activities mentioned by the respondents, divided further by area of activist effort).

2.4. Correlates of Activism

As can be seen from Table 2, high-activists generally do not differ from low-activists in terms of their personal characteristics. High-activists are around the same age as low-activists and are as likely as lowactivists to have been educated at a women's college. The two groups do not differ in terms of their sexual orientations. As well, they do not differ in terms of their institutional affiliations: It is not the case here that women's colleges are special hotbeds of activism. A significant relationship was found, however, between having a working class background and the number of activities one mentioned, $\Sigma^2 (1, N = 74) = 6.16$, $p < .05$. A higher percentage of women (92%) with a working class background than women (54%) not from a working class background cited many examples of social activism.

As to labels, either self-imposed or imposed by others, the association with activism is mixed. Although several of our measures showed no association with the labeling, two important findings emerged. One,

Table 2. Demographic and Attitudinal Correlates of Feminist Activism

	% always label self feminist	% who are always labelled feminist	% educated at women's colleges	% with working class background	% non-heterosexual	Average age[a]
Does respondent spontaneously mention activism in definition?						
yes	80.6[b]	56.7	20.0	24.1	22.2	49.3
no	60.0	53.5	25.6	11.4	9.1	50.2
Has she gone through a stage of activism?						
yes	74.1	57.1	23.2	16.4	13.0	49.2
no	53.8	50.0	33.3	23.1	0.0	52.2
When citing activities, does she cite many?						
many?	80.9**[C]	58.7	25.0	25.0*[d]	16.3	49.1
few?	50.0	46.4	20.0	3.3	10.3	51.0
Does she select social action as part of definition from a list of items?						
yes	71.2	59.4	23.1	18.5	12.5	49.4
no	50.0	16.7	33.3	0.0	40.0	55.8

Note. Cell values represent the percentage of respondents in each row category who endorsed the column variable.

[a]This value is the average age of those who endorsed each row category.

[b]Chi square analysis indicates the association between whether or not a respondent always labels herself a feminist and whether or not she spontaneously mentions activism approaches significance ($p=.057$).

[c]Chi square analysis indicates a significant association between whether or not a respondent always labels herself a feminist and whether she cites many or few activities.

[d]Chi square analysis indicates a significant association between whether or not a respondent has a working class background and whether she cites many or few activities, but note small cell size.

$* p$ .05. $** p$ .005.

Table 3. Pedagogical Correlates of Feminist Activism

	% making conscious effort to use values	% influenced by feminism	Average pleasure score	Average dificulties score	Average balance score
Does respondent spontaneously mention activism in definition?					
yes	51.6	61.3*a	8.4	3.8	5.1
no	45.7	33.3	8.8	3.4	5.5
Has she gone through a stage of activism?					
yes	50.0	44.8	8.6	3.4	5.4
no	46.2	38.5	8.2	4.7	4.2
When citing activities, does she cite					
many?	55.3	46.8	8.8	3.7	5.3
few?	33.3	40.0	8.4	3.4	5.4
Does she select social action as part of definition from a list of items?					
yes	43.9	42.4	8.5	3.8*	5.1*
no	50.0	33.3	9.2	2.0	7.2

Note. Cell values in columns one and two represent the percentage of respondents in each row category who endorsed the column variable. Cell values in columns three through five are average scores of those who endorsed each row category.
[a]Chi square analysis indicates a significant association between whether or not a respondent is influenced by feminism in her teaching and whether or not she spontaneously mentions activism in her definition of feminism.
[b]Using t-tests, significant differences were found between those who did and did not select social action. *p .05.

a significant relationship was found between women who always label themselves as feminist and those who report many activities, Σ^2 (1, N = 77) = 8.12, p < .005. Two, the relationship between always labeling oneself as a feminist and spontaneously mentioning activism in the definition of feminism approaches significance, Σ^2 (1, N = 76) = 3.62, p = .057. Seventy-two percent of those who always label themselves as feminist cited many activities, while only 37% of those who did not always label themselves as feminist cited many activities. Eighty-one percent of those who spontaneously mention activism in their definition of feminism also always define themselves as feminists, and only 25% of those who do not always label themselves as feminist spontaneously mention activism.

Table 3 shows some association between activism and teaching experiences among this sample of college and university professors. Those who spontaneously mention activism when defining what they mean by feminism are more likely than others to say that their teaching has been influenced by their feminism, Σ^2 (1, $N = 76$) = 5.8, $p < .05$. Women who select activism from a list of items as one feature of feminism differ from others in the sample in terms of their ratings of how difficult it is to be a feminist teacher, $t(65) = -2.11$, $p < .05$. Because they do not also experience greater pleasures in teaching, their "balance score" tips more toward displeasure than does the balance score of the other women. $t(65) = 2.19$, $p < .05$. However, none of the other indices of activism were related to differences between the pleasures and costs of feminist teaching.

3. Discussion

The primary purpose of this chapter was to shed some light on the debate between those who say that social activism among feminist psychologists is dead and those who say activism is alive and well. We review the results of a study of feminist psychology professors and their attitudes and behaviors related to activism in the hopes of further informing this debate.

Three measures of activism used in this study indicate that feminists in academia remain committed to engaging in change-agent types of activities that reflect their feminist beliefs and values. The vast majority (92%) endorsed social activism as part of their definition of feminism, 82% report having experienced a stage of social activism in their development as feminists, and 61% listed three or more examples of their own activism on and/or off campus.

The abundance and variety of examples of activist provided by the respondents also deepen the impression that activism is a thriving and enacted goal of feminist academics. The 246 activities reported underestimate the level of their involvement in social action. Often they named a general type of activity that encompassed numerous individual activities, such as serving on several committees or speaking with the media on several occasions or issues, and these were tallied as one activity. Further, from many of the responses, it was evident that the respondents' feminist attitudes influenced the nature of their role in many different, if not all, arenas of their lives. For example, in their involvement with boards and committees, their faculty leadership roles, or their interactions with students, they consistently raise feminist issues, challenging the status quo.

One measure of the salience of activism, that of spontaneously mentioning activism as part of their personal definition of feminism, is less easily interpreted. Fewer than half of our respondents spontaneously specified social action when asked to define feminism. Does this result suggest that for the majority of the respondents, social action is not an important part of feminism? If so, how can we account for the additional finding that 92% endorsed social action from a list of feminist principles and values? Perhaps for some, their feminist beliefs were readily accessible (Branscombe & Deaux, 1991) and for the others, it was necessary to activate their feminist beliefs. Once activated, they did endorse social action as an important part of being a feminist.

It is relevant, then, to consider other comparisons between those who spontaneously include social action as part of their definition and those who do not. The function of self-labeling seems to be important. We found that the relationship between those who spontaneously mention activism in their definition and those who always label themselves as feminist approached significance. Eighty-one percent of respondents who spontaneously mentioned activism always defined themselves as feminist. In comparison, of those who do not always label themselves as feminist, only 25% spontaneously mention activism. Perhaps those who label themselves as feminist in all situations have a deeper connection to their feminist identity. These individuals may have accessed more frequently their feminist beliefs, which for the large majority include promoting gender equality through social action.

We also found that those who spontaneously mention activism when defining what they mean by feminism are more likely than others to say that their teaching has been influenced by their feminist beliefs. Again, perhaps the unprompted recognition of activism as an essential part of feminism reflects the depth of the respondent's commitment to feminist values. The greater the commitment, the more integral feminist beliefs and actions will be to all aspects of the respondent's life, including her approach to teaching.

How we label ourselves also appears to impact how we behave with respect to promoting social justice. We found a significant relationship between always labeling oneself as feminist and citing many examples of academic and community activism. What is it about consistent self-labeling that might explain this relationship? Perhaps the public nature of identifying oneself as a feminist reflects the depth of commitment to the feminist movement. The greater the commitment, the more often we access our feminist beliefs, and thus, the more consistently we act in accordance with these beliefs. Or, perhaps having identified publicly as feminist, we then strive to achieve consistency between what we say and what we do, to fulfill that self-definition. One way to fulfill that definition is to behave as a feminist, that is, to act in such a way as to promote social and political changes for women.

As we anticipated, feminist beliefs are not the only precursor of social activism in behalf of women. Ninety-two percent of respondents who reported a working class background also participated in more activist efforts and groups. Women from working class backgrounds are likely to have experienced inequities and injustices related to both social class and gender. Because of their own experiences, they may be more willing, motivated, and committed to working for justice than those who have always been more privileged. We may also find a similar relationship between activism and women of color, but our sample was too small here to examine this possibility.

Finally, we were surprised to find that measures of activism did not support our speculation that activist academics will find more pleasure than costs in their teaching. To the contrary, the only significant result suggested that those who endorsed activism when prompted (92% of the sample) were less satisfied with their teaching than the small group who did not. Since this comparison represents a very skewed sample, it may not be very meaningful.

In closing, we return to the issue raised at the start of this chapter. How healthy is the feminist community in academia as measured by its commitment to advocacy and action toward social change? From our data compiled on a sample of 77 feminist psychology professors, we conclude that activism in its many forms and manifestations is alive and flourishing. Social action remains an important part of the definition of feminism and feminist psychologists continue to participate within their communities to promote political, economic, and social equality for women.

The variety and range of their interventions supports the contention of Verta Taylor (1989) that the feminist movement, far from being defeated, has been successful in expanding its efforts beyond the visible acts of marching and demonstrations. Feminists dedicated to social change have infused the community across many strata with strategic interventions that work from within, as well as from outside, social and political systems. For the feminists in our sample, their activism is clearly not revolutionary; rather it is a persistent, steady striving toward incremental structural changes in society that will result in the enhancement of the civil rights of all women.

Acknowledgments

Special thanks are due to Helen Astin, Patricia Atkins, Claire Etaugh, Lucia Gilbert, B.J. Hatton, Susan Jones, Jessica Kohout, Julie

Kmiec, Karen Lenhoff, Sandra Medley, Brenda Nash, Virginia O'Leary, and Abigail Stewart for their help on this project. We are also grateful to The Jessie Ball Dupont Fund and the Women's College Coalition as well as to Smith College, the J.L. Kellogg Graduate School of Management, and the University of Kentucky for their generous support of the work. We are most endebted to our respondents who shared their time, their stories, and their insights with us.

References

Astin, H.S & Leland, C. (1991). Women of influence women of vision: A cross generational study of leaders and social change. San Francisco: JosseyBass.

Branscombe, N. R. & Deaux, K. (1991). Feminist attitude accessibility and behavioral intentions. Psychology of Women Quarterly, 15, 411–418.

Daniels, A.K. (1991). Careers in feminism. Gender and Society, 5, 583—607.

Eagly, F. (June, 1993). The science and politics of comparing women and men. Invited address at the annual meeting of the American Psychological Society, Chicago.

Faludi, S. (1992). Backlash. New York: Simon & Schuster.

Hyde, J. (Spring, 1994). The little things. Psychology of Women Newsletter, 21 (2), 1–2.

Kahn, A. S. & Yoder, J. D. (1989). The psychology of women and conservatism. Psychology of Women Quarterly, 13, 417–432.

Kmeic, J., Crosby, F.J. & Worell, J. (In press). Walking the talk: On stage and behind the scenes. In K. Wyche & F. Crosby (Eds.), Women and ethnicity: Journeys through psychology. Boulder, Co: Westview.

Lalonde, R.N. & Cameron, J.E. (1994). Behavioral responses to discrimination: A focus on action. In M.P. Zanna & J.M. Olson (Eds.), The psychology of preludice: The Ontario Symposium (Vol. 7, pp. 257–288). Hillsdale, N.J.: Lawrence Erlbaum.

Lormier, L. (April 7, 1991). They are the best places. The Boston Sunday Globe, 1991, BlM, B4.

Reinhardy, L. (October, 1992). Feminist teaching: An outline and resource guide. Presented at the AAUW/Mills College conference, "Taking the Lead and Balancing the Educational Equation: Issues of Equity and Diversity for Women and Girls." Oakland, CA.

Stake, J.E. & Gerner, M.A. (1987). The women's studies experience: Personal and professional gains for women and men. Psychology of Women Quarterly, 11, 277—283.

Taylor, V. (1989). The future of feminism: A social movement analysis. In L. Richardson & V. Taylor (Eds.), Feminist frontiers II: Rethinking sex, gender, and society. New York: Random House.

Worell, J. (1991, March). The psychology of women vs. feminist psychology. Paper presented at the annual conference of the Southeastern Psychologi-

cal Association, as part of a symposium titled: How can we make the psychology of women more relevant to social change?, Arnie Kahn, Chair.
Worell, J., & Remer, P. (1992). Feminist perspectives in therapy: An empowerment model for women. Chichester: Wiley.
Worell, J. & Robinson, D. (1993). Feminist counseling for the 21st century. The Counseling Psychologist, 21(1), pp. 92–96.

Appendix A: Examples of Feminist Activism

On-Campus—With Groups and Committees

Women's Studies/Women's Centers
   participate on women's studies coordinating committee
   helped develop women's center on campus
Promoting/Supporting Women Faculty
   work with other departments to encourage hiring someone with
      a feminist perspective
   mentor women inside and outside my department
Committee Work
   raise feminist issues on campus committees on which I serve
   serve on committees on campus that deal specifically with
      women's issues
Leadership Roles in University Structure
   chair of department
   president of the Faculty Senate
Sexual Harassment
   wrote model sexual harassment policy and served on related
      subcommittee
   advocated for sexual harassment policy
Lesbian Issues
   work with lesbians on campus
   developed a course on lesbian psychology
Violence against Women
   supported developing programs on women's safety issues
   worked with counseling staff on dealing with acquaintance rape
Child Care
   helped to set up day care on campus
   actively support good nursery schools for the college
Women's Sports
   work to prevent cut-back of women's sports

fight injustices against women athletes on campus
Miscellaneous
    bring to campus symposia and visiting professors whose work is
        on feminism
    started a network on campus to bring women together to identify
issues the campus needs to address

Off-Campus—Speaks, Participates, Promotes
Community Boards and Committees
    participate on a number of different boards and committees and
        always raise issues that are feminist issues
    serve on committees in the community, such as child abuse
        council, domestic violence shelter, rape crisis center, Planned
        Parenthood
Public Speaking
    speak out for women on whatever panel or public forum I am
        invited to participate
    give community talks related to women's issues
Media
    speak with newspapers on women's issues
    talk to TV, radio, magazine, and newspaper reporters about rape
Consultant/Expert Witness
    go into court setting trying to educate judges
    act as expert witness on sexual harassment
Lesbian Issues
    work to facilitate creating community for new people in town
        who are lesbian or gay
    served on community board to set up health center with lesbian
        and gay focus
Psychology-Related Organizations
    on editorial board of feminist journal
    on task force of Division 35
School System
    speak with local and state school boards and with superinten-
        dents' offices regarding sexism
    work with school systems to introduce non-sexist curricula
Political Action
    work with political candidates
    organize women psychologists regarding electing women candi-
        dates

Donates Money

give contributions to political organizations that work on behalf
of women's rights (e.g., NOW, National Abortion League,
Planned Parenthood)
bring activist speakers and PAY them

Demonstrates

participate in marches and rallies (e.g., pro-choice rallies, Take
Back the Night, Gay Pride Day)
display signs and symbols that I am a feminist

Writes, Does Research

activist in my choice of research and reporting
take my research into the community to benefit women

With Students—Promote Change in Ideas and Behaviors

Encourage to Be Active
redefine activism for my students so they can recognize the many
things they can do
assign projects that require students to look into organizations
that are involved, one way or another, with women's issues
Link Classroom to Community
teach students about real cases
expose students to women in the community
Encourage Individually
advise women students—helping them set their goals to maximize their opportunities and potential

Challenges and Confronts Sexism and Injustice

don't stand by and let injustice occur, but call those things to
people's attention
alert people to inequality

7

From Is to Ought and the Kitchen Sink: On the Justice of Distributions in Close Relationships

Barbara Reichle

1. Introduction

As many theories in psychology, social exchange theory and equity theory (Adams, 1965; Blau, 1964; Homans, 1961; Thibaut, & Kelley, 1959) have started out with the aim to cover a rather broad area of human behavior. "Inequity in social exchange" (Adams, 1965) and "Exchange and power in social life" (Blau, 1964) are but a few examples for the rather all-encompassing nature of the original theories. In retrospect, the development of these theories seems to follow the same lines as described by Furnham (1990) for single trait personality theories. Today, three decades later, there is a wide variety of differentiations of the original theories, as is represented by the proposition of a multi-principle approach by several scholars which dates back to the late 70s (e.g. Deutsch, 1975, 1985; Lerner, 1981; Leventhal, 1980; Sampson, 1975). The original concepts have since gone through an advanced stage of "the development and refinement of more than one, often sphere-specific and multi-dimensional measures of the same concept" (which is stage six of the eight stages described by Furnham, 1990, p. 923). This is represented by studies like those conducted by Schwinger (1980), Schmitt and Montada (1982), Reis (1984), and Törnblom, Jonsson and Foa (1985). The

Barbara Reichle • Fb I - Psychologie, Universitaet Trier, D-54286 Trier, Germany.

Current Societal Concerns about Justice, edited by Leo Montada and Melvin J. Lerner. Plenum Press, New York, 1996.

results indicate that humans are able to use various principles in social justice judgments, and that judgments vary with personal factors like culture, values, class, gender, cognitive development, and even personality, as well as with situational factors like contexts, relationships, and objects to be distributed (overviews are given by Törnblom, 1992; Schmitt, 1994). The selection of the topic in this paper, the justice of role distributions among women and men who are spouses and parents, is yet another manifestation of the trend described.

If one considers the legal prescriptions in today's industrialized cultures as the Ought and existing social arrangements among men and women as the Is, a large discrepancy between Is and Ought can be found in the aggregate. The aggregate Ought bears the promise of equality, of an androgynous revolution (Badinter, 1991), and is represented in the verdict of any discrimination by gender (and race, and religion) in various preambles, constitutions and statutes. On the side of the Is, there are many differences correlated with gender: the average woman generally works more and earns less than the average man, is unemployed and works part-time more frequently, has less access to higher positions, will receive lower retirement benefits, and bears the brunt of the responsibilities in child care and domestic work (see Bundesanstalt für Arbeit, 1994, for an overview of the situation of women's employment in the European Community; Bundesministerium für Familie und Senioren & Statistisches Bundesamt, 1994; Erler et al., 1988; Gliedner-Simon & Jansen, 1995; Oberndörfer, 1993, for data on the distribution of employment, housework, child care, and leisure time in Germany; Institut für Praxisorientierte Sozialforschung Mannheim, 1992, for data on the distribution of housework in Germany; Wissenschaftlicher Beirat für Familienfragen beim Bundesministerium für Jugend, Familie und Gesundheit, 1984, for the German situation concerning retirement benefits; Engelbrech, 1991, and Reskin, 1994, for data and references on sex segration in the work place; Steil, 1994, pp. 230-233, for an overview of the US-American situation concerning housework, child care, employment).

Facing these differences between the Is and the Ought in the aggregate, one might ask whether there are corresponding differences in the individual couple. And if so, how are these differences experienced by the individual person? How do individuals cope with these differences? And finally, where do several ways of coping lead to in the long run? In the following I will try to clarify the Is-Ought discrepancies in gender-related distributions of modern Western societies. It will be specified under which conditions these discrepancies are experienced as injustice, and corresponding empirical research will be reported. In the second part, the experience of injustice in close relationships will be described, with its related cognitions, emotions, and more global correlates like marital quality and general well-being. Finally, the consequences of experienced injustice in marital relationships will be dealt with.

2. Distributions among Spouses and Parents: Objects, Subjects, and Norms

Compared to the original goals of equity and exchange theory (which can be considered the beginnings of a social psychology of distributive justice, cf. Törnblom, 1992, or the beginnings of the study of justice in close relationships, cf. Mikula & Lerner, 1994), justice of distributions among spouses and parents might seem like a very narrow focus. Yet at a closer look, these special distributions are just as difficult as the task of successfully allocating what needs to be done in the twenty-four hours each day between two adult persons who live together in a close relationship, day by day, over an entire family life cycle, in a time of rapid societal changes. From the beginning of a relationship until often times even beyond its termination, questions about "who does what, who gets what, and who omits what" are raised in many variations. These questions have to be answered several times a day, balanced between the personal Oughts and the Oughts of the partner, considering legal prescriptions and factual barriers. Throughout the family life cycle, established routines have to be changed for as many times as new tasks come up and old ones become obsolete. Finally, there is a complex interaction between changing sex-roles, new Oughts, and corresponding legal prescriptions that should induce changes in the decisions women and men make about their intramarital distributions.

Psychologically, if injustice means the experience that a person is not treated the way he or she is entitled to (with entitled defined as to have been given a rightful claim to possessions, privileges, mode of treatment, etc.; cf. Oxford English Dictionary), there are at least five parameters to consider: (1) the victim — the subject that is affected by the injustice, (2) the agent — the instance responsible for the injustice, (3) the object at issue, (4) the rule or norm that has been applied, (5) the rule or norm that has been violated. In other words, injustice can affect different subjects (oneself or others, a single person or a group, relatives or strangers, etc.) by the action or omission of some instance (a person, a group, an institution, a spiritual being) in giving or withholding a good, in acting or not in a way that corresponds with the personal norm of the victim and/or the observer for this particular distribution.

What does this mean when applied to the context of close relationships and the distribution of roles among men and women in this context? It first and foremost means a restriction to certain objects of the distribution, roles and related issues. Secondly, each spouse can be actor and victim alike. Then, there are different rules for the resulting distribution, the allocation, and the allocation process, that can be preferred, applied, or not applied, by each spouse, with legal norms and equity being just two among many others. And finally there is a host of related cognitions that influence the consequences of experiencing injustice, i.e., emotions and the more general consequences such as marital satisfaction, general well-being, and the like.

2.1. Objects and Goods

In the context of close relationships among spouses and parents, the objects and goods in question are limited to the roles of spouses and parents, and the corresponding tasks of maintenaning the conjugal relationship, household management and child care, of breadwinning, and own recreation. Consequently, the distribution of roles and corresponding tasks should be studied (Reichle, 1994a; Steil & Turetsky, 1987). Theoretically, the distribution of these roles can range from perfectly egalitarian to perfectly traditional, the first meaning a distribution of fifty-fifty in each role and related task to each spouse, the latter, perfectly traditional, meaning a distribution of all breadwinning to the husband and all child care, household and maintenance of the conjugal relationship to the wife (as can be derived from sex-role behavior inventories, cf. Beere, 1990, for an overview).

Such distributions are usually changed at transition points in the family life cycle, such as marriage, the coming or going of children, changes in employment of each family member, and others (Aldous, 1978). Changes can be the addition of a new role to the former role budget or relinquishing an old role. The first case can be represented by adding the role of a spouse after marriage, or by adding the role of a parent after the birth of the first child. The second case, the reduction of a role, is associated with the empty nest after the last child has left home, or with retirement, or with the death of a spouse. Through these different roles and related tasks, different needs are met. Therefore, changes in the distribution of roles will almost inevitably lead to changes in the fulfillment of needs. Such changes in the fulfillment of needs could also be an issue of justice in close relationships, as the following interview sequence with a first-time mother illustrates: "I'm lonesome, you know. And I'm envious because I would like to be doing a lot of things [that he does] too. And I'd rather that he be home with me, you know, doing things together rather than, you know, doing them separately ..." (LaRossa & LaRossa, 1981, p. 174).

The distribution of roles and related tasks is but one of the many possible classifications of objects and goods to be distributed, withheld, or withdrawn in close relationships — money and work, power, obligations, rights of spouses, intimacy, restrictions and gains, the ways of treating each other, are others (for an overview, see the edition by Lerner & Mikula, 1994). As well as specific objects and goods, global distributions were studied, leaving open what the relevant objects and goods are. The most prominent examples of such an open approach are the global equity measures of Hatfield and co-workers, which asks subjects to rate their overall balance of contributions and rewards in relation to their partner's balance (see Sprecher & Schwartz, 1994, p. 14, for a review of global measures of equity in close relationships).

2.2. Actor, Victim, and Responsibility

In studies of justice in close relationships it appears to be obvious that casting the roles of actor and victim occurs between the two spouses. Not only the victim of injustice in a marital relationship has to be a member of the dyad, but also the actor. This holds true primarily for studies which are based upon an equity-theoretical background and can be seen as a direct consequence of this particular background: In its basic assumptions, equity theory deals with the comparisons of inputs and outputs by two members of a dyad.

By definition, the victim of injustice in a marital relationship has to be a member of the marital dyad, yet one might ask whether there are good reasons for limiting the actor's role to the other spouse. There might, at least, be the possibility that the spouse *can* be the actor, but he or she *does not necessarily* have to be. In a close relationship, injustice might be experienced that is not caused or not exclusively caused by the spouse; a great many other instances can be blamed for it, e.g. one's own parents, the mother-in-law, men in the aggregate, the press, the state, the law, etc. Therefore, when asking for the actor who has produced the injustice, different instances should be considered.

Besides this, the actor can be a variable, and not only a dichotomous one, but a continuous variable ranking from zero to full responsibility.

As Shaver (1985) elaborated, when someone caused something negative without having foreseen it, there will be no further attribution of responsibility. Provided foreseeability can be attributed, however, the degree of ascribed responsibility increases with the attribution of knowledge of the consequences, of intentionality, of absence of coercion, and of appreciation of moral wrongfulness. Responsibility for negative outcomes leads to blame unless there are acceptable justifications and/or excuses, as has been elaborated for the context of close relationships by Fincham & Bradbury (1987). Thus, different reactions to injustice among spouses may occur depending on the attributions: If there is only causality ascribed to the spouse, the reaction is much less pronounced than if responsibility is ascribed. Anger about the spouse vis-à-vis an experienced injustice correlates with an ascription of causality at $r = .40$, even more with an ascription of responsibility at $r = .67$ (Reichle, 1994b), and it should be to a greater extent in case blame is ascribed. Thus, in this particular context, the attribution of responsibility will be a better predictor for almost any consequences of the perception of injustice than the classical causal attributions (e.g., Rotter, 1966; Levenson, 1972).

Why is the actor important? What difference does the distinction between injustice and attributions make? Reactions to inequity should depend on attributions in general, and especially on attributions of responsibility (Reichle & Montada, 1994; Utne & Kidd, 1980): As will be shown in the following, injustice experienced in the context of a marital relationship will lead to completely different reactions and long-term consequences depending on who is blamed for it.

Let us first consider the case of injustice with an attribution of responsibility to the spouse: Imagine a young couple who faces many restrictions in their daily lives since the birth of their first child a few months ago. The most likely restrictions are the resignment of the wife's employment, a decrease in sexual contact among the spouses, a decrease in leisure time, an enourmous sleep deficit, and others (Cowan et al., 1985; LaRossa & LaRossa, 1981; Reichle, 1994a). These restrictions can be evaluated in terms of justice and they can be attributed to someone. If they are evaluated as unjust and attributed to the spouse, negative emotions concerning the spouse will be experienced. As reported in a study of 190 first-time parents in their third month of parenthood by Reichle & Montada (1994), the *interaction of the experience of injustice with an ascription of responsibility to the spouse* predicts negative emotions about the spouse, and these negative emotions predict marital dissatisfaction. Injustice alone is a much less powerful predictor of anger, disappointment, and outrage about the spouse than it is in interaction with an attribution of responsibility to the spouse.

As a second case, one could imagine the same injustice with a different attribution of responsibility, since such an injustice does not necessarily need to be ascribed to the spouse. In this case, the consequences should be completely different: As has been reported for the case of relative deprivation in groups, collectively experienced injustice can lead to collective action (Martin, Brickman, & Murray, 1984). The same phenomenon might occur in a marital dyad if a mutually experienced injustice is attributed to an instance outside the dyad. In this case, it is likely that the couple responds collectively. It is similar if the injustice happens to only one of the two, but the other takes the role of the loyal observer and feels obliged to help. In both cases, the experience of injustice could even have stabilizing effects on the relationship, and strengthen it in the fight against adversity or in the shared experience of injustice. In the above mentioned study, 55% of the 108 first-time mothers thought a particular restriction was unjust, but only 35% blamed their husband for the restriction. Of the first-time fathers, 29% reported feelings of injustice vis-à-vis a particular restriction, but only 22% blamed their wife for it. The correlation between the experience of injustice and an attribution of responsibility to the spouse was not higher than $r = .43$ (Reichle, 1994a, p. 214). So, who else and what else can be responsible? In men and in women, most of the responsibility for the restriction was assigned to oneself, and the second most to other instances outside the dyadic relationship, and only the least amount to the spouse (Reichle, 1994a). If an experienced injustice is not ascribed to the spouse, there are statistically different effects: With a zero-order correlation of $r = -.46$, injustice is significantly correlated with marital satisfaction; when controlling for the variable of ascription of responsibility to the spouse the correlation is reduced to a first-order partial correlation of $r = -.35$ (Reichle, 1993). This means that in the prediction of marital satisfaction there is a considerable amount of shared variance between experienced injustice and responsibility attributed to the spouse. If injustice without responsibility of the spouse is considered, the correlation with marital satisfaction is reduced drastically, i.e., injustice attributed to the spouse is much closer related to lower marital satisfaction than injustice attributed to other instances.

Another illustration about the importance of the facet of attribution of responsibility comes from research on women's reactions to various unjust distributions. Women have many times been reported to not react in a way known from other deprived subjects, to not protest, to not divorce, to not feel outraged, resentful, angry, or disappointed, although objectively they are relatively deprived (Croghan, 1991; Crosby et al., 1989; Steil, 1994). It might be the attribution of responsibility that makes the difference. If responsibility is attributed to an employer, to the spouse, or to a particular person involved in the injustice, the reactions expected but not observed should occur. If, on the other hand, these women do not blame their spouses, employees, or other persons for the unequal share, although they feel themselves treated unjustly, (and the results cited indicate that they might not), but rather accept justifications, excuses, or even do not ascribe responsibility, they should not feel treated unjustly by these instances and therefore not show reactions to unjust treatment.

2.3. Rules and Norms

As a moral value, justice has a prescriptive component with a variety of possible rules and a selection of personal norms or principles that a person could expect as norms of just distributions in various contexts. Such rules can be legally prescribed or they can be of informal character; they may concern the process of distribution, the criteria to be applied in distributions (sometimes called allocation rules), or the resulting distribution itself, as will be outlined in the follwing sections.

Before turning to these aspects in detail, it should be noted that concepts of justice underly development. If different people were asked to judge different distributions, individuals could be encountered who, at the very extreme, did not have developed any sense of justice or injustice in a particular context, or even in general. On the other side of the developmental continuum, in analogy to moral development in terms of Piaget and Kohlberg, there might be individuals with highly differentiated concepts (e.g., Kohlberg, & Lickona, 1986; Piaget, 1965). Such a difference might reflect different stages of individual moral development (Montada, 1980). Besides this, distributions are certainly based on other rules or norms, such as utility, economy, tradition, or others (see Harsanyi, 1991, for a critical discussion). In the special case of distributions in close relationships, this is reflected by the fact that, for a long time, these distributions were not considered matters of justice at all (cf. Mikula & Lerner, 1994). Rather, raising the question of justice was considered an indicator of a deteriorating relationship (Kirchler, 1989), from "self-sacrifice" to "formal contest" and even "fight" (Desmarais & Lerner, 1994). When asking subjects to rate different distributions, we should be aware of these aspects and provide the respective alternatives for them. Such alternatives could be other rules or norms, or, at least, the information that a certain distribution is not considered a matter of justice.

Another distinction seems in order in this place. As psychologists, we are mainly concerned with the personal norms individuals have about just distributions, and less with the legal norms that could exist for these distributions. Legal injustice arises when a distribution is different from the distribution one is legally entitled to. If we consider the factual distributions among men and women, we might find many legal injustices with respect to income, work, status, retirement benefits, and the like, all being unequally distributed between men and women (references see above). Yet frequently, there seem to be discrepancies between legal norms and personal norms, about what one *is entitled to* and what one *feels to be entitled to*. Uninformedness, stage of moral development, socialization, and coping are but a few explanations for this discrepancy. The history of equal rights' legislation in Germany might serve as an example: While the post-war German statute of 1949 prescribed equal entitlement for both women and men, many subordinate laws dating from pre-war times were still being adapted and therefore not abolished (cf. Mitleger & Rathgeber, 1988). This adaptation took as long as 44 years and was finally completed with the legislation concerning the name of married spouses in 1993. It is highly unlikely that many citizens have followed this process in detail, although they were concerned not only by their own rights, but also as socializing agents for later generations. Other individuals might have established their own norms in the course of their personal moral development (in terms of Schwartz, 1978), aware of the laws or not, and last but not least, by being confronted not only with norms, but also with the possibilities of their realization. Therefore, studies of transitions seem to be the royal road in justice research: It is a fact that the probability to observe reactions to injustice without much coping should be highest, when new distributions have just occurred.

There is no need to consider discrepancies between the legal Ought and the individual Is unjust as long as they do not violate the personal norms of an individual. Or, in other words, as long as the legal norm is not the personal norm of an individual, inequalities like the ones cited in the beginning of the chapter must not be considered unjust. When asked to rate the egalitarian distribution of a fictive couple ("...they aim for a distribution of responsibilities that is at equal as possible. She is equally responsible for family income, household, child care and maintaining their relationship as he is.") which comes the closest to the purport of the law of the past four decades, ten percent of the men and six percent of the women (of 82 men and 108 women from West Germany, all cohabitating, in the third month after transition to parenthood) said that this distribution was unjust. When asked to rate the procedural norm of the men's casting-vote ("... they decide according to the principle 'the head of the family has to decide'"), two percent of the women versus six percent of the men regarded this procedure as just (Reichle & Gefke, 1995). So, even with the most difficult item, the question about a norm and an instance that has legally been abolished, there exist minorities with seemingly different norms.

What are the rules? In the beginnings of justice research, with equity and exchange theories in the 1960s, there was just one all encompassing principle: equity. Gradually, more principles were identified, with a total of 17 principles collected by Reis (1984). At the same time, different classifications of principles were developed (see Törnblom, 1992, for an overview). For our purpose, a distinction between the following three categories of principles might be helpful: allocation rules, procedural rules, and rules concerning the resulting distribution. Allocation rules concern the characteristics of the potential recipient that are relevant for the distribution; procedural rules (Lind & Tyler, 1988; Thibaut & Walker, 1975) concern the process by which decisions about allocations are made; distributional rules concern the resulting distribution itself (similar to what Brickman, Folger, Goode, & Schul, 1981, call macro justice).

(1) Allocation rules

The most prominent allocation principle of equity involves proportionality of one's social rewards to one's costs and investments (Homans, 1961). When applied to the context of close relationships, the perspective of the other spouse's inputs and outcomes is added and compared to the own balance (Hatfield & Traupman, 1981; Walster, Walster & Berscheid, 1978). If the comparison of the two balances results in the perception of inequity, the theory predicts distress and dissatisfaction. Hence the rule is equity in balances. The relevant characteristic for the distribution is the amount of a person's input.

In the alternative framework of the multiprinciple approach, equity is not considered as the sole principle of justice but rather as a rule among others; this rule is sometimes labeled as proportionality principle, sometimes as merit principle. Another prominent principle is equality, meaning an equal distribution regardless of inputs. Applied to distributions in close relationships, equality would be represented in the perfectly egalitarian distribution where each spouse has an equal share of the objects and goods in question, independently of inputs (as could be income in the domain of breadwinning, or quality of work performed in any domain).

The third most frequently cited principle is the one of need, favoring the person whose need is greatest in the distribution. According to the need principle, a couple distributes its objects and goods in a way that each gets what she or he needs most for her or his development, well-being, health, etc..

What do we know about these three different allocation principles in close relationships? First, there seem to be differences in the preference for one or another principle depending upon the context of a distribution: Contrary to equity, equality was seen to be associated with interpersonal harmony and status congruence, an need should have the closest association to caring-oriented relationships with an emphasis on the well-being or positive development of the members of the relationship (Deutsch, 1975; Mikula, 1980; Sampson, 1975; for empirical evidence, see Schmitt & Montada, 1982; Schwinger, 1980). The third principle, equity, is associated with the goal of economic utility, and with relationships of rather competitive and impersonal character, since "the basis of mutual and self-respect is undermined because equity suggests that the different participants in a relationship do not have the same value" (Steil, 1994, p. 238, citing Deutsch, 1985, and Lerner & Whitehead, 1980). In a between-subjects design, Steil & Makowski (1989) assessed the context specifity and differential feelings related to the outcomes of each principle. In this study, individuals were more likely to associate the need principle with incidents related to nurturance or personal development, while equity as well as equality were more likely to be related to incidents concerned with the allocation of responsibilities. In comparison to equity, equality was associated with more positive feelings about the decision, about oneself and the partner, and with less negative feelings toward the partner. Contrary to expectations, the most positive and least negative feelings were not associated with need; rather, with equality. Following Mikula (1980), the authors assume that the application of the need principle is a source of tension: "When allocations according to need cannot be reciprocated, especially among those of otherwise relatively equal status (e.g., two adults as compared to an adult and child), the use of need emphasizes the differences in dependency between the giver and the receiver" (Steil & Makowski, 1989, p. 136).

This is in line with results from a study by Reichle & Gefke (1995) with 190 first-time parents in the third month of parenthood. In this study, respondents were asked to rate the justice of different principles for allocating rights and obligations among women and men. Equality was found to be superior to need, with 83% of the subjects rating equality as just and 73% rating need as just. The percentage of men who reported to practise equality and need in their everyday-decisions was about equal, while the percentage of women who reported practising equality and need was between seven and ten percent less.

When asking couples why they distribute their roles, tasks, objects, goods, obligations, rights, etc. the way they do, the answer was frequently that one should take advantage of tradition. Tradition could be considered another effective allocation rule in the context of close relationships. If a couple decides to distribute the traditional way, this might reflect a utilitarian attitude as is described by Lerner & Whitehead (1980) for unit relationships. Applied to the distributions a couple makes, it might be of high utility to take the traditional route, since this means to take maximal advantage of the given societal infrastructure. In the study mentioned above, 7% of the women and 9% of the men rated tradition a just principle for distributions among women and men. The percentage of men who indicated to distribute in a traditional way was about the same. With women, the percentage of those who distributed traditionally was about twice as high as the percentage of those who had rated the norm as just (Reichle & Gefke, 1995).

In sum, large majorities of between seven and more than eight out of ten respondents, irrespective of gender, endorsed equality and need, and a minority of under ten percent with significantly more men than women endorsed tradition. The percentage of women who rated equality, need, bargaining, and lottery as just was higher than the percentage of women who practised these principles, and a higher percentage of women indicated to practise tradition than those who actually rated tradition a just principle. In men, the percentages of endorsers and the percentages of those practising the norm in question were about equal. This, however, does not mean that men were more consistent in their practise than women, since endorsing a norm must not mean to practise it. This aspect, consistency, will be considered later. A final word on the normative character of allocational rules seems to be in order: Instead of asked to rate the degree of justice of the rules discussed, respondents were given the alternative of indicating whether this rule, in their opinion, had nothing to do with justice. With the allocation rules, between six and 17% chose this alternative. This is to say that for significant minorities justice does not seem to be an issue in their everyday distributions with their spouse.

(2) Procedural rules

In her 1991 theoretical paper, Thompson comes to the conclusion that "women often accept the justifications because they like it that their husbands consult them, even if outcomes are to the advantage of husbands. ... In sum, although the distribution of outcomes is unfair, women may not sense the injustice because they accept as appropriate the participatory process by which the outcomes were created" (see also Cohen, 1985). This leads us to the question of procedural justice, namely, the fairness of the rules regulating the allocation process (Leventhal, 1980); a question that arises in cases of disputable allocations only and which is separate from the question of allocation (Thibaut & Walker, 1975). So far, procedural justice has been studied in the context of law, in the political arena, and in organizations (cf. Lind & Tyler, 1988). In most of these studies, an important variable was the amount of control assigned to the individual. In the ground-breaking research by Thibaut and Walker (1975), the amount of third-party control was considered one of the most important variables, and this selection mirrors the contexts studied — in law, politics, business, and other formal organizations, third-party control is one of *the* issues.

This is different in the context of close relationships and families. It is socially rather undesirable to have and show conflicts over distributions in close relationships, and, therefore, it will be unlikely that a couple seeks third-party control in the process of distributing roles, tasks, obligations, rights, etc. Thus, no procedure reported from the contexts of law, politics, and formal organizations involving third-party control can be applied to this context.

Among the few who have studied procedural justice in the family context, Fry and Leventhal were among the first (Fry & Leventhal, 1979, reported in Lind & Tyler, 1988). The rules studied were products of analytically elaborated dimensions of fairness in procedures. Similarly, a study by Barrett-Howard & Tyler (1986) used scenarios with systematically varied dimensions. Opposed to this strategy, I shall present some procedural rules that were derived from everyday life observation and family legislation. The guiding question leading to these rules was: Which procedural rules could be important when it comes to the distribution of objects and goods in close relationships, such as roles, tasks, obligations, or rights?

First and foremost, there is the ideal of bargaining, which under certain circumstances can be considered a highly democratic procedure: In contrast to many other procedures in conflict resolutions, there is no third-party control in this procedure and a maximum of participants' control. If compared with four other procedures (which all had more or less third-party control), bargaining was the most preferred principle as long as there were no standards for judging the merits of rival claims, no temporal urgency to resolve the dispute, and a cooperative orientation within the group (Thibaut & Walker, 1975). In a study by Gefke and myself, bargaining was the favorite procedural principle with an equal 93% of both genders rating it as a just principle. When it comes to the actual practise, however, an equal amount of men report practising bargaining while about ten percent less women reported applying this procedure (Reichle & Gefke, 1995).

One of the oldest and simplest procedures in conflict resolutions is the lottery or balloting. In contrast to any other procedures, in balloting there is absolutely no control by the disputants, justice is found in the equality of absence of control. Alternating solutions over equal periods of time can be considered a variation of this principle. An application of alternation can be found in Scandinavian and German legislation about the parental leave during the first years of parenthood, with father and mother being equally eligible for the leave as well as having the given right to alternate this leave. When asked about the justice of lottery in close relationships, 24% of the men and 35% of the women said it was just, but only 17% reported to use this procedure in their daily distributions (Reichle & Gefke, 1995).

A third principle for the ruling of conflict in close relationships is the casting-vote with male privilege. A rather informal account of this principle comes from a popular Mexican mariachi song, saying "Con dinero o sin dinero, hago siempre lo que quiero, Y mi palabra es la ley" (Whether I have money or not, I always do what I want, and my word is the law). On more formal grounds, German legislation might not be the only one with an institutionalization of this principle. Although gradually abolished from 1949 to 1993,[1] this principle is still effective, especially among members of the older generation. In a study with 190 German new parents aged 18 to 42 years, the casting-vote principle was rated as just by two percent of the women and six percent of the men. This was the only principle of the ones studied with about an equal amount of endorsing and practising by both genders (Reichle & Gefke, 1995).

To summarize, bargaining as a procedural rule was found just by the great majority of the responding spouses, followed by a minority of between one-fourth of the males and one-third of the females who found

[1] Until 1958, the husband was given the right to decide about all matters concerning the marriage, the woman's property, employment, and decisions about the children. Until 1958, the wife was legally obliged to run the household, however, this was liberated in 1958 by the addition of the woman's right to employed work "if it doesn't conflict with her obligations in marriage and family". In 1977, this restriction was abolished (cf. Mitleger & Rathgeber, 1988). A final adaptation was the legislation concerning the surnames of married spouses and their children in 1993.

lottery just, and finally another minority of up to five percent who endorsed the casting-vote principle.[1] Significantly more women than men rated bargaining and lottery as just and casting-vote as unjust. The amounts of endorsement and practise were equal in casting-vote for both genders, and almost equal in bargaining for men. The percentage of women who rated bargaining as just was ten percent higher than the percentage of women who indicated to practise bargaining. In both genders, lottery was rated as just by between 8 to 17 percent more than it was indicated to be practised. The normative character of the rules in question was assigned by 60% to 95%, or, in other words, between 5% to 40% indicated that the rule in question for them was not a question of justice; with a maximum at the lottery principle and a minimum at bargaining. Thus, in this particular context, lottery seems to be a rather unlikely procedure.

(3) Distributional rules

When allocation and procedure are being decided upon, it remains open what the resulting distribution will look like. Imagine a newlywed couple distributing their roles and tasks: In a bargaining-like procedure, they decide that roles and tasks should be distributed according to the need principle. Each spouse has the same amount of time to spend with obligations, tasks, and leisure. The resulting distribution, however, is different from their ideals, either too traditional, or too equal.

The resulting distributions among a couple seem to have two dimensions at least: equality vs inequality and conformity vs nonconformity with the existing societal standards. Perfectly equal means the distribution that was named perfectly egalitarian before, with every spouse holding exactly the same amount of every distributable item. The opposite pole is the perfectly unequal distribution, with every spouse being highly specialized on mutually exclusive items. On a metadimension, however, perfectly unequal can be equal — if one imagines the perfectly specialized distribution with every spouse having own areas of responsibilities (e.g., one is responsible for breadwinning, the other for household maintenance, etc.), both shares can be equal in amount of time necessary for the fulfillment of duties and tasks, both shares can leave

---

[1] Social desirability was assessed by a German version of the Marlowe-Crowne-scale (Crowne & Marlowe, 1960; Lück & Timaeus, 1969). With the exception of the men's ratings of practising lottery, there were no significant effects of social desirability on the ratings of justice and practise. Those scoring high on social desirability indicated to practise the lottery principle less than those scoring low on social desirability.

equal amounts of leisure time, both shares can be equally respected, etc. The second dimension, conformity vs nonconformity, is not orthogonal to the first one. While there are no degrees of freedom for casting roles in the egalitarian distribution, the specialized distribution does not automatically dictate the who does what. Rather, specialized can mean the traditional distribution described above, with all breadwinning to the husband and all child care, household, and maintenance of the conjugal relationship to the wife. Specialized can also mean the opposite, i.e., the single-earner wife and the primary caregiving father, a distribution practised by not more than one percent (see Statistisches Bundesamt, 1991, for data from Germany).

Empirically, there is a rather consistent inconsistency between the amounts of those endorsing the norms and the amounts of those who indicate practising them. In her review of the literature, Steil (1994) reports that 57% of adult citizens in the United States prefer an egalitarian distribution, with between 2% to 20% to actually practising in an egalitarian way. Representative data from West Germany show that 70% of the respondents favor the egalitarian solution in caring for small children (Institut für Praxisorientierte Sozialforschung Mannheim, 1992), but in more than 98% of the cases it is the woman who stays home or cuts back her employment (Statistisches Bundesamt, 1991). Most of the shopping, cooking, and cleaning was done in one-half to two-thirds of the families by women, while equality in these tasks was reported by 13% to 34%, depending on the task (Institut für Praxisorientierte Sozialforschung Mannheim, 1992). In a study of 190 first-time parents, an equal two-thirds of both sexes opted for an egalitarian distribution, but only 22% of the women and 28% of the men reported to really distribute responsibilities and goods that way. The specialized distribution, in which each spouse has his or her own domains of responsibilities, was rated just by 55% of the women and 66% of the men, and claimed to be practised by an equal 63% of both genders. The nonconform variant of the specialized distribution was rated as just by 38% of the women and 32% of the men, and reported to be practised by a maximum of four percent (all data from Reichle & Gefke, 1995).

To summarize what has been reported about preferences and practise of distributions among spouses, the egalitarian distribution with a maximally equal share of all rights and obligations between the spouses is the most favored mode, at least for women (and in some studies also for men), followed by the specialized distribution and then the variant of the nonconform specialized distribution. With men, there is no clear majority for a certain distribution. If asked about several alternatives independently, an equal amount of men opt for the egalitarian and the specialized distribution, with a considerable overlap of two-thirds that judge both principles as just (in women, this overlap was about equal in size). Significantly less men than women rated the nonconform specialized distribution as just. The amounts of endorsement and practise were equal only in men concerning the specialized distribution. In all other distributions, there were substantial discrepancies between the rates of endorsers and those of practitioners — most pronounced in the nonconform specialized distribution, and secondmost in the egalitarian distribution, with far more endorsers than practitioners. The opposite was true for women in the specialized distribution, where the rate of endorsers was lower than the rate of those who indicated practising that distribution. Thus, in the egalitarian or the nonconform specialized distribution, there are much higher percentages of justice ratings than of practise ratings: Two-thirds find the egalitarian distribution just, but only one-fifth to one-fourth claim practising this sort of distribution. The nonconform specialized distribution was almost never practised but rated just by around one-third of the subjects. Finally, the distributions presented posed the most problems to the respondents when it came to the question of justice: With between 18% and 52%, significant proportions of the respondents indicated that the distributions in question were not a matter of justice to them — the most at the nonconform distribution, and the least at the specialized distribution. Thus, for a majority, a nonconform distribution among spouses with a primary caregiving father and a primary breadwinning mother is not a question of justice. Rather, such a distribution might be dictated by utility, necessity, or other principles, with the unemployed or student husband of an employed wife taking primary responsibility for child care and household.

2.4. Normative Patterns

The patterns of preferred norms are gender specific (see table 1). The endorsement of the egalitarian distribution in women is correlated with a preference for the specialized nonconform distribution, and a preference for equality. For men, endorsement of the egalitarian distribution is correlated with a preference for equality, and a rejection of tradition and casting-vote. Endorsement of a specialized distribution yields no significant correlations with any other distributional forms — which is not surprising, since the direction of the specialization is not specified. It is specified, however, in the phrasing of the nonconform specialized distribution, and the endorsement of this distribution in women is correlated with a preference for equity. For men, a preference for equality

Table 1: Correlations Between Norms of Justice[a]

	Egalitarian	Specialized	Non-conform	Equality	Need	Tradition	Lottery	Bargaining
Women:								
Specialized	.12							
Nonconform	.45**	.28						
Equality	.51**	.01	.47**					
Need	−.16	.23	−.15	−.11				
Tradition	−.13	.02	−.26	−.38**	−.06			
Lottery	−.06	.05	−.08	−.01	.04	.12		
Bargaining	.19	.22	.13	.21*	−.03	−.05	.03	
Casting-vote	.15	.01	.01	.04	−.02	.42**	.17	.02
Men:								
Specialized	−.02							
Nonconform	.29	.10						
Equality	.35**	.02	.17					
Need	.05	−.11	.06	−.21				
Tradition	−.42**	.06	−.24	.03				
Lottery	−.11	.02	.34	−.04	.24	−.02		
Bargaining	.18	.16	.08	.29*	.12	−.13	.20	
Casting-vote	−.55**	.03	−.23	−.29*	−.01	.57**	−.03	−.16

[a] $36 \leq n(\text{females}) \leq 92$; $31 \leq n$ (males) ≤ 74. Ratings of (in)justice, scale ("If my spouse would propose this model to me, I would find it ...") ranging from 0 ("this has nothing to do with justice") resp. 1 ("completely injust") to 6 ("completely just"), with all ratings of 0 excluded.

is negatively correlated with tradition and positively with bargaining. For women, a preference for equality is also positively correlated with bargaining and negatively with casting-vote. For women, tradition is positively correlated with casting-vote and negatively with equality. For men, tradition is also positively correlated with casting-vote and negatively correlated with the egalitarian distribution. For both genders, need as well as lottery do not significantly correlate with any other principle.

By means of factor analysis, the following patterns of normative preferences are obtained: A three-factor solution of the women's preferences accounting for 65% of the variance of all preference items yields a first factor with high loadings on the nonconform specialized distribution, equality, the egalitarian distribution, and with a negative loading, tradition. The second factor is represented by the specialized distribution, bargaining, and need; the third factor by lottery and casting-vote. The first factor could be interpreted as the liberal attitude, the second one as the conservative attitude, and the third one as a victim-like attitude, externally controlled, with a preference for those two rules that for women contain the least personal impact. For men, the three-factor solution accounts for 59% of the variance of all prefer-

ence items. A first factor with equality, the egalitarian and the nonconform distribution could be interpreted as the representation of a liberal
attitude. A second factor contains tradition, casting-vote, and with
negative loadings, need and lottery, and a third factor contains the
specialized distribution only (with a factor structure coefficient for
bargaining of under .50). Thus, for men, the liberal factor does not
contain the rejection of tradition, and the conservative factor is represented by the sole principle of specialization. The third factor in
women, interpreted as a representation of external control, is mirrored
in men as the decidedly priviledged, with the right of a casting-vote, of
tradition, and a rejection of lottery and need. For men, bargaining is not
represented in this solution. Explorative analyses with other solutions
show, however, that in both genders, bargaining almost always appears
on the same factor as the specialized distribution.

2.5. From Ought to Is: Norms and Practise

If it comes down from Ought to Is, four different types of consis-
tency-inconsistency can be observed: First, there is the consistency
between the norm one holds for just and one's own practise — these are
the persons who practise what they think is just; i.e., consistent practise.
The second form of consistency, consistent rejection, is between a norm
one thinks is unjust and not practising it. The first form of inconsistency
is not practising what one rates as just, and the second form is practising
what one rates as unjust. Table 2 summarizes the different constellations.

The highest percentages with majorities of consistent practise can
be found in the two allocation principles of equality and need, in the
distributional principle of bargaining, and in the specialized distribution, with consistently higher percentages of men than women indicating that they practise what they think is just. Majorities of consistent
rejections are reported with the allocational rule of tradition, and with
the distributional rules of lottery and casting-vote, with higher percentages of men in two of these three cases. Majorities in the inconsistency
condition of not practising what one finds just can be found in the
egalitarian and in the nonconform specialized distribution, with consistently higher percentages of women indicating to not practise what they
rate as just. Only minorities report practising what they decidedly find
unjust, with a maximum of nine percent of women and of eight percent
of men at the specialized distribution, and of eight percent of the women
at tradition. Thus, the rates of reported consistency is almost always
higher in men, as well in doing what they find just as in not doing what

Table 2: Percentages of Reported Consistencies/Inconsistencies between
Justice Ratings and Application of Different Principles[a]

Principle		Consistency		Inconsistency	
		just & practised	unjust & not pract.	just & not pract.	unjust & practised[b]
Equality	females	77	2	19	1
	males	83	1	13	3
Need	females	64	11	23	2
	males	66	22	8	4
Tradition	females	5	84	2	8
	males	7	88	3	2
Bargaining	females	86	1	13	0
	males	91	1	6	1
Lottery	females	24	47	29	0
	males	20	60	20	0
Casting-Vote	females	0	97	2	1
	males	3	94	3	0
Egalitarian	females	30	6	64	0
	males	37	10	53	0
Specialized	females	58	18	16	9
	males	63	12	18	8
Nonconform specialized	females	2	21	77	0
	males	7	38	55	0

[a]$52 \leq n_{(females)} \leq 101; 42 \leq n_{(males)} \leq 78$. Ratings of (in)justice, scale ("If my spouse would propose this model to me, I would find it ...") ranging from 0 ("this has nothing to do with justice") resp. 1 ("completely unjust") to 6 ("completely just"), with all ratings of 0 excluded. Ratings of current practise, scale ("This model corresponds to our current distribution...") ranging from 1 ("not at all") to 6 ("exactly").

they find unjust. In women, the discrepancies between norm and practise almost always seem to be larger, which is partly due to their more
liberal attitudes concerning their Oughts, and partly due to their more
negative views of their Is: As has been reported before, significantly more
women than men opt for a nonconform distribution, against tradition
and against casting-vote. When it comes to their Is, significantly less
women than men report to really distribute in an egalitarian way.
Inspections of the data on the distributions practised indicate that the
female view is the more realistic: Women who report practising in an
egalitarian way report significantly less differences between their own
and their partner's amount of child care and household chores than
women who report not practising according to egalitarian ideals (how-

ever, the respective difference between own and spouses' employment hours in those who report somewhat egalitarian practise is not significantly different from the self-partner-difference reported by those who indicate to not practising an egalitarian way). On the other side, the only significant difference between men who report practising an egalitarian way and men who report not practising that way is in the sharing of child care, with the first ones yielding less a difference between their own and their wife's share than the latter ones. [1]

3. Is-Ought-Discrepancies: Do They Matter?

Much justice research in the area of close relationships has been devoted to the question of justice and relationship satisfaction. That equity be associated with rather competitive relationships fits with the judgmental connotations that were mentioned above when it comes to the question of equity in close relationships. On the other side, there is some empirical evidence for a positive, although weak relationship between perceived equity and relationship satisfaction, at least cross-sectionally (see Mikula, 1992; VanYperen & Buunk, 1990 for overviews). These somewhat contradictory valuations might be explained by moderating variables, like different stages of relationships, with irrelevance or even rejection of equity considerations during the romantic stage of a relationship and equity becoming more important in later stages. Or, similar, as has been reported by Buunk and VanYperen (1991), the relationship between equity and relationship satisfaction might be moderated by individual differences in exchange orientation, with equity being predictive for relationship satisfaction only in individuals high in exchange orientation.

In her review on equality and entitlement in marriage, Steil (1994, p. 243) concludes that "Despite the methodological limitations, ... more equal relationships were characterized by more mutually supportive communication, less manipulative forms of influence, and greater sexual

---

[1] For women who indicated at least to some extent to practise according to an egalitarian distribution, the mean of the differences between own and spouse's share of household chores was $M_{Diff(egalit)}=2.6$, for women who indicated to, at least to some extent, not practise according to an egalitarian distribution, the respective mean was $M_{Diff(nonegalit)}=3.4$ (p(t)1-tailed=.00), similarly for child care, $M_{Diff(egalit)}=3.3$ vs $M_{Diff(nonegalit)}=3.8$ (p(t)1-tailed=.02). For men who indicated at least to some extent to practise according to an egalitarian distribution, the mean of the differences between own and spouse's share of child care was $M_{Diff(egalit)}=-.91$, for women who indicated at least to some extent not to practise according to an egalitarian distribution, the respective mean was $M_{Diff(nonegalit)}=-1.47$ (p(t)1-tailed=.02).

and marital satisfaction. Greater equality was also consistently associated with less dysphoric symptomatology for wives who were usually the underbenefited when relationships were unequal." The methodological limitations mentioned mainly concern the validity of equality. Thus, inequity does not seem to be an injustice for everybody, same as inequality does not seem to be an injustice for everybody, but given some validity of what has been operationalized as injustice, the experience of injustice in close relationships at least seems to correlate with relationship satisfaction.

But how are injustice and relationship satisfaction related? After what has been said before, injustice must be of some importance for the individual. One way of assuring subjective importance is by studying emotions (Arnold, 1960; Lazarus, 1975). If in reaction to an unjustice there are emotions to observe, we can feel to be on somewhat safe grounds about the validity of the injustice studied. In the following, the experience of injustice, attribution of responsibility and several reactions to it will be linked to several emotions on the basis of cognitive emotion theory (Averill, 1978, 1980; Frijda, 1986, 1987; Lazarus, 1975; Montada, 1989; Ortony, Clore, & Collins, 1988; Roseman, 1984; Scherer, 1984; Smith & Ellsworth, 1985; Weiner, 1986). On the basis of the emotions thereby predicted, different predictions of relationship satisfaction will be worked out later.

3.1. Emotional Reactions to Injustice

For the socially and morally educated, inconsistencies between own norms, be it to help, not to be aggressive, or to distribute in a just way and the respective behavior should be a rather noxious state and require resolution. Thus, as has been stated long ago by theorists in moral development as well as in equity, the experience of injustice is distressing and motivating, and it may lead to various reactions depending upon one's role: The responsible harmdoer could fear retaliation and feel a threat to self-esteem, the observer could sense his/her own vulnerability, the victim could feel deprivation, a loss in self-esteem, derogation, stigmatization (Steil & Slochower, 1985, for an overview). The observer as well as the harmdoer could feel empathy (Hoffman, 1982). Finally, attempts to restore justice will be observed, objectively or psychologically (Walster, Walster, & Berscheid, 1978). As is resumed by Steil and Slochower (1985), on the side of the harmdoer and the observer, such attempts are helping, assuming responsibility, compensation, and distortion, blaming, and derogation. The victim could attempt to secure restitution, to retaliate against the harmdoer, to gain self-enhancement by minimizing or even denying their lot, or to regain a sense of control by means of self-blame. All these reactions were shown to be accompanied or even motivated by emotions — fear and anxiety, guilt, anger, moral outrage, disappointment, disdain, and sadness (Martin, Brickman & Murray, 1984; Mikula, 1987; Montada, Schmitt & Dalbert, 1986; Montada & Schneider, 1990, Reichle & Montada, 1994).

Most of these reactions to the experience of injustice are resumed from other contexts. Since empirical evidence from the context of close relationships is rather sparse, the application of the reactions reviewed is largely of hypothetical nature.

3.1.1. The Victim

This person, deprived, could either feel anger, outrage, disappointment at the instance responsible for the injustice, or sadness and regret. If the spouse is ascribed some responsibility for the experienced injustice, i.e., the spouse is perceived as the harmdoer: anger, outrage, and disappointment will be directed towards him or her.

If there is no ascription of responsibility to the spouse, the victim of the injustice will experience sadness (Reichle, 1994a; Reichle & Montada, 1994). If responsibility for the injustice is ascribed to oneself, negative emotions will be directed towards onself. If an instance outside the conjugal relationship is made responsible for the injustice, the victim's anger and similar emotions will be directed towards this instance.

3.1.2. The Bystanding Observer

When it comes to injustice in close relationships, the role of the victim's spouse will either be the one of harmdoer or the one of bystander, less likely the one of the observer, as there is a close relationship between the spouses. More so than observers, bystanders have to assume some responsibility. To illustrate this case, imagine a husband observing his wife to suffer from a distribution of roles among them that she herself has worked out before, as is often the case around family life transitions. In practise, she gradually recognizes injustice, with herself assuming more obligations, less attractive ones and less valued ones than he does.

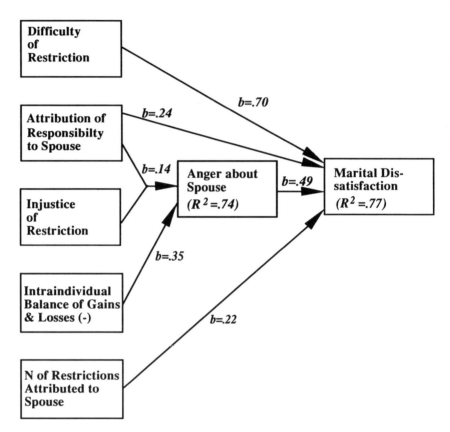

Figure 1. Prediction of marital satisfaction in men three months after the birth of a first child.

If she has worked out the distribution with the feeling of having no degrees of freedom, she won't assume responsibility. Maybe she can identify a responsible instance outside the relationship, e.g. her mother or mother-in law who unexpectedly had decided not to help with some obligations. In this case of outside attribution of responsibility, the spouse's role is the one of a more or less compassionate observer. If the spouse shares the perspectice of the victim, he should feel empathy. If the injustice to him seems to be not compensable, his belief in a just world could come into play, similarly, if he ascribes some responsibility for the injustice to his wife, with the consequence of derogation and disdain as was reported from other contexts (Lerner, 1970, 1981; Lerner & Miller, 1978; Lerner, Miller & Holmes, 1976). Finally, if there is some probability for the injustice to happen to the husband, too, defensive attribution as another motivational distortion could lead to similar results (Shaver, 1970).

Still another case is the victim assuming responsibility for the injustice — the wife in the example has worked out the distribution as a decision among alternatives, she has foreseen some of the consequences and, negligently, has taken the risk. In this case, it will depend on past actions and omissions by the spouse whether he blames his wife or feels compassion, pity, or the like: If he had tried to prevent the solution and with it, the injustice, and she has been negligent, blame should be maximal. If, on the other hand, he admits having been negligent too, compassion will be more likely.

3.1.3. The Harmdoer

Harmdoers have the alternatives to either assume responsibility or to deny it, to distort, blame, or derogate. With an assumption of responsibility, guilt will be experienced and compensation will be sought.

3.2. Emotions and Relationship Satisfaction

Depending upon whether or not there is a responsible instance other than the victim and whether there is a chance of compensation and the like, we expect anger as an attempt for an objective restoration of justice (Averill, 1978), or anger directed towards oneself, or simply sadness. In a next step, the experience of compensation is crucial. If it takes place then things are set right. If not, things still have to be set right, with various distortions and symptomatology as reported by Steil & Slochower (1985) being one possibility. Other possibilities are summed up in Rusbult's "exit-voice-loyalty-neglect model" (1987), with all except the one of voice bearing a high probability of a future deterioration of the relationship.

Anger, disappointment, and moral outrage on the side of the victim towards the responsible spouse affect marital satisfaction (Reichle & Montada, 1994), even over and above a host of other variables (Reichle, 1994a). Figure 1 gives an example of these relationships. It shows a model of the prediction of men's marital satisfaction in dependence of restrictions experienced three months after the birth of their first child, of

Table 3: Comparisons Between Still Cohabitating and Separated Couples Over a period of Four and a Half Years (Mann-Whitney U-Tests)

Predictor	Mean Rank	n	Group	U	p (2tld.)
Injustice of	61.90	120	Together		
Restriction (t_1)	103.50	8	separated	168.0	.0020
Responsibility of	61.82	120	Together		
spouse(t_1)	104.63	8	separated	159.0	.0015
Disappointment	61.72	120	Together	146.0	
about spouse (t_1)	106.25	8	separated		.0008
Anger about	62.01	120	Together		
spouse (t_1)	101.81	8	separated	181.5	.0028
Family Income	65.14	118	Together		
(subj. rating; t_1)	39.38	8	separated	279.0	.0409

various cognitions and emotions related to these restrictions and finally, of several other possible stressors that have been controlled for. [1]

The emotional correlate of an injustice for which the victim ascribes some responsibility to himself or herself is anger about oneself. This emotion is closely and negatively related to marital satisfaction in men ($r = -.45$), but unrelated to marital satisfaction in women (Reichle, 1994a).

Feelings of guilt on the side of the bystanding observer, as well as on the side of the harmdoer, can lead to excuses, restitution, and compensation. Even simply the perception of an excuse given by a spouse can be a significant predictor of marital satisfaction with accounting for a significant proportion of three percent of the variance explained in marital satisfaction (Reichle, 1995).

Finally, all the distortions and cases of disagreement among the spouses are left. Disagreement in many cases might intensify the experience of injustice and will lead a couple towards more conflict or distortion. Concerning distortions, there is some empirical evidence for symptomatology from a study by Steil & Turetsky (1987, also reported

---

[1]The following predictors were considered for inclusion: (1) Cognitions: difficulty of restriction, extent of restriction, anticipation of restriction, prospective stability of restriction, injustice of restriction, attribution of responsibility to spouse, number of restrictions attributed to spouse, number of restrictions in positively valued needs, number of restrictions in positively valued needs in the domain of relationship. (2) Emotions: anger about spouse, disappointment about spouse, moral outrage about spouse, sadness about restriction, hopelessness concerning future improvement. (3) Control variables: social desirability, security of income, family income, vicarious experience of transition to parenthood in others, couple's sum of hours spent with employment, employment constellation (dual- vs single-earners), planned parenthood, extent of help available, spouse's share of child care, spouse's share of household chores, child's temperament, child's health, balance of own vs spouse's restrictions, balance of own gains and losses.

in Steil, 1994). The results are mixed and not entirely clear. It is clear, however, that perfectly just solutions are frequently not the most effective ones.

All that has been reported so far is cross-sectional. Empirical evidence for a causal relationship between injustice and marital satisfaction or other longitudinal consequences of injustice, like symptomatology, is very sparse. VanYperen and Buunk (1990) report a longitudinal effect of inequity on relationship satisfaction over the period of one year. In a longitudinal study by Montada and myself which followed the transition to parenthood of 128 originally cohabitating women and men over a period of four and a half years, significant differences were found between those who had later separated and those still living together: At the time of first measurement, the later separated subjects had reported not only a significantly lower family income, but also significantly more injustice vis-à-vis restrictions in their life, significantly more attributions of responsibility to their spouse, disappointment, and anger (see Table 3).

4. Conclusion

In sum, then, there is some evidence for injustice not only happening but also being recognized in close relationships — not everybody, but a majority seems to have some concept of justice in close relationships. These concepts are far from being uniform, different persons have rather quite different perceptions of what is just, ranging from the fundamentalist ideals of casting-vote and tradition to egalitarian utopias. Norms and practise are more often inconsistent than consistent, with more liberal norms being less frequently put into practise than more traditional ones, women mostly being the ones with the more liberal norms and, consequently, also the ones with the larger discrepancies between their Ought and Is.

An attempt of linking injustice, emotions, behavioral reactions and marital satisfaction together seems to be promising, in not only explaining and understanding the relationships between injustice and various reactions and their consequences for the marital relationship, but also in predicting some long-term consequences of injustice in close relationships. It is the emotions of anger, disappointment, and outrage that are the most potent predictors of marital satisfaction. It still remains open whether the respective emotions such as anger about oneself on the side of the victim and guilt on the side of the harmdoer have a similar potential.

Acknowledgments

Own cross-sequential empirical research reported in this chapter was partly supported by a fellowship for doctoral study awarded to the author from the Stiftung Volkswagenwerk and the country of Rhineland-Palatinate. Longitudinal research reported was funded by a grant from the Deutsche Forschungsgemeinschaft (DFG, German Research Association) to Leo Montada, whose support is gratefully acknowledged.

References

Adams, J. S. (1965). Inequity in social exchange. In L. Berkowitz (Ed.), Advances in experimental social psychology (Vol. 2, pp. 267-299). New York: Academic Press.

Aldous, J. (1978). Family careers. Developmental change in families. New York: John Wiley & Sons.

Arnold, M. B. (1960). Emotion and personality. Vol. 1: Psychological aspects. New York: Columbia University Press.

Averill, J. R. (1978). Anger. In R. A. Dienstbier (Ed.), Nebraska Symposium on Motivation (pp. 1-81). Lincoln: University of Nebraska Press.

Averill, J. R. (1980). A constructivist view of emotion. In R. Plutchik & H. Kellerman (Eds.), Theories of emotion (pp. 305-339). New York: Academic Press.

Badinter, E. (1991). Ich bin Du. Die neue Beziehung zwischen Mann und Frau oder Die androgyne Revolution. München: Piper.

Barrett-Howard, E. & Tyler, T. R. (1986). Procedural justice as a criterion in allocation decisions. Journal of Personality and Social Psychology, 50, 296-304.

Beere, C. A. (1990). Gender roles: A handbook of tests and measures. Westport: Greenwood Press.

Blau, P.M. (1964). Exchange and power in social life. New York: Wiley.

Brickman, P., Folger, R., Goode, E. & Schul, Y. (1981). Micro and macro justice. In M. J. Lerner & S. C. Lerner (Eds.), The justice motive in social behavior: Adapting to times of scarcity and change (pp. 173-202). New York: Plenum.

Bundesministerium für Familie und Senioren & Statistisches Bundesamt (1994). Wo bleibt die Zeit? Die Zeitverwendung der Bevölkerung in Deutschland. Wiesbaden: Statistisches Bundesamt.

Bundesanstalt für Arbeit (Ed.) (1994). Arbeitsmarktreport für Frauen. Berufliche Bildung und Beschäftigung von Frauen. Situation und Tendenzen. Nürnberg: Bundesanstalt für Arbeit.

Buunk, B. P. & VanYperen, N. W. (1991). Referential comparisons, relational comparisons, and exchange orientation: Their relation to marital satisfaction. Personality and Social Psychology Bulletin, 17, 709-717.

Cohen, R.L. (1985). Procedural justice and participation. Human Relations, 38, 643-663.

Cowan, C. P., Cowan, P. A., Heming, G., Garrett, E., Coysh, W. S., Curtis-Boles, H. & Boles, A. J., III. (1985). Transitions to parenthood: His, hers, and theirs. Journal of Family Issues, 6, 451-481.

Croghan, R. (1991). First-time mothers' accounts of inequality in the division of labour. Feminism and Psychology, 1, 221-246.

Crosby, F. J., Pufall, A., Snyder, R. C., O'Connell, M. & Whalen, P. (1989). The denial of personal disadvantage among you, me, and all the other ostriches. In M. Crawford & M. Gentry (Eds.), Gender and thought: Psychological perspectives (pp. 79-99). New York: Springer.

Crowne, D. P. & Marlowe, D. (1960). A new scale of social desirability independent of psychopathology. Journal of Consulting Psychology, 24, 349-354.

Desmarais, S. & Lerner, M. J. (1994). Entitlements in close relationships: A justice-motive analysis. In M. J. Lerner & G. Mikula (Eds.), Entitlement and the affectional bond. Justice in close relationships (pp. 43-63). New York: Plenum.

Deutsch, M. (1975). Equity, equality, and need: What determines which value will be used as the basis of distributive justice? Journal of Social Issues, 31, 137-149.

Deutsch, M. (1985). Distributive justice: A social psychological perspective. New Haven: Yale University Press.

Engelbrech, G. (1991). Berufsausbildung, Berufseinstieg und Berufsverlauf von Frauen. Empirische Befunde zur Erklärung beruflicher Segregation. Mitteilungen aus der Arbeitsmarkt- und Berufsforschung, 24, 531-558.

Erler, G., Jaeckel, M., Pettinger, R. & Sass, J. (1988). Brigitte Untersuchung 88. Kind? Beruf? Oder beides? Eine repräsentative Studie über die Lebenssituation und Lebensplanung junger Paare zwischen 18 und 33 Jahren in der Bundesrepublik Deutschland im Auftrag der Zeitschrift Brigitte. Hamburg & München: Redaktion Brigitte und Deutsches Jugendinstitut e.V.

Fincham, F. D. & Bradbury, T. N. (1987). Cognitive processes and conflict in close relationships: An attribution-efficacy model. Journal of Personality and Social Psychology, 53, 1106-1118.

Frijda, N. H. (1986). The emotions. Cambridge: Cambridge University Press.

Frijda, N. H. (1987). Emotion, cognitive structure, and action tendency. Cognition and Emotion, 1, 115-143.

Furnham, A. (1990). The development of single trait personality theories. Personality and Individual Differences, 11, 923-929.

Gliedner-Simon, A. & Jansen, M. (1995). Neue Wege der Vereinbarkeit von Beruf und Familie für Frauen und Männer. Pfaffenweiler: Centaurus (in press).

Hatfield, E. & Traupmann, J. (1981). Intimate relationships: A perspective from equity theory. In S. W. Duck & R. Gilmour (Eds.), Personal relationships. Vol 1: Studying personal relationships (pp. 165-178). London: Academic Press.

Harsanyi, J. C. (1991). Equality, responsibility, and justice as seen from a utilitarian perspective. Theory and Decision, 31, 141-158.

Hoffman, M. L. (1982). Development of prosocial motivation: Empathy and guilt. In N. Eisenberg (Ed.), The development of prosocial behavior (pp. 281-313). New York: Academic Press.

Homans, G. C. (1961). Social behavior: its elementary forms. New York: Harcourt, Brace & World.

Institut für Praxisorientierte Sozialforschung Mannheim. (1992). Gleichberechtigung von Frauen und Männern - Wirklichkeit und Einstellungen in der Bevölkerung. (Schriftenreihe des Bundesministers für Frauen und Jugend, Bd. 7). Stuttgart: Kohlhammer.

Kirchler, E. (1989). Interaktionsprozesse in Liebesbeziehungen. Von der kühlen Geschäftslogik zur spontanen Gefälligkeit. Zeitschrift für Familienforschung, 1, 77-102.

Kohlberg, L. & Lickona, T. (1986). The stages of ethical development: From childhood to old age. San Francisco: Harper.

LaRossa, R. & LaRossa, M. M. (1981). Transition to parenthood. How infants change families. Beverly Hills: Sage.

Lazarus, R. S. (1975). A cognitively oriented psychologist looks at feedback. American Psychologist, 30, 553-561.

Lerner, M. J. (1970). The justice motive: Some hypotheses as to its origins and forms. Journal of Personality, 45, 1-52.

Lerner, M. J. (1981). The justice motive in human relations. Some thoughts on what we know and need to know about justice. In M. J. Lerner & S. C. Lerner (Eds.), The justice motive in social behavior (pp. 11-35). New York: Plenum.

Lerner, M. J. & Miller, D. T. (1978). Just world research and the attribution process: Looking back and ahead. Psychological Bulletin, 85, 1030-1151.

Lerner, M. J., Miller, D. T. & Holmes, J. G. (1976). Deserving and the emergence of forms of justice. In L. Berkowitz & E. Walster (Eds.), Advances in Experimental Social Psychology (Vol. 9, pp. 134-162). New York: Academic Press.

Lerner, M. J. & Mikula, G. (1994) (Eds.), Entitlement and the affectional bond. Justice in close relationships. New York: Plenum.

Lerner, M. J. & Whitehead, L. (1980). Procedural justice viewed in the context of justice motive theory. In G. Mikula (Ed.), Justice and social interaction: Experimental and theoretical contributions from psychological research (pp. 219-256). Bern: Huber.

Leventhal, G. S. (1980). What should be done with equity theory? In K. J. Gergen, M. S. Greenberg & R. Willis (Eds.), Social Exchange: Advances in theory and research (pp. 27-55). New York: Plenum.

Levenson, H. (1972). Distinctions within the concept of internal-external control: Development of a new scale. Proceedings of the 80th Annual Convention of The American Psychological Association, 7, 261-262.

Lind, A. E. & Tyler, T. R. (1988). The social psychology of procedural justice. New York: Plenum.

Lück, H. E. & Timaeus, E. (1969). Skalen zur Messung Manifester Angst (MAS) und sozialer Wünschbarkeit (SDS-E und SDS-CM). Diagnostica, 15, 134-141.

Martin, J., Brickman, P. & Murray, A. (1984). Moral outrage and pragmatism: Explanations for collective action. Journal of Experimental Social Psychology, 20, 484-496.

Mikula, G. (1980). On the role of justice in allocation decisions. In G. Mikula (Ed.), Justice and social interaction: Experimental and theoretical contributions from psychological research (pp. 127-166). Bern: Huber.

Mikula, G. (1987). Exploring the experience of injustice. In G. R. Semin & B. Krahé (Eds.), Issues in contemporary German social psychology: History, theories, and applications (pp. 74-96). London: Sage.

Mikula, G. (1992). Austausch und Gerechtigkeit in Freundschaft, Partnerschaft und Ehe: Ein Überblick über den aktuellen Forschungsstand. Psychologische Rundschau, 43, 69-82.

Mikula, G. & Lerner, M. J. (1994). Justice in close relationships. An introduction. In M. J. Lerner & G. Mikula (Eds.), Entitlement and the affectional bond. Justice in close relationships (pp. 1-9). New York: Plenum.

Mitleger, R. & Rathgeber, R. (1988). Der mühsame Weg zur Gleichberechtigung. Das Eherecht. In K. Leube, L. Pagenstecher, R. Rathgeber, J. Stich & K. Wahl (Eds.), Wie geht's der Familie? Ein Handbuch zur Situation der Familien heute (pp. 415-424). München: Koesel.

Montada, L. (1980). Developmental changes in concepts of justice. In G. Mikula (Ed.), Justice and social interaction: Experimental and theoretical contributions from psychological research (pp. 257-284). Bern: Huber.

Montada, L. (1989). Bildung der Gefühle? [On the formation of emotions]. Zeitschrift für Pädagogik, 35, 292-312.

Montada, L., Schmitt, M. & Dalbert, C. (1986). Thinking about justice and dealing with one's own privileges: A study of existential guilt. In H. W. Bierhoff, R. Cohen & J. Greenberg (Eds.), Justice in social relations (pp. 125-142). New York: Plenum.

Montada, L. & Schneider, A. (1990). Justice and emotional reactions to the disadvantaged. Social Justice Research, 3, 313-344.

Oberndörfer, R. (1993). Aufgabenteilung in Partnerschaften. In B. Nauck (Ed.), Lebensgestaltung von Frauen: eine Regionalanalyse von Familien- und Erwerbstätigkeit im Lebensverlauf (pp. 145-175). Weinheim: Juventa.

Ortony, A., Clore, G. L. & Collins, A. (1988). The cognitive structure of emotions. Cambridge: Cambridge University Press.

Piaget, J. (1965). The moral judgement of the child. New York: Free Press.

Reichle, B. (1993). Injustice does not always matter: The case of restrictions in the course of first childbirth. Paper presented at the IVth International Conference on Social Justice Research, Trier, Germany, July 2nd, 1993.

Reichle, B. (1994a). Die Geburt des ersten Kindes - eine Herausforderung für die Partnerschaft. Bielefeld: Kleine.

Reichle, B. (1994b). Die Zuschreibung von Verantwortlichkeit für negative Ereignisse in Partnerschaften: Ein Modell und erste empirische Befunde. Zeitschrift für Sozialpsychologie, 25, 227-237.

Reichle, B. (1995). Lebensveränderungen nach der Geburt des ersten Kindes: Reaktionen und Bewältigung. Paper presented at the VIIIth Coping Workshop, Mannheim, Germany, March 24th, 1995.

Reichle, B. & Gefke, M. (1995). Just distributions among spouses: Preferences and patterns. Unpublished manuscript.

Reichle, B., & Montada, L. (1994). Problems with the transition to parenthood: Perceived responsibility for restrictions and losses and the experience of injustice. In M. J. Lerner & G. Mikula (Eds.), Justice in close relationships: Entitlement and the affectional bond (pp. 205-228). New York: Plenum.

Reis, H. T. (1984). The multidimensionality of justice. In R. Folger (Ed.), The sense of injustice: Social psychological perspectives (pp. 25-61). New York: Plenum.

Reskin, B. F. (1994). Sex segregation: Explaining stability and change in the sex composition of work. In P. Beckmann & G. Engelbrech (Eds.), Arbeitsmarkt für Frauen 2000 - Ein Schritt vor oder ein Schritt zurück? Kompendium zur Erwerbstätigkeit von Frauen (pp. 97-115). (Beiträge zur Arbeitsmarkt- und Berufsforschung 179). Nürnberg: Institut für Arbeitsmarkt- und Berufsforschung der Bundesanstalt für Arbeit.

Roseman, I. (1984). Cognitive determinants of emotion. A structural theory. In P. Shaver (Ed.), Review of personality and social psychology, Vol. 5: Emotions, relationships, and health (pp.11-36). Beverly Hills: Sage.

Rotter, J. B. (1966). Generalized expectancies for internal versus external control of reinforcement. Psychological Monographs, 80, (Nr.1, whole Nr. 609), 1-28.

Rusbult, C. (1987). Responses to dissatisfaction in close relationships: The exit-voice-loyalty-neglect model. In D. Perlman & S. Duck (Eds.), Intimate relationships (pp. 209-237). Newbury Park: Sage.

Sampson, E. E. (1975). On justice as equality. Journal of Social Issues, 31, 45-64.

Scherer, K. R. (1984). On the nature and function of emotion: A component process approach. In K. A. Scherer & P. Ekman (Eds.), Approaches to emotion (pp. 293-317). Hillsdale: Erlbaum.

Schmitt, M. (1994). Gerechtigkeit [Justice]. In M. Hockel, W. Molt & L. von Rosenstiel (Eds.), Handbuch der Angewandten Psychologie (Kap. VII.10) [Handbook of Applied Psychology] (Chap. VII.10). Munich: Ecomed.

Schmitt, M. & Montada, L. (1982). Determinanten erlebter Gerechtigkeit [Determinants of experienced justice]. Zeitschrift für Sozialpsychologie, 13, 32-44.

Schwartz, S. H. (1977). Normative influences on altruism. In L. Berkowitz (Ed.), Advances in experimental social psychology (Vol. 10, pp. 221-279). New York: Academic Press.

Schwinger, T. (1980). Just allocation of goods: Decisions among three principles. In G. Mikula (Ed.), Justice and social interaction: Experimental and theoretical contributions from psychological research (pp. 95-125). Bern: Huber.

Shaver, K. G. (1970). Defensive attribution: Effects of severity and relevance on the responsibility assigned for an accident. Journal of Personality and Social Psychology, 14, 101-113.

Shaver, K. G. (1985). The attribution of blame. Berlin: Springer.

Smith, C. A. & Ellsworth, P. C. (1985). Patterns of cognitive appraisal in emotion. Journal of Personality and Social Psychology, 48, 813-838.

Sprecher, S. & Schwartz, P. (1994). Equity and balance in the exchange of contributions in close relationships. In M. J. Lerner & G. Mikula (Eds.), Entitlement and the affectional bond. Justice in close relationships (pp. 11-41). New York: Plenum.

Statistisches Bundesamt (Ed.). (1991). BMFuS Erziehungsgeld-Statistik 1989 vom 18.2.1991. Unpublished Tables. Wiesbaden: Statistisches Bundesamt.

Steil, J. M. (1994). Equality and entitlement in marriage: Benefits and barriers. In M. J. Lerner & G. Mikula (Eds.), Entitlement and the affectional bond. Justice in close relationships (pp. 229-258). New York: Plenum.

Steil, J. M. & Makowski, D. G. (1989). Equity, equality, and need: A study of the patterns and outcomes associated with their use in intimate relationships. Social Justice Research, 3, 121-137.

Steil, J. M. & Slochower, J. (1985). The experience of injustice. Social psychological and clinical perspectives. In G. Stricker & R. H. Reisner (Eds.), Form research to clinical practise (pp. 217-242). New York: Plenum.

Steil, J. M. & Turetsky, B. (1987). Is equal better? The relationship between marital equality and psychological symptomatology. In. S. Oskamp (Ed.), Applied Social Psychology Annual (pp. 73-97). Beverly Hills: Sage.

Thibaut, J. W. & Kelley, H. H. (1959). The social psychology of groups. New York: Wiley.

Thibaut, J. W. & Walker, L. (1975). Procedural justice: A psychological analysis. Hillsdale: Erlbaum.

Thompson, L. (1991). Family Work. Women's sense of fairness. Journal of Family Issues, 12, 181-196.

Törnblom, K. Y. (1992). The social psychology of distributive justice. In K. R. Scherer (Ed.), Justice: Interdisciplinary perspectives (pp. 177-284). Cambridge: Cambridge University Press.

Törnblom, K. Y., Jonsson, D.R. & Foa, U.G. (1985). Nationality, resource class, and preferences among three allocation rules: Sweden vs. USA. International Journal of Intercultural Relations, 9, 51-77.

Utne, M. K. & Kidd, R. F. (1980). Equity and attribution. In G. Mikula (Ed.), Justice and social interaction: Experimental and theoretical contributions from psychological research (pp. 63-93). Bern: Huber.

VanYperen, N. W. & Buunk, B. P. (1990). A longitudinal study of equity and satisfaction in intimate relationships. European Journal of Social Psychology, 20, 287-309.

Walster, E., Walster, G. W. & Berscheid, E. (1978). Equity: Theory and research. Boston: Allyn & Bacon.

Weiner, B. (1986). An attributional theory of motivation and emotion. New York: Springer.

Wissenschaftlicher Beirat für Familienfragen beim Bundesministerium für Jugend, Familie und Gesundheit. (1984). Familie und Arbeitswelt. Schriftenreihe des Bundesministers für Jugend, Familie und Gesundheit; Bd. 143). Stuttgart: Kohlhammer.

8

Justice and Leadership: A Social Co-Constructionist Agenda

James R. Meindl and Karen J. Thompson*

Issues of justice are integral to social, political, and economic change. And so are matters of leadership. While justice, on the one hand, and leadership, on the other, have both received massive research attention by scholars over the years, few efforts have focused explicitly on how these two broad issues commingle, either during times of change or under more placid circumstances. Is there a social psychology which links them? What are the dynamics involved? Surely such questions are reasonable ones for justice researchers to ask. After all, post-industrial nations are increasingly described as "societies of organizations", in which economic and political power rests less with individuals, and more with formal organizations and organized interest groups in both the public and private sectors (e.g., Drucker, 1988; Zucker, 1983). This being the case, an understanding of justice, particularly during times of turbulence and revolutionary change, cannot be complete without being informed by those sciences which are dedicated to understanding and improving human organizations. Organizational science has a number of priorities, often conflicting. But in the pantheon of organizational concepts, leadership is seen as central (Hollander, 1986), with great relevance and importance for organizational forms, processes, and outcomes.

*This paper was supported by an endowment from Marine Midland Bank.

James R. Meindl and Karen J. Thompson • School of Management, State University of New York at Buffalo, Buffalo, NY 14260

Current Societal Concerns about Justice, edited by Leo Montada and Melvin J. Lerner. Plenum Press, New York, 1996.

These two domains—justice and leadership—have only occasionally been joined over the years, with few researchers bothering to foray beyond their topical territories, into the domain of the other. The low and sporadic frequency of such boundary-spanning activity is, no doubt, the result of many factors, but nevertheless surprising given the great significance that each topic is independently accorded, especially around matters of social change.

The social construction of reality is an integrative process, and its study must address the complex weaving-together of multiple experiences (Berger & Luckman, 1966). If justice can be considered a social construction, as many would argue, then as justice researchers we ought to more seriously consider that the sense of fairness, what one deserves and is entitled to, is not established in a vacuum devoid of the social constructions that give meaning to other aspects of an individual's experiences. Justice and other things—such as leadership—are similarly constructed, and when woven together—form a coherent patchwork, if not a seamless, interpretive, subjective clothing of events and circumstances, and our relationships to them. *The construction of justice, as important as it is, co-occurs and becomes part of other, important, salient, and perhaps more general social constructions of experience.* The underlying thesis of this paper is that justice and leadership can be though of, and fruitfully examined, as social "co-constructions," with theoretical and empirically verifiable linkages between their constructed features.

As a first step toward developing a fuller description of how these two constructive domains are linked, we identify and review a few issues, themes, and concepts that, over the years, have preoccupied researchers in each domain. We hypothesize how they might be related to one another. In doing so, we cast justice constructions as dependent on the constructions of leadership that emerges among members of group and organizations. We sought to address basic questions about how alternative constructions of leadership influence the way followers think about justice; that is, how common leadership concepts "map" onto issues of enduring interest to justice researchers. One could just as easily have done it the other way around. The few modest ideas we present here regarding these connections are by no means definitive; rather, this is a speculative, cursory exercise, which is intended to demonstrate, by example, the possibilities for more articulated and substantial work in the future. Because a social constructionist view of leadership is likely to be somewhat alien to the typical justice researcher, we first provide a brief review of what it is. The particular brand of social construction with respect to leadership presented here is one which emanates from previous work on something which has been labeled the "romance of leadership" notion (see Meindl, in press, for a more extensive description).

1. The Social Construction of Leadership

People develop thought systems to deal with the complexities of organizational life. These "implicit theories of organizations" (e.g., Downey & Brief, 1986) become manifested in the concepts and processes used to understand and give meaning to organizational events and occurrences, and to convey that understanding to others. Evidence suggests that leadership factors are of paramount importance in these shared, implicit organizational theories (Meindl, Ehrlich & Dukerich, 1985). The emphasis on leadership is both cause and consequence of a social construction process, heavily influenced by social interactional (Meindl, 1990), organizational (Pillai & Meindl, 1994)and media-related (Chen & Meindl, 1991) factors.

There is a long tradition of leadership studies which has become quite variegated and elaborated over the years, enriched by the participation of many scholars, of various disciplinary stripes, including psychology, sociology, anthropology, and political science (see Bass, 1990, for a review). The traditional study of leadership phenomena has not emphasized the subjective, interpretive, and social construction view. It is only recently that such perspectives have gotten a foothold on the dominant, more objective, positivist approach. The hallmark of a social constructionist view of leadership is an emphasis on followers. Leaders—who they are, what they are doing—are of interest only insofar as they are the focal objects in follower's thought systems. While traditional views of leadership concentrated on the personas and behaviors of leaders, a social constructionist view shifts the study of leadership away from leaders toward a focus on followers. In a social constructionist view, whatever the personality and behavioral characteristics of the leader, leadership is something which exists in the "eyes of the beholder"— socially constructed in the minds of followers and observers. These social constructions are intersubjectively shared understandings of what leadership is, and what criteria are to be used to evaluate those in positions of power and authority. And while all leadership research is ultimately interested in followership outcomes—that is, the performance, commitment, satisfaction, etc. of followers—a social constructionist view focuses on the processes throuqh which images of specific leaders and more generalized conceptions of leadership itself, are generated. These images and the social processes which produce them are treated as the most immediate and powerful precursors for the onset of followership, in terms of its qualities, but more basically in terms of its occurrence at all. In this view, leadership—and by implication followership—is an emergent phenomenon, which may or may not develop as an aspect of the constructed relationships qroup members develop with one another.

This perspective on leadership emphasizes social psychological processes and concepts. It also embeds the leader-follower relationship within a broader network of social relationships and cultural contexts than more traditional perspectives on leadership. It recognizes that the development of leadership-followership as an important characteristic of any given relationship between actors is, by and large, a product of a social system which includes other followers, and not simply a product of the dyadic, vertical linkages (behavioral, psychological) that exist bctwccn, say a supcrvisor and his/her subordinate.

Leadership, as a socially constructed product, is by no means given by virtue of the occupancy of hierarchical roles, and the asymmetrical power-dependency relationships which describe them. A social constructionist view separates formal role designations from the informal development of leadership-followership as a way to understand relationships. The roles of "leader" and "follower" are creations that, for the most part, describe an informal overlay that actors place onto an otherwise formally defined hierarchical relationship. The emergence of leadership implies more than subordination: it represents an elaborated conceptualization of that relationship, central to the understanding that group members have of one another, the task activities facing the group, and their relationships to them.

Leadership can be analyzed from a power point of view (Hollander & Offerman, 1990), and indeed many traditional definitions of leadership have power and influence at their core. However, the separation of power and leadership that is achieved in a social constructionist view is crucial to understanding how leadership is connected to justice. Justice researchers who mistakenly equate the two are likely to be blinded by an overly deterministic connection between leadership power and justice: Leaders are those in positions of power who possess the capacity to control resources. Since leaders control resources, they are obviously in a position to determine how fairly others will be treated. Thus, in this deterministic view, power, not leadership, appears as the more critical variable. Some equity theorists appear to adopt this perspective regarding the connection between power/status and justice (e.g., Austin & Hatfield, 1980), by emphasizing that leaders are in a

Table 1: Co-constructive Aspects of Justice and Leadership

Justice domain	Leadership domain
Forms of Justice	Leadership Styles
Distributive/Procedural	Transaction/Transformation
Justice Motives	Charismatic Leadership

position to reinforce their status quo domination by influencing the justice constructions of their followers. In this perspective, leadership-followership is a proxy for power relationships. As such, the study of "leadership" as it relates to justice, is little more than an examination of power dynamics as it affects the allocation of resources, and the manner in which they are construed. This is a restrictive view which fails to take into account that considerable variations in leadership can and do occur, given equal power, and that those variations have significant implications for justice. Furthermore, whereas the restricted view emphasizes power and control as the precursors for assuming and maintaining positions of leadership (i.e, formal, legitimate positions of authority), a social constructionist view emphasizes that the increased potential for power, and the ability to influence, emerges out of followers' prior constructions of leadership.

Within a broad social constructionist framework, there are any number of alternative possibilities for linking leadership and justice. Our approach is simply to identify several key issues and themes in leadership studies and describe for readers how they may be linked to, and correspond with a few themes/issues that are of great familiarity to justice researchers. These are outlined in Table 1, and we will cover each in turn.

2. The Forms of Justice

Considerable attention over the years has been devoted to understanding the variety of ways in which justice is manifested in the rules that individuals and groups use to allocate material and other kinds of rewards (e.g., Deutsch, 1975; Lerner, 1975; Leventhal, 1976; Reis, 1986). For our purposes here, these rules can be classified into three categories. Non-differentiating rules which tend to minimize the differences in outcomes people receive and differentiating rules which tend to favor uneven distribution of outcomes on the basis of any variety of evaluative criteria which allow an allocator or recipient to justify and rationalize variances in the distribution of resources. An important subclass of these differentiating rules to an organizational scientist is one which includes rules whereby resources such as salary and bonuses are merited on the bases of performance and/or productivity measures. Such performance-contingent or "pay-for-performance" rules are the basis of meritocratic systems, and are included in theories of work motivation, such as expectancy theory (e.g., Vroom, 1964). Perhaps the most prominent contrast between these types is the one that is captured in the equity-parity contrast. Studies have examined the managerial use and implications of the equity-parity contrast (e.g., Meindl, 1989; Kabanoff, 1991), the social construction of justice involves the negotiations among organizational members regarding their understanding of the appropriate rules by which they deserve various outcomes. While the allocation of resources by managers may be driven by their own philosophies, values, and understanding of what is appropriate, a social constructionist view suggests that followers view of what is or is not appropriate depends on the manner in which they construct the leader. These constructions are central to the way in which followers view their relationship to one another, to the leader, and to the tasks facing the group. These constructs reveal the culture and psychological climate of the group, creating an ambiance from which appropriate notions of justice are derived. Notions of appropriate justice will be consistent with the incipient social order within the group (Deutsch, 1985). Leadership constructions are an important part of that incipient order.

We speculate here that equity and parity rules, as alternative constructions of what is an appropriate formulation of fairness can be linked with alternative constructions of leadership, around the concept of behavioral styles. The traditional concept of leadership styles focuses on the behavior of managers and supervisors vis a vis their subordinates. In some theories, these styles are seen as general behavioral tendencies which describe patterns of behavior that leaders may exhibit irrespective of situations and contexts, whereas others see more flexibility, with the leader possessing a multiplicity of styles which are displayed contingent on various contextual cues, including subordinate characteristics—such as competency and motivation. The most prevalent, well-known portrayal of leadership styles suggests that style variances can be captured in a two dimensional space defined in terms of a "people orientation" dimension and a "task orientation" dimension (e.g., Fleishman, 1953). These two dimensions correspond roughly to the task versus maintenance functions identified by small group researchers. The task dimension (high versus low) includes directive, controlling, and structuring behaviors, while the people dimension includes supportive behaviors intended to enhance the morale, comfort, and satisfaction of subordi-

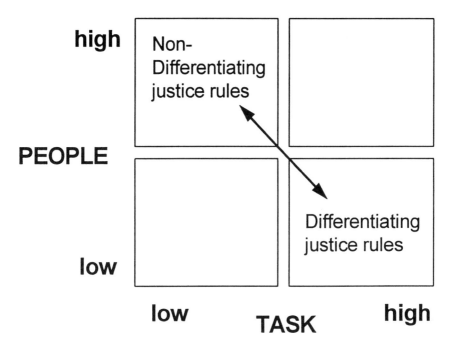

Figure 1. The Co-Construction of Justice Rules and Leadership Styles

nates. The standing of leaders on these two dimensions (high versus low task, high versus low people) combine to produce stylistic variations, describable in terms of four "archetypes", as summarized in Figure 1.

It can reasonably be speculated that as the construction of a leader becomes more people-oriented and less task-oriented, constructions of justice will favor non-differentiating forms of justice. Conversely, as the construction of leaders becomes more task oriented and less people-oriented, the more differentiating, performance contingent justice constructions will occur. The suggestion here is that as followers define their leaders as being more concerned with issues of morale, cohesion, and acceptance, on the one hand, or with direction, obedience, and control on the other, satisfaction with the distribution of rewards will tend to be greater when such allocations are based on rules that "fit" with those leadership constructions.

As justice researchers know, solidarity/social cohesion values are congruent with non-differentiating allocation rules, whereas productivity values are congruent with differentiating, performance-contingent allocation patterns. These alternative values have their counterpart in task and people oriented leadership constructs. Of course, the construction of any given leader involves a weighting of both task and people oriented features, and the resultant construction of justice would perhaps correspondingly reflect a weighted blending of the rules of justice as well (e.g., Leventhal, 1976). In some models of leadership style, effectiveness is linked to the capacity of a leader to be seen as high on both people and task dimensions (e.g., Blake and Mouton, 1966). Rather than blending, the resultant justice constructions may be contingent ones, with the expectation that the allocations will reflect the alternating use of equity and parity based logic to fit various other situational requirements.

The general notion here is that one of the main preoccupations of justice researchers—the exploration of alternative forms of justice, the so-called justice rules—can be examined within the context of followers' alternative constructions of leadership styles. Justice rules can be thought of as being more or less consistent with, or wedded to, particular stylistic images that followers generate of their leaders.

3. Distributive versus Procedural Justice

Whereas the work on the forms of justice concerns itself with the allocation/distribution of outcomes, social justice researchers have become comfortable making the distinction between distributive and procedural justices, the former weighted heavily to the patterning of outcome allocations, the latter more heavily focused on the fairness of proccessual variables and practices which determine what outcomes recipients will receive. Much work and effort has gone into discovering what procedural practices are likely to generate greater feelings of justice and fair treatment, independent of the outcomes that are produced. Indeed, there is evidence that the perceptions of processes and of distributed outcomes both independently contribute to a resultant sense of justice having occurred: People care about the distribution of outcomes they and others receive, but are also concerned with the procedures used to determine those outcomes.

Although issues of justice will be generally important within the context of leadership, contributing to the legitimacy and endorsement of a leader by followers (e.g., Tyler, 1986; Martin, Scully & Levitt, 1990; Hollander & Julian, 1970; Michener & Lawler, 1975), the salience of justice-related concerns can be variable across situations, circumstances, and contexts (Prentice & Crosby, 1987). On occasion, the actions and decisions of institutions and/or of individuals in authority can cause followers to be more vigilant of, and sensitive to, potential transgressions and insults to notions of fairness. Some researchers have suggested that relatively stable patterns exist regarding such sensitivities (Huseman, Hatfield & Miles, 1987), highlighting the individual difference counterpart to more situated sensitivities.

We speculate that alternative leadership constructions may cause followers to be hyper-sensitive to alternative types of justice-related concerns, roughly equivalent to the distributive versus procedural justice arenas. What is it about the constructions of leadership that might influence the relative sensitivity of followers to distributive versus procedural matters? The answer to this question lies in much broader distinctions and definitions of leadership than that which was focused on by our previous analysis of leadership styles. Just as the forms of justice lie within the domain of distributive justice, the concept of behavioral styles lies within an equally circumspect domain of leadership constructions. In order to accommodate the higher order distinction between distributive and procedural justice, we can refer to a higher order cleavage in the way leadership is constructed by followers: the so-called transactional versus transformational domains of leadership (e.g., Bass, 1985).

The transactional ("TA") domain of leadership deals with the day-to-day transactions that occur between leaders and followers. The guiding principle is that leaders and followers are engaged in an exchange of goods, services, and behavioral styles with one another. In this exchange, the rules and procedures which govern the rate of return, so to speak, that each party can expect is paramount. Concepts such as Individualized Consideration and Management by Exception (Bass, 1985), and frameworks such as path-goal theory (House, 1971), two-factor (behavioral styles) theory (Fleishman, 1953), and LMX—leader-member exchange—theories (Graen & Cashman, 1975) are all included as a part of the TA domain.

Whereas TA emphasizes the workings of leadership within some preexisting, status-quo organizational structure and culture, Transformational ("TF") leadership is more closely aligned to notions of organizational change and revolution. Rather than emphasizing the tit-for-tat transactions between leaders and followers, the TF construal of leadership deals with creative issues of values and vision, purpose and commitment. Concepts related to charismatic leadership (e.g., Weber, 1947; House, 1977; Conger, 1992), visionary leadership (Conger & Kanungo, 1989), and inspirational leadership (Bass, 1985), are among those connected with this domain. These two domains can be taken as alternative constructions that followers can generate for one another, suggesting various criteria they will employ to evaluate the effectiveness

and attractiveness of their leaders (Meindl, 1990, 1993). The development and application of one or the other set of leadership criteria is
influenced by contextual factors. For example, Pillai and Meindl (1993a,
b) found that more transformational constructions of leadership tend to
emerge among group members under conditions of crisis and threat,
whereas more transactional constructions are more likely when crisis
and threat are minimal.

We speculate here that the relative salience to followers, of distributive versus procedural justice, will, to an extent, be conditioned by their
constructions of leadership in transactional versus transformational
terms. That is, if and when followers develop an image or construal of
leadership in transactional terms, they will tend to be more sensitive to
procedural justice issues. In contrast, constructions of leadership emphasizing transformational criteria will tend to cause followers to down-
play procedural issues, and lead them to place greater weight on matters
of distributive justice.

The rationale for this lies with the relative congeniality of TA and
TF concepts to efficiency and effectiveness criteria. The TA domain has
leaders and followers operating with a predefined, status-quo system of
assumptions. The orientation is toward perfecting the system at is it,
making it more efficient. Such leadership constructions are likely to
fixate followers on operational issues involving the refinement of rules,
regulations, policies, and practices. "How to do things right" (i.e.,
operational means) will be a more salient concern. The TF brand of
leadership concepts are oriented toward breaking with status quo assumptions, and to creating a "new order". TF leadership constructions
are likely to keep questions of ultimate missions, purposes, and values
most prominent in followers mind, with procedural matters being relatively less important. "Doing the right things" (i.e., strategic ends) will
be the important concern.

Thus, procedural issues will preoccupy followers working with TA
constructions of leadership, whereas distributive, outcome issues will
dominate groups of followers working with strong TF constructions.
There is some indirect evidence to support this speculation. A study of
revolutionary leaders (Martin, Scully & Levitt, 1990), for example,
showed that such leaders tend to make use of language which ignores or
leaves vague procedural justice issues, but rather focuses attention on
the sheer redistribution of resources, and fairer outcomes. While that
study did not examine the constructions made by followers, it is a
reasonable surmise that revolutionary leaders the likes of Mao, Peron,
Castro, and others, are often constructed by their followers in transformational terms and that these leaders were responding in part to their

concerns. A study by Pillai (1993) examined the emergence of TA and TF leadership constructions among various units of a large social services agency. As hypothesized, that study found that TF was more likely to emerge in organic organizational structures—systems in which matters of routines, standard operating procedures, formal policies, rules, and regulations are generally weak—in comparison to more mechanistic organizational arrangements where such factors are strongly emphasized.

4. Justice Motives

As Lerner described it, people are motivated to believe that the world is basically a just place in which to live. Such beliefs allow actors to maintain a sense that they can deserve and earn the resources they desire, and avoid negative fates. Evidence of injustices—when people clearly do not get what they apparently deserve and are entitled to—threatens this belief. Knowledge of the victimization of others is important because it questions the viability of one's own personal "contract" with the world: that if I work hard, if I do the rights things—I will get my just deserts. In this theory, the justice motive is the key, organizing feature of social relationships, a pre-eminent concern influencing the evaluation and conduction of social relationships.

Although justice motives are thought to operate across a wide array of social situations, settings, and relationships, are there occasions of behaviors—some special, unique relationships—where the normal operation of justice motives is suspended? We have not yet considered the possibility that the emergence of alternative leadership constructions may interact with more basic concerns about the role of justice and personal deservingness in social relationships. The focus here is on the strength of the justice motive itself, given one or another construction of leadership. A point that unifies our previous two speculations about the co-occurrence of a leadership and justice construct is the suggestion that leadership constructions will increase the chances that certain justice-related concerns/issues will become more or less prominent in a follower's experiences. There is, however, a special case of leadership constructions which may very well have the opposite effect: rather than raising the prominence of some aspect of justice, this type of construction may work to keep all justice-related concerns in abeyance.

One of these occurs with the development of charismatic leadership, involving members of groups who construct their leaders in charismatic terms, and who see themselves as a charismatic following. While the previous analysis suggests that distributive issues are likely to be a greater concern than procedural ones for those who construct leadership in transformational terms—which includes charisma—there is another, more basic phenomenon that may come into play when a charismatic following develops—that is, when charismatic criteria are applied by followers to evaluate their leaders, *and* when those leaders are found to be extremely appealing and attractive in those terms. Charismatic leadership is evidenced by its effects on followers (House, 1977). These effects can be thought of as a syndrome (Meindl, 1990), a cluster of attitudinal and behavioral outcomes that followers experience and display as a result of following a charismatic leader. Elements of the charismatic syndrome among followers include reactions such as heightened sense of commitment, loyalty, strong sense of purpose, identification with the leader and the cause, the exertion of extra effort, above and beyond the call of duty performances, and the like.

Under the more typical construal of leadership in transactional terms, justice motives may operate as they normally do, orienting followers to the typical transactions and exchanges which take place as a part of the daily social encounters groups members have with one another. It may even be that transactional constructions of leadership keeps justice motives at or near the top of the hierarchy of other, potentially competing motivations. However, the powerful, charismatic construction of leadership that emerge within a group of followers may be one of the few factors which can reduce the governing effect of justice motives on interpersonal relationships. Compelling anecdotal evidence—from Jim Jones in Guyana, to David Koresh and the Branch Dovidians in Texas—suggests that members of organized, charismatic followings suspend secular ideals of justice and fair treatment. This type of leadership construction may be more congenial to the ascension of other social motives, linked to the heroic pursuit of holy causes and great missions (e.g., Meindl & Lerner, 1983; 1984).

This speculation could be tested in a modified version of the now classic victim-derogation study conducted by Lerner and Simmons (1966). The logic of that study was as follows. Justice motive theory suggests that people are concerned about each others fates because of the general implications it holds for a just world order, and the ability for any actor to reap just deserts.

The theory states that when people are confronted with undeserved suffering, the belief in the just world is threatened, and the observer will act to reestablish a sense of justice. One way of accomplishing this is to derogate the victim—make it seem that the victims, because of what they did, or who they are—deserved their negative fate. In their classic study

Table 2: Conceptual Replication and Extension of Lerner and Simmons (1966) Victim Derogation Study

	Condition	
Context	Subject can help victim	Subject cannot help victim
Original Lerner and Simmons	No Derogation	Derogation
Non-charismatic leadership	No Derogation	Derogation
Charimatic leadership	No Derogation	No Derogation

Lerner and Simmons confronted observers with the suffering of an innocent victim. In one set of conditions, the observers were provided with a low cost, legitimate opportunity to help the victim. Under these circumstances, no derogation is necessary because justice can be reestablished, and the threat to the belief in a just world minimized. In another condition, though, observers witnessed the victim's suffering without a legitimate means of helping. In that case, the belief in the just world is threatened, and, as a consequence, the victim is derogated by the observer. This pattern of results provided compelling evidence of a justice motive at work.

Imagine a conceptual replication of this study: one that would retain the crucial features—observers witnessing the suffering of an innocent victim under similar sets of circumstances—but shifted into a group leadership context, in which observers are members in transactional versus charismatic followings. This design is depicted in Table 2. In this crossed, 2x2 design, we expect an interaction between leadership context and the help versus no help conditions.

That is, the typical derogation effect, wherein the victim is seen in more negative terms when the witness cannot act to aid or terminate the suffering of the victim, will be replicated in the transactional leadership context. This would be evidence of the normal operation of the justice motive. However, we would expect that the derogation effect would be much weaker, if it occurs at all, for those observer/followers operating under the spell of charismatic leadership constructs. This would occur only if, as we speculate, such leadership constructions disrupt or suspend normal justice motives, and the desire to believe in a just world.

5. Conclusion

To study social justice is to explore one of the most fundamental aspects of the human condition. To study leadership is to gain an insight into a significant part of the way people normally constructs the collective issues facing groups and organizations. In this paper we draw attention to the potential linkages that exist between justice and leadership as two co-related constructions. As change and upheaval seem to raise the salience of justice-related concerns, the profile of leadership issues are similarly heightened under such conditions.

There are large bodies of work devoted to each domain—justice on the one side, leadership on the other. Surprisingly, research with the expressed purpose of examining the connection between them has been very limited. Leadership researchers have had only a passing, tangential interest in justice, and justice researchers are largely ignorant of the work being produced on topic of leadership. The result is that the connection between leadership and justice is poorly understood. Given the prominence of each during times of change, we ought to know more. What is their relationship to each other? What implications does one have for the other? How do they interact with one another to determine human behavior? For anyone interested in gaining a better understanding of the role of justice in human affairs, some knowledge of leadership processes ought to be central. In this chapter, we have laid out some simple ideas as a first, broad-based cut at exploring the linkages. Our hope is that readers will, as a result, be sufficiently interested to consider undertaking their own explorations of these significant co-constructions. While this analysis has been limited by our particular social constructionist bent, other approaches and perspectives may also be useful.

References

Austin, G. W. & Hatfield, E. (1980). Equity theory, power, and social justice. In G. Mikula (Ed.), Justice and social interaction (pp. 25-61). New York, NY: Springer-Verlag.

Bass, B. M. (1985). Leadership and performance beyond expectations. New York, NY: Free Press.

Bass, B. M. (1990). Bass & Stogdill's handbook of leadership, 3rd edition. New York, NY: Free Press.

Berger, P. L. & Luckman, T. (1966). The social construction of reality. Garden City, NY: Irvington.

Blake, R. R. & Mouton, J. S. (1964). The managerial grid. Houston, TX: Gulf.

Calder, B. J. (1977). An attributional theory of leadership. In B. M. Staw & G. R. Salancik (Eds.), New directions in organizational behavior (pp. 179-204). Chicago: St. Clair.

Chen, C. C. & Meindl, J. R. (1991). The construction of leadership images in the popular press: The case of Donald Burr and People Express. Administrative Science Quarterly, 36, 521-551.

Cropanzano, R. & Folger, R. (1990). Procedural justice and worker motivation. In R. Steers & L. Porter (Eds.), Motivation and work behavior (5th edition, pp. 131-143). NY: McGraw-Hill.

Deutsch, M. (1975). Equity, equality, and need: What determines which value will be used as the basis off distributive justice? Journal of Social Issues, 31, 137-149.

Deutsch, M. (1985). Distributive justice. New Haven, CT: Yale University Press.

Downey, H. K. & Brief, A. P. (1986). How cognitive structures affect organizational design: Implicit theories of organizing. In H. P. Sims & D. A. Gioia (Eds.), The thinking organization (pp. 165-190). San Francisco: Jossey-Bass.

Drucker, P. M. (1988). Management and the world's work. Harvard Business Review, 65-76.

Fiedler, F. E. (1964). A contigency model of leadership effectiveness. In L. Berkowitz (Ed.), Advances in experiemental social psychology (pp. 150-191). New York, NY: Academic Press.

Fleishman, E. A.(1953). The description of supervisory behavior. Personnel Psychology, 37, 1-6.

Folger, R. & Greenberg, J. (1985). Procedural justice: An interpretive analysis of personnel systems. In K. Rowland & G. Ferris (Eds.), Research in personnel and human resource management (pp. 141-183). Greenwich, CT: JAI Press.

Graen, G. & Cashman, J. F. (1975). A role making model of leadership in formal organizations: A developmental approach. In J. G. Hunt & L. L. Larson (Eds.), Leadership frontiers (pp. 143-165). Kent, OH: Kent State University Press.

Greenberg, J. (1982). Approaching equity and avoiding inequity in groups and organizations. In J. Greenberg & R. L. Cohen (Eds.), Equity and justice in social behavior (pp. 389-436). New York, NY: Academic Press.

Hersey, P. & Blanchard, K. H. (1969). Life cycle theory of leadership. Training and Development Journal, 23(2), 26-34.

Hollander, E. P. (1986). On the central importance of leadership processes. International Review of Applied Psychology, 35, 39-52.

Hollander, E. P. & Julian, J. W.(1970). Studies in leader legitimacy, influence, and innovation. In L. Berkowitz (Ed.), Advances in experimental social psychology (pp. 33-69). New York, NY: Academic Press.

Hollander, E. P. & Offerman, L. R. (1990). Power and leadership in organizations. American Psychologist, 45, 179-189.

House, R. J. (1971). A path-goal theory of leader effectiveness. Administrative Science Quarterly, 16, 321-339.

House, R. J. (1977). A 1976 theory of charismatic leadership. In J. G. Hunt & L. L. Larson (Eds.), Leadership: The cutting edge (pp. 194-205). Carbondale, IL: Southern Illinois University Press.

Kabanoff, B. (1991). Equity, equality, power and conflict. Academy of Management Review, 16, 416-441.

Lerner, M. J. (1975). The justice motive in social behavior: Introduction. Journal of Social Issues, 31, 1-19.

Lerner, M. J. (1977). The justice motive: Some hypotheses as to its origins and forms. Journal of Personality, 45, 1-52.

Lerner, M. J. (1980). The belief in a just world. New York, NY: Plenum.

Lerner, M. J. & Lerner, S.C. (Eds.). (1981). The justice motive in social behavior: Adapting to times of scarcity and change. New York, NY: Plenum.

Lerner, M. J., Miller, D. T. & Holmes, J.G. (1976). Deserving and the emergence of forms of justice. In L. Berkowitz and E. Walster (Eds.), Advances in experimental social psychology (pp. 133-162). New York, NY: Academic Press.

Leventhal, G. S. (1976). The distribution of rewards and resources in groups and organizations. In L. Berkowitz & E. Walster (Eds.), Advances in experimental social psychology (pp. 91-131). New York, NY: Academic Press.

Lind, E. A. & Tyler, T. R. (1988). The social psychology of procedural justice. New York, NY: Plenum.

Martin, J., Scully, M. & Levitt, B. (1990). Injustice and the legitimation of revolution: Dammning the past, excusing the present, and neglecting the future. Journal of Personality and Social Psychology, 59, 281-290.

Meindl, J. R. (in press). The romance of leadership as follower-centric theory: A social constructist approach. Leadership Quarterly.

Meindl, J. R. (1982). The abundance of solutions: Some thoughts for theoretical and practical solution seekers. Administrative Science Quarterly, 27, 670-685.

Meindl, J. R. (1989). Managing to be fair: An exploration of values, motives, and leadership. Administrative Science Quarterly, 34, 252-276.

Meindl, J. R. (1990). On leadership: An alternative view of the conventional wisdom. In B.M. Staw and L. L. Cummings (Eds.), Research in organizational behavior (Vol. 12, pp. 159-203). Greenwich, CN: JAI Press.

Meindl, J. R. (1993). Reinventing leadership: A radical, social psychological approach. In K. Murnighan (Ed.), Social psychology in organizations (pp. 89-118). Englewood Cliffs, NJ: Prentice Hall.

Meindl, J. R., Ehrlich, S.B. & Dukerich, J. M. (1985). The romance of leadership. Administrative Science Quarterly, 30, 78-102.

Meindl, J. R. & Lerner, M. J. (1983). The heroic motive: Some experimental demonstrations. Journal of Experimental Social Psychology, 19, 1-20.

Meindl, J. R. & Lerner, M. J. (1984). The exacerbation of extreme responses to an outgroup. Journal of Personality and Social Psychology, 47, 71-84.

Michener, H. A. & Lawler, E. J. (1975). Endorsement of formal leaders: An integrative model. Journal of Personality and Social Psychology, 31, 216-223.

Pillai, R. & Meindl, J. R. (1991). The impact of a performance crisis on attributions of charismatic leadership: A preliminary study. Best Paper Proceedings of the 1991 Eastern Academy of Management Meetings, Hartford, CT.

Pillai, R. & Meindl, J. R. (1991). The effects of a crisis on the emergence of charismatic leadership: A laboratory study. Best Paper Proceedings of The 1991 Academy of Management National Meetings, Miami, FL.

Prentice, D. A. & Crosby, F. (1987). The importance of context for assessing deservingness. In J. C. Masters & W. P. Smith (Eds.), Social comparison, social justice, and relative deprivation: Theoretical, empirical, and policy perspectives (pp. 165-182). Hillsdale, NJ: Erlbaum.

Reis, H. T. (1986). The multidimensionality of justice. In R. Folger (Ed.), The sense of injustice (pp. 25-61). New York, NY: Plenum.

Thibaut, J. & Walker, L. (1975). Procedural justice: A psychological analysis. Hillsdale, NJ: Plenum.

Tyler, T. R. (1986). The psychology of leadership evaluation. In H. W. Bierhoff, R. L. Cohen, & J. Greenberg (Eds.), Justice in social relations (pp. 72-81). NY: Plenum.

Vroom, V. H. (1964). Work and motivation. NY: Wiley.

Weber, M. (1921). The sociology of charismatic authority. In H. H. Gerth & C. W. Mills (trans. & Eds.), From Max Weber: Essays in sciology (pp. 245-252). New York: Oxford University Press, 1946.

Witt, A. & Wilke, H. (1988). Subordinates' endorsement of an allocating leader in a commons dilemma: An equity theoretic approach. Journal of Economic Psychology, 9, 151-168.

Zucker, L. G. (1983). Organizations as institutions. In S. Bacharach (Ed.), Research in the sociology of organizations (Vol. 2, pp. 1-47). Greenwich, CT: JAI Press.

9

Victims without Harmdoers: Human Casualties in the Pursuit of Corporate Efficiency

Melvin J. Lerner

In response to economic market pressures, many Western societies have created new categories of innocent victims. These include members of the work force participating in the process of corporate restructuring, and the younger generations denied access to secure employment. To promote better understanding of the implications of this contemporary tragedy, this chapter highlights and examines the sense of justice as it appears in the lives of the participants: the victims, survivors, harmdoers, and the generation entering the workforce.

1. Corporate Restructuring: What Happens When "Good" Managers Harm "Good" Employees for "Good" Reasons?

According to a recent survey of companies in the United States (Smith, 1994), almost half had reduced their work force from mid 1992 to mid 1993 and for two thirds of them this was at least their second year of downsizing in a row. In this process of "restructuring" their means of production, companies notify their affected employees that their jobs will be terminated within a period of months. Although the companies

Melvin J. Lerner • Department of Psychology, University of Waterloo, Waterloo, Ontario, Canada N2L 3G1

Current Societal Concerns about Justice, edited by Leo Montada and Melvin J. Lerner. Plenum Press, New York, 1996.

may provide some of the discharged employees with a severance and compensation package including out-placement counseling, the vast majority enter the ranks of the unemployed with only the assistance governmental programs provide for anyone who loses their job. Under ideal conditions being layed off in this manner might mean nothing more than a shift in employment from one company to another; however, the sinister contemporary reality is that the discharged employees are forced to compete for jobs in a labor market that has become globalized and where production is increasingly automated. As a consequence, if they find reemployment, they will often have to settle for considerably lower wages with less, if any, job security. Their subsequent losses, however, only begin with the degrading of their economic well-being. The increasing numbers of North Americans who experience this downward economic mobility move from a middle class to a marginal lower socioeconomic status life-style, with essentially no hope of future upward mobility, either for themselves or their children. Depression, family abuse, and increased use of alcohol, and drugs, are among the more obvious signs of suffering that have been traced to this form of victimization (see Kozlowski et al., 1993).

But victimization implies not only that people are deprived and suffering but that an injustice has been commmitted, harm has been done. In this case, the injustice appears in multiple forms. It is commonly understood that in the typical corporate restructuring the discharged employees are innocent of any prior wrongdoing or failings. In violation of the implicit social contract between employers and workers, the employees' income and security were taken from them through no failure of performance or fault on their part. This undeserved deprivation appears even less equitable when compared with the fate of the corporate stakeholders who are enjoying growing prosperity. That prosperity, gained at least in part through the corporate restructuring, makes the discharged employees' deprivation and suffering appear less fair. It also raises the specter of earlier labor policies when it was commmon practice for corporations to use their economic and political power to exploit their workers in the search for greater profits.

Given this history it is particularly noteworthy that for the most part, the accusation of managements' unjust exploitation of labor has not been part of the public dialogue surrounding these issues. In fact, quite the contrary seems to be the case. The norms of the present free market economy legitimize corporate stakeholders' pursuit of a reasonable rate of return on their investments. Added to that is the general recognition that the globalizing of the free market requires the corporations to become more efficient in order to maintain their share of the market or, in many cases, to survive. As a consequence, corporate management can claim a legal and moral responsibility to adapt to this increased competition by reducing production costs. Their ethical posture is unassailable as long as the corporate restructuring resulting in wide spread job loss is justified by the demands of these market forces, and their procedures fall within the rules of law and normal practice. The paradoxical social reality, then, is that many people, the discharged employees and their families, have been victimized by the acts of others, corporate management, but in terms of the public dialogue, there are no harmdoers to blame. The responsibility for the victimization has been externalized by blaming impersonal economic market forces for creating the need for corporate restructuring.

This tragic situation raises theoretically challenging and practically serious questions for those who study the justice motive in human relations. No reliable observer would deny the severe injustices experienced by the increasing numbers of discharged employees and their families. How, then, do these innocent victims deal with this crisis and the ensuing deprivation? Societal norms deny them any legitimate bases for blaming their harmdoers or themselves. Without having a harmdoer to blame, and only able to attribute their fates to a form of natural economic disaster, do they experience the emotions of anger, resentment, sadness, and outrage (Smith & Ellsworth, 1985)? How do their feelings about justice enter into their coping reactions? Without an identifiable harmdoer do justice-related emotions and thoughts become irrelevant in their lives?

In responding to these and related questions we will focus on how the discharged employees' sense of justice, and especially their belief in a just world influences their reactions to the job loss. Then, we will consider the "survivors", who by virtue of a more or less fair procedure, escaped being victimized and were able to remain employed. Of particular concern is how their view of the justness of the restructuring process —who was discharged, and how they were treated by the company— influences their subsequent reactions including their confidence about what the future holds for them.

The managerial staff, of course, plays a major role in the entire process, and one that is most challenging for contemporary theories concerning how and in what ways people actually care about justice. Of particular importance is how these managers react to the socially constructed moral paradox described above, whereby their decisions were the direct proximal causes of their employees' undeserved suffering, but according to societal norms they were not harmdoers, they were simply doing their duty. And finally, although they are not directly involved in the restructuring and job loss process, the present and future generations of job entrants will be profoundly affected by a labor market with relatively few high-paying jobs requiring exceptional intellectual abilities while the vast majority of them compete for low-paying jobs with little security. How will they react to having less income and security than their parents and, no matter how hard they work, remarkably less than the highly educated and talented members of their generation?

2. Employees Reactions to Their Victimization: To Believe or Not to Believe in a Just World

When we focus on those most directly victimized by the corporate restructuring we quickly discover that, contrary to the social norms, they do not uniformly accept the moral innocence of those causally responsible for or implicated in their victimization. For example, the workers in one plant closure, who had recently been informed of their impending job loss, generally considered the company somewhat blameworthy, but they claimed the government, not the company, had treated them least fairly during this crisis in their lives (Lerner & Somers, 1989). There were also important individual differences among the employees' blaming reactions and their stress-related symptoms. Those who felt they had been treated unfairly, especially by the company, and who felt the company had some responsibility to help them become reemployed, were most distressed by the prospect of losing their jobs (Lerner & Somers, 1989, 1992). This finding leads to the more general questions of the relations among the employees' morale, belief in the justness of their treatment, and subsequent coping efforts. Considerable prior research has documented people's desire to find a harmdoer to blame for a victim's suffering (see, for example, Montada, 1994).

For the sake of their own future security, most people do not want to believe that uncontrollable or random forces can inflict undeserved suffering. They would much prefer to believe that injustices do not occur - innocent people do not suffer. Therefore, any evidence of suffering or deprivation implies that the victims might have merited their fates by virtue of their behaviors or their character - the kind of person they are. Or, when constrained from blaming the victim, people may convince themselves that the victims' unjust fate is only temporary, and ultimately the undeserved suffering will be compensated and the harm-doer punished (Lerner, 1980). The evidence also indicates that, although people differ reliably in the extent to which they hold on to the simplest and most direct forms of this "belief in a just world", victims as well as observers and harmdoers engage in this same motivated blaming process (Lerner, 1980; Rubin & Peplau, 1973).

These earlier findings have been corroborated in the recent research examining the coping reactions of the unemployed. For example, one study of a random sample of Northern Ireland adults (Benson & Ritter, 1990) revealed that among those who had recently lost their jobs, those who held a high belief in a just world were more likely to experience depressive symptoms than those who had little belief that their world was just. But, the *Belief in a Just World* is less likely to induce this form of demoralization and self-blame, among those whose unemployment was caused by corporate restructuring. The obvious reality of their own innocence, as well as the recognition that many others were similarly affected, should enable the victims of restructuring to avoid self-blame and provide support for externalizing the blame, or remaining optimistic about their ultimate fate. The results of laboratory and field research reveal that people who generally believe their world is just and people get what they deserve, are more likely to respond optimistically to impending crises and threats.

Tomaka & Blascovich (1994) carefully documented these stress moderating effects. They found that when faced with a threatening, difficult task their experimental subjects with relatively strong just world beliefs rated the task as less stressful, had autonomic reactions that were consistent with this appraisal and subsequently performed better than than the subjects who held weaker just world beliefs.

These experimental findings are consistent with the recent survey research of Hafer and Olson (1993) and Dalbert (1993). Hafer and Olson found that among their sample of working women, the greater their belief in a just world the less group and personal discontent they reported. Dalbert (1993) reported that among her heterogeneous sample of women, including teachers threatened by job loss, and unemployed workers, there was a positive relation between the belief in a just world and their positive mood level and satisfaction with their lives, even when controlled for self-esteem. It seems that the belief in a just world can provide a buffer between the crises people face and the threats they experience.

But it also appears that whatever initial protective confidence and trust in their future this belief provides, more dysfunctional consequences may follow. Lerner and Sommers (1992) found that shortly after being informed of the impending plant closure, there was a positive relation between the employees' beliefs in a just world and their efforts to find another job. Several weeks later, however, just prior to the actual closure there was a reversal in this relationship, especially among those employees for whom reemployment would be problematic. Among these workers, the less they believed in the justness of their world, the more upset and frightened they were, and the greater their efforts to find work. This pattern is consistent with Hafer and Olson's (1993) report that the women who initially had less belief in a just world and greater discontent with their job situation were more likely than their more trusting and contented coworkers to be actively engaged in efforts to improve the situation for themselves and the other employees in the subsequent month. Apparently, the belief in the justness of their world can provide some comfort for the threatened employees, but that sense of well-being may reduce the incentive to engage in the costly efforts of directly coping with the crisis. And, it may eventually lead to an even greater sense of loss and despair.

In sum, the evidence indicates that some discharged employees may feel they have been victimized by others not simply by natural forces over which no one had control. Initially, the belief that people generally get what they deserve can provide them with a degree of support and optimism concerning their ultimate fates. They believe that having done no wrong, everything will turn out right for them in the end. Over time, this belief can take the form of a groundless optimism and become a comforting alternative to the more difficult and often frustrating efforts to find reemployment. Whereas, those victims who admit to themselves that they do not live in a just world, and that they were treated unjustly, though more emotionally distraught and angry, they are also more likely to do something to improve their lots, both individually and collectively. It is a familar trade-off: the short term gains of comforting illusions, in this case of living in a just world, or directly confronting a painful and threatening reality with efforts to find reemployment, in a rather "non-just" world.

3. The Survivors' Reactions to the Victimization: The Paradoxical Effects of Procedural Fairness without Distributive Justice

If the discharged employees blaming reactions and belief in a just world influence their emotional well-being and coping responses, how are the remaining employees affected by their having witnessed the restructuring process in which some of their fellow employees lost their jobs through no fault of their own?

In a recent manuscript, Brockner (1994) summarized the findings of contemporary research on "survivors" reactions to their jobs and their employers after the restructuring had occurred. Apparently, the survivors' judgments of the fairness of the compensation received by those discharged made a considerable difference in their remaining allegiance to the company as measured by various indices, including productivity.

Even more important, however, were the survivors' assessments of management's procedural fairness in selecting which employees were to be discharged and how the company treated them during the discharge process, i.e. to what extent they were treated with dignity and respect. Not surprisingly, the survivors' prior relations with the victims and with the company had significant postrestructuring consequences, but these were considerably weaker and often overridden by the procedural fairness issues. Most noteworthy is the finding that, similar to the reactions of the victims, survivors who believed their companies engaged in unfair procedures during the restructuring were more likely than the others to be actively engaged in job seeking efforts. A central finding of this research revealed that companies that engage in, or at least create the perception of, fair procedures in the restructuring process are more likely to maintain the morale and allegiance of the remaining employees.

But there is reason to believe the matter may be more complex than that. The research of Buck & Miller (1994) on "reactions to incongruous negative life events" suggests that it is important to consider the residual effects of seeing one's coworkers become innocent victims of a "good" company employing fair procedures. The basic question is whether that would be more or less threatening to the survivor's ultimate sense of job security than being able to attribute some portion of the blame to the company's failures. Is it possible that finding the company blameless may provide immediate reassurance and comfort for the survivors, but believing that uncontrollable and unpredictable forces are in control of one's job security, would create greater threats to their confidence in the future, especially as the incidence of closures and downsizing increases?

Armstrong-Stassen and Latack (1992), in their study of the survivors of a restructuring of a major corporation in the telecommunication industry, found some evidence for this implicit delayed threat. For example, those who had been exposed to prior layoffs, felt more powerless than those for whom this was a first experience. They were also more likely to report having expected it. Apparently, even when prior downsizings had been done fairly, the experience of witnessing their fellow employees victimization left the survivors with less security and greater pessimism about their own futures. If the survivors come to believe they, and the company, are powerless to avoid these catastrophes, how can they fully regain a sense of security about their own futures?

One of them described the subsequent reactions of alienation and withdrawal: "I will try to find security in myself and my family because

I don't think I will ever trust my company again." (p. 210). It is important to recognize that this distrust comes not from the companies' devious or unfair practices, but from their inability to protect their competent employees from the disastrous and demoralizing consequences of losing their jobs, presumably caused by unpredictable market pressures beyond their control.

4. Managers: The Entrapped Victims of a Hidden Moral Dilemma

Focusing on the reactions of corporate managers during the restructuring process leads to unexpected and extremely important insights into the nature of the senses of justice. In particular, it appears that the normatively based rules of moral reasoning interact with the psychologically based intuitively experienced sense of justice to influence the managers' decision making process and their subsequent emotional reactions to having done harm to innocent people. In effect, the managers may become the innocent victims of their own senses of justice.

This process begins with the recognition that societal norms for determining blameworthiness clearly distinguish between causality and culpability. According to these conventionally accepted standards, in order to find someone blameworthy for another person's suffering, the perpetrator must be judged causally responsible and have been negligent or intentionally violated an ethical norm (Shaver, 1985). If the key issue, in the ethical evaluation of those who engage in corporate downsizing is whether that practice is normatively sanctioned, then managment should be completely exonerated of any wrongdoing. Their ethical posture is morally acceptable as long as the restructuring, including widespread job loss, is justified in terms of market forces and the mechanisms of implementation fall within the rules of law and normal practice; in other words, what all the other corporations do. According to these conventionally accepted rules for the assignment of culpability, management has done no "harm" in restructuring their means of production and providing services. Even though their decisions led to considerable suffering for the discharged employees and their families, the norms absolve the managers of any moral wrongdoing. They need experience no guilt or shame because of the consequences of their actions.

Recent reports, however, strongly suggest that this normative-legal model of culpability does not adequately explain the managers' postrestructuring experiences. These often include feelings of considerable guilt and subsequent demoralization. The lead article and cover story of Fortune, (July 25, 1994), "Burned-Out Bosses", portrays management as the unexpected victims of the restructuring. According to Smith (1994), the author of the article: "nothing - not overwork, not confusion, not lost perks, not apprehension - is as deadening to a manager's morale as firing subordinates. To do it once is traumatic enough, but subsequent dismissals wear down one's resilience". (p. 46). The role of guilt feelings in this demoralization process is explicit in the conclusion: "What makes the flood of dismissals in recent years especially distressing for managers is that so often workers have been fired not for cause but because their skills were no longer needed. "(p. 2). And poignantly described by an IBM executive: "Every year we'd call it something different - early retirement, reorganization, reengineering ... it was slow water torture ... I came home every night worried how this one or that one was going to support himself." (p. 46).

Although there must be individual differences in the way managers react to these events and there are no available figures on the incidence of guilt and "burn-out" among managers involved in downsizing, experienced consultants have recognized the prevalence of these unanticipated strong emotional reactions following corporate restructuring and the serious problems they create for managment. In his address upon receiving a "Distinguished Professional Contribution to Knowledge Award" from the American Psychological Association (Toronto, 1993), Harry Levinson (1994) recommended that following restructuring the participants openly face the reality of what has occurred and deal with the emotional consequences. He proposed that this should include a mourning process so that people can detach themselves from the old and confront the realities of the new, and supportive procedures for coping with the increased sense of helplessness. Levinson also recommended that these coping efforts be supplemented with means for reducing the sense of guilt, especially among the executives: "The conscious guilt any manager of conscience has about terminating someone else without cause is compounded by the unconscious guilt that arises from the sense that he or she is destroying the other" (1994, p. 429).

Whether or not one accepts these diagnoses or recommended treatments for managment's postrestructuring demoralization, the main point for present purposes is Levinson's (1994) compelling observation that the commonly accepted rules for determining blameworthiness and innocence did not protect the managers from strong feelings of guilt and self-blame. A court of law and public consensus would find them innocent of wrongdoing and yet these managers blamed themselves for having personally harmed the discharged employees and their families.

It is also important to recognize that these self-inflicted painful feelings clearly contradict the common assumption that whenever possible people will employ self-serving and defensive attributions to avoid responsiblity for undesirable and blameworthy outcomes (Shaver, 1985). In this case, the managers not only had the opportunity they also had full normative support for not blaming themselves. By conventional standards their self-blame was "irrational" and undeserved. Apparently, that was not sufficient to protect them from whatever it was that was driving their subsequent guilt feelings. The fundamental question here is: What do we know about the psychology of harmdoing that might explain what led these managers to take on the painful burdens of guilt when society's norms and laws told them they had no obligation to do so?

Two recent theoretical models integrating cognition and emotion suggest the general outlines of an explanation. They have in common the proposition that people encode and respond to important events through two separate, though related systems. Epstein (see e.g., Epstein, Lipson, Holstein & Huh, 1992) terms these the "rational system" and the "experiential system". The first operates primarily at a conscious level and functions according to conventionally established rules of evidence, while the second is "experienced passively and preconsciously, and encodes reality in concrete images, metaphors, and narrative systems". Similarly, Shweder & Haidt (1993) refer to "fast and slow" cognitive processes. They distinguish between "moral reasoning" which involves relatively slow ex post facto propositional reasoning and "moral intuition" which is rapid and "introspectively opaque" (p. 364). The moral intuitions, consisting of self-evident moral truths, generate the emotions which typically are not accessible to conscious introspection, while the logical, slow thought processes provide the post hoc normatively understandable explanations. Both Shweder and Epstein suggest that the fast automatic processing of the experiential system often leaves people "seized by our emotions," but they appear to differ in important ways concerning the nature of these emotions. Epstein portrays the experiential system as essentially "pleasure-pain oriented," what feels good or not. On the other hand, Shweder and Haidt (1993) find a strong and pervasive moral dimension in these preconscious processes with distinct emotional reactions such as anger, sympathy, shame, guilt, and disgust as automatic intuitive reactions to elemental signs of injustice, harm, or degradation.

These theories are consistent with the propositions Lerner (1987) developed to explain a series of experimental findings that revealed systematic discrepancies between people's reactions to injustices and their ways of publicly portraying them. On the basis of such evidence, Lerner (1987) contends that people are emotionally aroused by signs of unjust suffering and their virtually automatic reaction is to eliminate the injustice. If their initial appraisal of the situation includes themselves as the harmdoer, then they are vulnerable to guilt-related emotions, which may not be automatically eliminated by the appeal to normatively "good" or innocent intentions (Lerner, 1980). One consequence of this limited ability of moral norms to provide emotional absolution appears in people's reluctance to engage in, or excuse, violations of the simple rules of fairness such as equal pay for equal work; people should get what they deserve. The explanation for the manager's guilt begins with the recognition that people have at least two senses of justice and morality that influence their reactions to harmdoing and victims. These include the automatic intuitive reactions to emotion-arousing cues of injustice, and the moral reasoning based on societal rules for assigning blameworthiness on the basis of negligence or bad intentions.

The operation of these two systems and the different procedures for processing information makes the decision to engage in corporate restructuring an entrapping form of conflict between two moral values: one, intuitive and preconscious, and the other, rational and consciously understood. (see Tetlock et al., forthcoming). Managers recognize their obligations to the corporate stakeholders which require that they restructure the organization. This potential harm to the stakeholders for failure to restructure is consciously understood and drives their decisions. Typically, during this decision process their intuitive moral obligation that they cause no harm to their employees remains unconscious, "introspectively opaque"(Shweder & Haidt, 1993), only to appear subsequently in their emotional reactions when their employees' suffering, as a consequence of their job loss, is vividly documented. Although consciously justified in their decisions by societal norms, the managers unknowingly remained vulnerable to the signs of injustice and the associated experiences of guilt, regret, sadness, for having victimized their employees. According to Levinson (1994) and Smith (1994) the subsequent efforts to cope with these unanticipated," irrational", distressing emotions are often costly to themselves and others.

5. The Next Generation of Employees: Young People Coping with the Injustice of Relative Deprivation

The net effect of the the wide spread "reengineering" of the manufacturing and service sectors of the economy, in the form of plant closures, downsizing, and the replacement of unionized permanent jobs with those offering low wages, with no security and benefits, has been to progressively change the nature of the North American job market. As a consequence, those entering that job-market now and in the future will have increasingly fewer opportunities to realize what previous generations had taken for granted: A secure job with enough income to support a "nice life" for one's self and a family. Will these young people then raise the question of "fairness", and, if so, what are the predictable consequences of the answers they find or are given?

In the Work of Nations (1991) Robert Reich described a North American society of the immanent future as becoming increasingly stratified into a virtual caste system. The "fortunate fifth" of the population, primarily composed of "symbolic analysts" (his terms), will enjoy the profits of an increasingly efficient and productive economy. The remaining four fifths who engage in routine production, or provide inperson services, will face continually reduced real wages and job insecurity. They will be increasingly at risk of being replaced by advanced machinery or those willing to work for lower wages. The "fortunate fifth", symbolic analysts, will maintain or increase their market value because of their ability to deal with abstractions, engage in system thinking, experimentation, and collaboration - and thus design and creatively employ the advanced technology. These are the brightest, best educated, and personally gifted 5-20% of each generation.

But what about the lives of the remaining 80%, especially those who do not inherit considerable capital? How will they cope with their absolute and relative deprivation, the insecurities associated with their economic futures? From the perspective of justice theorists, those entering the labor force who grew up in a middle class environment, but who do not have the personal qualifications to become one of the fortunate fifth symbolic analysts, are of particular concern. These are young people of average to somewhat above average intelligence whose bedrock expectations and sense of self-worth are tied to having a "nice home" in a "nice area", with enough stable income to have a "comfortable" family life with a "good future" for their chidren. If Reich and others (see, e.g., Aronowitz & DiFazio, 1994; Krugman, 1994) are correct and the present trends continue, there is little chance of their realizing those expectations either alone or with a partner. It is reasonable to expect that at some point in time they will conform to the demoralizing limitations they face, while recognizing that others, some of their interpersonally and intellectually gifted previous classmates and neighbors, are doing very well.

The anthropologist Katherine Newman (1993) described early signs of this awareness. On the basis of her interviews she concluded that" The baby-boom generation does not resent its parents per se for coasting into the propertied class ... they just want to know why the gravy train gave out before it got to their doorstep and who is responsible for the unfairness they have been subjected to" (p. 131). If the trends continue, the children of the baby-boom generation now beginning to enter the labor force will face considerably greater obstacles and disappointments. Unfortunately, the most obvious and familar means of reducing the individual and structural strains associated with the inability to find a secure place in the economy may not be applicable with the failed children of the middle class. For example, the "fortunate fifth" might be willing to allocate sufficient resources to the unfortunate four fifths, in terms of guaranteed income, welfare, etc. to provide them with some reasonable degree of economic security. However, that would still leave these next generations, the beneficiaries, with the problem of how to find ways of maintaining their feelings of self-worth. For the middle classes, in particular, self esteem as well as public status depend upon one's position in the economy, the job one holds. That may well change, but to what, and after how much human suffering?

The immediately pressing question is how will this majority of job entrants explain and deal with their personal "failures", while others succeed in a thriving economy? To what extent will they define themselves as innocent victims of an unjust society, or rather, find justice in blaming themselves for their relatively deprived circumstances (Lerner, 1980)? Given their "middle-class" socialization, they can be expected to go to considerable lengths to maintain a positive self-image and an optimistic view of their future (see Montada et al., 1992). As a consequence, the threatening and unyielding economic realities make them prime candidates for adopting any belief system that provides the needed ego-enhancing explanations for their state of deprivation and the promise of a rosy future.

However comforting at the time, these coping responses pose serious risks for the individual and society. The societal dangers of chauvinism are implied when young people reach the point where after several economic threats or setbacks they decide, as cited earlier: "I will try to find security in myself and my family because I don't think I will ever trust my (any) company again" (Armstrong-Stassen & Latack, 1992 p. 210). The dependence upon ingroup identities, e.g., family, religion, ethnic group, for a sense of self-worth and a pervasive distrust of "them" can activate the psychological roots of bigotry and racism (Meindl & Lerner, 1984) with serious consequences for the social fabric of North American society.

6. Concluding Thoughts

The emerging scenario for the North American societies projects an increasingly productive economy in absolute terms, with a minority of the population gaining the most benefit from that productivity. Whatever direct benefits this increased productivity offers for the minority of corporate stakeholders and possibly the majority of citizens at some future point in time, they need to be considered in light of the destructive effects on those who participate in and witness the requisite corporate "restructuring" in the interest of increased competitive efficiency. Mainly, the human sense of justice seems to be pervasively violated by these efforts to restructure our means of production in order to success-fully compete in the global markets. As described in this manuscript, the "costs" of these violations include the managers' destructive guilt feel-ings, the survivors' increased anxiety and distrust of the world they live in, the victims' anger and grief over what their job loss has done to them and their families, and the next generations' problematic struggles to achieve a decent, secure life and a sense of selfworth. And, there are potential sociopolitical dimensions to these "costs" of economic restruc-turing that might threaten the very fabric of our democratic institutions. Rosenthal (1995) succinctly portrays the concern shared by many con-temporary social analysts when he observes that: "The working middle class now take out their resentments on the very poor, very foreign, or very democratic. They will discover that this will help them as much as aspirin helps a corpse. Neither welfare recipients, neither Mexican immigrants nor their local democratic assemblyman have much to do with an economic-technological revolution that pushes hardworking people from the campfire. Many of them could turn against a society that broke its deal and stuck a 'loser' sticker on their foreheads. They may vote for demagogues who reject the society that has turned away from them."

References

Armstrong-Stassen, M. & Latack, J. C. (1992). Coping with work-force reduction: The effects of layoff exposure on survivors' reactions. Best paper proceed-ings, 1992, Academy of Management, 207-211.

Aronowitz, S. & DiFazio, W. (1994). The Jobless Future: Sci-tech and the dogma of work. Minneapolis, MI: University of Minnesota Press.

Benson, D. E. & Ritter, C. (1990). Belief in a just world, job loss, and depression. Sociological Focus, 23, 49-63.

Brockner, J. (1994). Perceived fairness and survivors' reactions to layoffs, or how downsizing organizations can do well by doing good. Social Justice Research, 7, 345-364.

Buck, M. L. & Miller, D. T. (1994). Reactions to incongruous negative life events. Social Justice Research, 7, 29-46.

Dalbert, C. (1993). Gefaehrdung des Wohlbefindens durch Arbeitsplatzunsicherheit: Eine Analyse der Einflussfaktoren Selbstwert und Gerechte-Welt-Glaube. Zeitschrift fuer Gesundheitspsychologie, 4, 294-310.

Epstein, S., Lipson, A., Holstein, C. & Huh, E. (1992). Irrational reactions to negative outcomes: Evidence for two conceptual systems. Journal of Personality and Social Psychology, 62, 328-339.

Hafer, C. J. & Olson, J. M. (1993). Beliefs in a just world, discontent, and assertive actions by working women. Personality and Social Psychology Bulletin, 19, 30-38.

Kozlowski, S. W. J., Chao, G. T., Smith, E. M. & Hedlund, J. (1993). Organizational downsizing: Strategies, interventions, and research implications. International review of industrial and organizational psychology. New York: John Wiley.

Krugman, P. (1995). Peddling prosperity: Economic sense and nonsense in an age of diminished expectations. New York: W.W. Norton.

Lerner, M. J. (1980). The belief in a just world: A fundamental delusion: New York: Plenum.

Lerner, M. J.(1987). Integrating societal and psychological rules of entitlement: The basic task of each social actor and fundamental problem for the social sciences. Social Justice Research, 1, 107-125.

Lerner, M. J. & Somers, D. G. (1989). Worker responses to plant closures. Final report submitted to Plant Closure Review and Employment Adjustment Branch of the Ontario Ministry of Labour. Toronto, Ontario, Canada.

Lerner, M. J. & Somers, D. (1992). Employees reactions to an anticipated plant closure: The influence of positive illusions (Chapter 13). In Montada, L., Filipp, S-H. & Lerner, M. J. (Eds.). Life crises and the experience of loss in adulthood Hillsdale, N.J.: Erlbaum.

Levinson, H. (1994). Why the behemoths fell: Psychological roots of corporate failure. American Psychologist, 49, 428-436.

Meindl, J. R. & Lerner, M. J. (1984). Exacerbation of extreme responses to an outgroup. Journal of Personality and Social Psychology, 47, 71-84.

Montada, L. (1994). (Volume Editor). Experiencing and observing victimization. Social Justice Research, 7, 1-91.

Montada, L., Filipp, S.-H. & Lerner, M. J. (1992). (Eds.) Life crises and experiences of loss in adulthood. Hillsdale, N.J.: Erlbaum.

Newman, K. S. (1993). Declining fortunes: The withering of the American dream. New York: Basic Books.

Reich, R. (1991). The work of nations: Capitalism in the 21st century New York: A.A. Knopf.

Rosenthal, A. M. (1995). Profit up and employment down, anger up and civility down. International Herald Tribune, January 7-8.

Rubin, Z. & Peplau, L. A. (1973). Belief in a just world and reactions to another's lot: A study of participants in the national draft lottery. Journal of Social Issues, 29, 73-93.

Shaver, K. G. (1985). The attribution of blame: Causality, responsibility, and blameworthiness. New York: Springer-Verlag.

Shweder, R. A. & Haidt, J. (1993). The future of moral psychology: Truth, intuition, and the pluralist way. Psychological Science, 4, 360-365.

Smith, C. A. & Ellsworth, P. C. (1985). Patterns of cognitive appraisal in emotion. Journal of Personality and Social Psychology, 48, 813-838.

Smith, L. (1994). Burned-out bosses. Fortune, 130, 44-52.

Tetlock, P. E., Peterson, R. & Lerner, M. J. (Forthcoming). Revising the value pluralism model incorporating social content and context postulates. In C. Seligman, J. Olson & M. Zanna, (Eds.). Values: Eighth annual symposium on personality and social psychology. Hillsdale, N.J.: Erlbaum.

Tomaka, J. & Blascovich, J. (1994). Effects of justice beliefs on cognitive appraisal of and subjective, physiological, and behavioral responses to potential stress. Journal of Personality and Social Psychology. 67, 732-740.

10

Mass Unemployment under Perspectives of Justice

Leo Montada

1. Unemployment—A Personal Hardship and a Social Evil

Mass unemployment is a central problem in most OECD states. It destroyed the dream of full employment which was more or less realized in the growth period after World War II and which was theoretically nourished by Keynesianism. The mean rate of registered unemployed people is over 10% in most OECD countries, it is significantly less in the US and Japan (OECD, 1994). Not counted are those who receive welfare benefits, those in the "quiet reserves" not registered as unemployed or job seeking, and those involved in an "active labor market measure", e.g. those in early retirement or retraining programs.

While the injustice of unemployment is frequently deplored, it is rarely explicated what exactly the basis for this judgment is (Montada, 1994a) nor what measures and policies might be the right ones to provide more justice (Montada, 1994b). Occupational policies to solve this problem are controversially discussed. The "justice-gab", "new poverty", "working poor", "the two-third societies", "the excessive costs for communal welfare", "deregulation", "defense of acquired entitlements", "second labor market" are keywords in the public debate.

Judging unemployment unjust implies to consider it an undeserved disadvantage, hardship or loss. While wealthy nations can afford a

Leo Montada • Professor of Psychology, Fb I - Psychologie, Universitaet Trier, D-54286 Trier, Germany

Current Societal Concerns about Justice, edited by Leo Montada and Melvin J. Lerner. Plenum Press, New York, 1996.

material buffering of unemployment, it still means a critical life event for quite a few implying reductions in material resources and a threat to self-esteem, self-efficacy, social status, and life goals (Fryer, 1988; Montada, 1994a; Brinkmann & Wiedemann, 1994; Kieselbach, 1994). Though in the majority of cases, new employment is found within the relatively short period of several months (Franz, 1994), the number of long-term unemployed people is steadily growing (Siebert, 1994). And this, above all, is the subgroup at risk (Brinkmann, 1984; Franz, 1994). The risks are loss of human capital like professional expertise, health impairments, and social discrimination which in combination lead to the "hysteresis", meaning that long-term unemployment causes continued unemployment (Brinkmann, 1989).

Every overgeneralization is inadequate as empirical studies show (Brinkmann, 1984; Fryer, 1988; Montada, 1994a). For instance, the frequency of somatic and psychic health problems resulting from unemployment is significantly increased in long-term unemployment, but not regularly (Banks & Jackson, 1983; Fryer & Payne, 1984). Majorities of elderly employees would prefer an early retirement (long before the official age limits) if adequate retirement benefits could be guaranteed (Schmal, 1993) which quite a few of them raise by additional work on the gray market (Kohli, 1995). For many in the "quiet reserve", paid work is neither the only nor the preferred option in planning their life (Ambos, Gertner & Schiersmann, 1989). Empirical research has helped to identify the risk factors in unemployment: high subjective importance of professional work (which is more common in qualified professions), resulting poverty, and long-term unemployment without meaningful alternative commitments (Fryer, 1988). Youth unemployment holds specific risks: Young people cannot compensate lacking employment by a rich professional, familial or social biography and a stabilized personal identity (Lerner in this volume).

Even if overgeneralizations are avoided, there is evidence that unintentional unemployment is frequently experienced as a serious loss and as a victimization. It is hypothesized that the degree of victimization depends on causal attributions among other factors: Internal explanations threaten the self-esteem more than external ones (Kieselbach, 1994). Mass unemployment is less likely to be explained by internal causes than individual unemployment. However, provided a majority of unemployed people were successful in finding a new job within a relatively short period of time, long-term unemployment would be explained by internal causes. This, at least, is always insinuated by parts of the public who tend to blame the long-term unemployed for lacking qualifications or efforts (Montada & Schneider, 1990a). These judgments may well be experienced by the unemployed as secondary victimizations (Kieselbach, 1994).

Aside from the fact that unemployment is frequently a personal hardship, it is a social evil. It does not only cost a mint of money in benefit payments, it may also threaten the social cohesion and leave a society susceptible for political radicalism what is convincingly demonstrated by the German history in the early thirties (Brinkmann & Wiedemann, 1994). And, of course, the effects are not only on the unemployed themselves but also on those close to them: their children (Madge, 1983), their spouses (McKee & Bell, 1986), their parents, and also their former colleagues, the survivors of lay offs (Brockner, 1990).

It might be that the value paid work has gained in our societies is dangerously high -dangerous with respect to the low chances in our society to realize full employment (Lepenies, 1984) and we should look for alternatives with equivalent functions for self-esteem and a meaningful life. Yet, until we will have available alternatives we have to take every effort to avoid or reduce unemployment.

2. Is Mass Unemployment an Injustice?

Considering the implied losses and risks, long-term unemployment in particular is in many cases a serious jeopardy to life quality and life chances. This fact provokes questions about justice and injustice. To approach the question of whether or not mass unemployment is an injustice, my first suggestion would be to distinguish between *undeservedness* and *injustice* (Montada, 1994c). Every loss or disadvantage is undeserved as long as it is not self-inflicted or voluntarily accepted by the subjects themselves. A loss or disadvantage, such as unemployment, is unjust when other actors (persons, institutions) are responsible for having caused it, for not having prevented it, or for not rectifying it without having a convincing justification for their actions or omissions. The attribution of responsibility presupposes that these actors have control over means or ways to get more people employed and that they ought to use these means.

I will try to outline some aspects which seem important to me for a reasonable reflection about the justice problems implied in unemployment as well as about justice problems implied in policies aimed at reducing it. Any analysis of justice has to refer to reasonable entitlements and corresponding responsibilities and obligations. Therefore, I will start with discussing the concept of a civil right to employment.

3. The Claim for a Civil Right to Employment and Responsibility Attributions to the State

Reflections about mass unemployment under justice perspectives are rooted in conceptions of a desirable constitution of the state and the economy. Liberal constitutions with market economies and communist constitutions offer different solutions. In the formerly communist part of Germany, the civil right and the obligation for every adult citizen to work was part of the constitution. Consequently, providing jobs and distributing them rested with the state who also determined the amounts of working hours and income. As in other communist states, employment was a matter of distributive justice.

Advocates of a free market economy deny the idea that unemployment has anything to do with justice, as long as there really is free competition among employers as well as among the job seeking which can be expected to exclude exploitative use of power-imbalances. Some people might not have to offer useful qualifications that are demanded on the labor market or they do not offer them for prices employers are willing to pay. That, however, is not considered a matter of justice (Keynes, 1960; Merklein, 1994). Granting welfare benefits is another question: Even Hayeck (1991) admits that those who are not able to compete successfully on the labor market to earn their living by employment should be supported by the state.

In free market economies, employment and unemployment are not considered belonging to the domain of distributive justice and to the redistributive responsibilities of the state: Everybody has the basic right to freely chosen economic activities but nobody has the right to become employed. Instead, it is a matter of exchange to be negotiated between employers and employees. Unemployment in a free market society is primarily explained by the fact that prices demanded for work offered are too high. Unfairness in exchange (in contracts) results from imbalances of power between the parties demanding and offering work. The foremost responsibility of the state is to prevent power inbalances. Historically, such imbalances did not only lead to the founding of labor unions, they, furthermore, did condition the conception of the "social market economy". These economies - the West European model - combine components of state controlled economies and free market economies insofar as competition as well as freedom of exchange are basically preserved yet restricted by laws and contracts which mainly aim at the improvement of employees' security (Schlecht, 1994).

The welfare state guarantees participation in general prosperity and culture for every citizen (Timmins, 1995). The paramount importance of professional life obligates the welfare state to intervene into the free market in order to ensure an adequate participation of more citizens for the benefit of general welfare and social goods. It is evident that having employment not only yields a better material basis for life, but also mediates quite a few additional immaterial resources such as social status and prestige, self-esteem, and a meaningful life. Therefore, material benefits or welfare payments might possibly not be considered sufficient compensation for unemployment. As long as professional work cannot be replaced with respect to these immaterial functions, these advocates will hold the state responsible for providing work for everybody who needs it. The big question is how? There is a variety of possible state interventions: protective laws, subsidies for companies, individual branches of business, regions and jobs, takeover of companies by the state, expenditure programs to start economic growth or to stop decline. Even measures such as a temporary freezing of wages and banning of dismissals by law are occasionally claimed.

Concerning these basic philosophies people have widely differing views (Pioch & Vobruba, 1994; Nullmeier & Vobruba, 1994). There are differences between societies as well as within societies. Lane (1986), for instance, reported that majorities in the US rated the justice of the market economy higher than the justice of redistributive activities of the state. However, with respect to the reduction of unemployment, many more considered the state responsible. Still, the view that individuals themselves are responsible for their welfare and not the state, seems to be prevailing in the US whereas state responsibility for individual welfare is rated significantly higher in European countries with a welfare state tradition or a communist past (Wegener, 1994). The intracultural differences are interesting, too. For example, state responsibility is rated higher in East Germany than in West Germany, especially in the "service" class (i.e., the category of professionals).

4. Responsibility Reconsidered

Of course, the state is not the only actor on the market. The national bank, the business banks, the employers and their associations, the unions, the employees, the consumer, the unemployed are some others. Moreover, the national economies are not isolated but internationally linked together. It is not only the state that is able to take measures against unemployment. All other actors can do so, too. Every actor can be considered responsible to take efforts that can achieve improvement and that can reasonably be expected to be followed through. The attribution of responsibility requires assumptions about causes of unemployment, about the controllability of causes, about effective measures to reduce unemployment, and about the control of these measures (Montada, 1994b).

4.1. Causes of Mass Unemployment

What are the experts' views about causes of mass unemployment in the "first world", the OECD countries? The OECD report on unemployment (1994) emphasizes the following causes (see also Siebert, 1994; Kommission der Europäischen Gemeinschaften, 1994):

1. There is an increasing demand for jobs because of the growing participation of women on the labor market and because of immigration from poor countries. It is a fact that even in those countries where the number of jobs substantially grew in the 80s, it did not fit the growing demand.
2. The increase in wage levels and additional labor costs (employers' share in social security, severance payments, medicare) causes pressure to rationalize and to replace labor by capital (machines), especially under the condition of international competition.
3. The *globalization of product markets* produces higher competition especially with economies who have lower labor costs.
4. The internationalization of the labor market facilitates the transfer of jobs from higher wage economies to lower wage economies. To illustrate this: In 1993, hourly wages including social security and medicare in German currency were 41.53 in West Germany, 33.00 in The Netherlands, 27.00 in the US, 9.00 in Taiwan, 2.34 in Poland, and 0.73 in China. Exporting routine industrial jobs to countries with lower wage levels is the consequence which cannot even be criticized since it might well be the most effective kind of foreign aid.
5. The resulting problem for occupational politics in the OECD states is to determine which kind of jobs will be productive in economies with high wage levels, well aware that a substantial part of the population does not have the abilities to perform high-tech jobs or - as Robert Reich (1992) called them - the creative jobs in technology, science, and organizations. We have to look for occupational alternatives for those parts of the popu-

lation that are less qualified or else provide possibilities for them to achieve higher qualifications.

6. In some branches there is currently a mismatch between offered and required qualification profiles (Buttler & Cramer, 1991).

5. Economies are in a continuous process of modernization. Some are behind with these transformations and are lacking modern products, modern technologies, currently needed services, and modern forms of organization (Giersch, 1984).

8. International competition is hampered by tax burdens (Siebert, 1984).

9. High interest rates may prevent necessary investments and reduce consumptive demands (Hoffmann & Scheremet, 1994).

10. Many countries - not so much the United States - have a heap of regulations in labor laws and labor contracts between unions and employers' associations regulating working hours, wages, wage supplements, social security plans, paid vacation, plant operation times, layoff protection, specific requirements for trade and industry, rights of the employed and rights of the dismissed (e.g. amount of unemployment benefits, the right to refuse offered jobs which are less attractive than the former ones), and so forth. All of these are considered by some experts as barriers for higher employment rates (Kommission der Europäischen Gemeinschaften, 1994).

This look at causal hypotheses is incomplete, yet it still allows for an analysis and a discussion of perceived injustices on the labor market.

4.2. Who Is Responsible? The Construction of Reality

A look at the list of possible causes allows the attribution of responsibilities to several actors on the market. The *parliament* is responsible for labor laws and tax rates. The government, together with the *parliament*, is responsible for education, the allocation of social security benefits, granting and allocating subsidies, and the immigration politics. The *national bank* is coresponsible for interest rates and exchange rates. *Employers* are responsible for necessary modernizations, the *employees*, together with the unions, are responsible for labor costs, the employees and the *unemployed* for maintaining and increasing their qualification level and their readiness to mobility and flexibility.

Of course, there are trends and events which do not fall in the responsibility of identifiable actors: The growing demand for employment by women is part of the *Zeitgeist* (spirit of the age), the *immigration* from poor countries into wealthier ones cannot be controlled perfectly, *economical* crises seem to be international and are hard to prevent, and the *internationalization of the labor market* simply has to be accepted as a fact.

Given the diversity of responsible actors and the fact that some causes of unemployment are objectively not controllable, the attribution of responsibility becomes an act of individual or social construction of the reality. The same is true for the allocation of obligations to agents or institutions.

5. The (Social) Construction of Justice

Is mass unemployment unjust? Many say yes, quite a lot of them with emphasis, with emotional impetus and outrage. Others say no, and it is interesting to determine empirically what these judgments and feelings depend on: the social position of respondents, the security of their job, their political orientation, the individually preferred justice principles, their attributions of responsibility or personal traits like belief in a just world, sensitivity to befallen injustice, self-efficacy, and control beliefs, etc. All of the variables mentioned are moderately correlated with judgments about the injustice of mass unemployment (Montada & Schneider, 1990a).

When studying perceptions and feelings of injustice it becomes obvious that the implied cognitions are frequently not well articulated and reflected. This is demonstrated by the fact that general judgments and feelings about injustice are only moderately high correlated with statements about specific aspects when much closer connections are expected on the bases of conceptual implications. Psychology can help subjects to explicate their feelings in the sense of articulating the implicit cognitions and assumptions which might be necessary to test their validity and to possibly change them in the light of economic knowledge.

When dealing with perceptions of the injustice of unemployment, with the responsibilities of various actors on the labor market, and with the efficiency and justice of occupational policies, we actually need interdisciplinary cooperation in order to put the assessed individual views into the perspective of expert knowledge even if this is not consensual.

Outrage about the injustice of unemployment does not a priori convey an ethical truth. It has to be seen in the light of facts which are described by different disciplines: economy, sociology, medicine, psychology. The same holds true when the jobless are blamed for self-infliction of their situation. We have to explore subjects' explanations of unemployment, their responsibility attributions, and their ascriptions of duties if we want to understand their feelings of injustice or their reproaches. But then we will have to reflect their judgments in the light of scientifically proven knowledge about facts and knowledge about the controllability and effectiveness of the means that we intend to apply.

What we can observe in Germany and elsewhere is a prevailing tendency to attribute responsibility for the causation of mass unemployment to the industry and to attribute responsibility for its remedy to the government (Montada & Mohiyeddini, 1995). But there are significant interindividual differences: blaming the jobless, the unions, and denying all responsibility also occurs (Montada & Schneider, 1990b; Montada & Mohiyeddini, 1995). Frequently, the attributions are biased or made without sound economic knowledge. Efforts to improve the knowledge and to reduce biases are helpful in starting a fair public debate about what can be done, what should be done, and who can contribute to it.

In the light of economic analyses, the list of factors that contribute to unemployment is impressively long as was reported above: interest rates; currency exchange rates; lack of innovative products and services; the state of the economy to do this; demand for goods and services which again depends on income, prices, and interest rates; levels of qualification by employees and those who are looking for jobs, employees' mobility; flexible working hours; costs for dismissals which prevent new hiring; protective rules for layoffs which constitute a handicap for entering the labor market, and so forth. All in all: a complex network of interrelated factors which are only more or less controllable is presented.

Some factors can be controlled by the state, others by the economy, still others by the unions, by financial politics regulated by the national banks, and, last not least, there are also some factors that can be controlled by the employees and the job seeking themselves because they have some control over their qualifications, their mobility, and their readiness to share working time and income.

Few people have sufficient knowledge and are sufficiently free of bias to make fair responsibility attributions. There seems to be a tendency to charge the state and the industry which is understandable in the light of Judith Shklar's thesis to search for responsible agents when threatening things happen (Shklar, 1991). The market—Adam Smith's invisible hand—cannot be used for responsibility attributions since it is not an agent. However, there are other agents that can be charged with responsibilities. To arrive at fair solutions all possible agents have to be charged. Biased responsibility attributions allow denial and defense and are an obstacle for common efforts.

Those who perceive mass unemployment as unjust tend to acknowledge a causal relationship between their own favorable professional life and the unemployment of others, they tend to favor the need principle over the equity principle in the allocation of jobs (and dismissals), they tend to experience existential guilt feelings and resentment vis a vis the fate of jobless people, and they tend to show readiness to prosocial commitments for the unemployed. At the same time, it is less likely that they will blame the unemployed for self-infliction and that they will attribute negative traits to them. (Montada & Schneider, 1990a; 1990b).

Interestingly, the readiness to individually realized renounciations in terms of reducing working hours and wage reductions in order to save jobs or create new ones is not well predicted by resentment about injustice. It seems more likely to be motivated by existential guilt feelings. Resentment is rather related to claiming activities from others like the state and the industry (Montada & Schneider, 1990b).

Those employees who perceive mass unemployment as unjust and those who are resenting this injustice do not tend to hold the jobless or the unions and their policy responsible for the unemployment. Instead, they tend to blame the government, the employers and their policy of rationalization as well as the internationalized economy. The exact opposite pattern of relationships was found for those who blame the jobless for self-infliction. These differences are partly mirrored in the attributions of responsibility for the reduction of unemployment (Montada & Schneider, 1990b; Montada & Mohiyeddini, 1995).

Those who judge mass unemployment unjust tend to dispute that employers are free to hire and fire employees as they seem fit. Claiming a general entitlement to obtain employment is correlated with judging unemployment as unjust Montada & Mohiyeddini, 1995).

Resentment about the injustice of unemployment is correlated with a positive view of the following measures to reduce unemployment: stop of rationalizations and automatizations in companies, granting state subsidies to support the maintenance of jobs and the creation of new jobs, freezing higher wages, claiming job splitting, and cancelling overtime work. All these measures are rejected by those who blame the jobless and the unions for having caused unemployment. (Montada & Schneider, 1990b).

6. The (In-)Justice of Occupational Policies

I want to outline the discussion about efficiency and justice of a few measures proposed in the current discussions. I will do so in a somewhat simplified manner. In fact, I will focus on the basic conflicts without making further reference to other more marginal viewpoints.

Every single measure (and every group of measures) has to be evaluated under two perspectives: the perspective of justice and the perspective of efficiency. Traditionally, efficiency in the sense of maximizing common goods and justice are considered independent dimensions. In political and economic philosophy there are, of course, efforts to integrate both. Pareto's optimality criterion and Rawls' theory of justice are prominent examples for putting efficiency on the chain of justice. I am convinced that it should also be possible to chain justice to efficiency: It is common sense knowledge that it is unjust to deny the population higher prosperity provided it can be realized without unreasonable risks and and one-sided allocation of costs. Suppose, that equality would be the preferred principle of justice, then equal prosperity and equal poverty were equally just, yet, when applying a productivistic principle of justice (Vobruba 1994), withholding higher prosperity could still be judged as unjust.

Concerning occupational policies the justice is judged by considering the relation and the distribution of gains and costs.

6.1. General Reduction of Working Hours

The basic, yet disputable idea is that there is a total amount of work available. A normative reduction of working hours for all employees would allow a broader distribution of working time and thus, reduce unemployment (Kommission der Europäischen Gemeinschaften, 1994). Provided a sufficient number of equally qualified applicants were available, the logic would be appealing. The question is, whether the majority of employees who are not afraid to lose their jobs would be ready to accept a proportional cutback in income.

Currently, having the attitudes of their members in mind, the unions claim more or less full compensation of income which implies a proportional increase in hourly wages. The basis of this claim for compensation is the principle of preservation of acquired entitlements which allows the defense of current income and favorable privileges. Were this request accepted, it would mean an increase in labor costs for employers with all the possible consequences already mentioned (e.g. pressure to rationalize instead of creating new positions) (McKee & Bell, 1986; Siebert, 1994).

Basically, two justice problem arise with this measure: (1) the distribution of costs for new jobs between employers and employees, (2) the distribution of working time and income between employees and the unemployed. There are rare examples of solidarity and of readiness to share both working time and income. Volkswagen, in Germany, is an already famous example. In 1993, when business was slow, the complete staff accepted a cut in working hours and in annual income in order to avoid dismissals. The reduction in income was less than a proportional cut would have been, meaning that the company also assumed a share of the costs.

The readiness to accept reductions in working time without full financial compensation varies interindividually. It is positively correlated with the perception of a causal relation between ones' own favorable life situation and the unfavorable situation of the unemployed, with judging unemployment as unjust and resenting this injustice, and with existential guilt feelings about own advantages that are not fully deserved. It is negatively correlated with blaming the unemployed for having self-inflicted their failure on the labor market (Montada & Schneider, 1990b)

6.2. Creating More Part-time Positions

In many, if not in all OECD countries, preferences for part-time employment significantly surpass the number of currently available part-time positions. Mainly women who care for a family are forerunners for this preference, yet the number of men with the same preference is increasing. This preference is documented among both people seeking jobs and full-time employees (Deutsches Institut für Wirtschaftsforschung, 1992). Part-time employment might also be preferred frequently by elderly employees who favor a stepwise transition into retirement (Bäcker, 1994) as well as by younger people who want more time for educational, familial, and personal commitments (Schmal, 1995). Others would be willing to reduce their working time to help create jobs for the unemployed.

To split full-time positions would increase the number of jobs. If all those who want one would get a part-time job, unemployment could be substantially reduced. As long as part-time employment is individually preferred, no justice problem will arise by reductions in working time and income (Nozick, 1974).

There are two major barriers against part-time work. Where social security insurance is bound to wages, part-time work will mean reduced benefits. A government supported increase in social security dues would make the voluntary decision to reduce a full-time position to part-time a lot easier (Bäcker & Stolz-Willing, 1994). On the side of the employers, however, the organizational load would be higher and some other difficulties might arise (e.g. to have an equal distribution of part-time employees available over the whole period of time), and there is considerable reluctance to offer more part-time jobs. Since there are neither serious efficiency problems nor serious justice problems, splitting jobs could be an important contribution to reduce umemployment (Bundesministerium für Arbeit und Sozialordnung, 1994).

6.3. Flexibilization of Working Times

In many OECD countries typical labor contracts stipulate a fixed weekly working time. Flexible working time would mean a reduction in labor costs. Employers would not have to pay for times where no work is available, and they would not have to pay overtime for extra working hours needed. There is growing insight that high labor costs jeopardize jobs (Hoffmann & Scheremet, 1994; Siebert, 1994). Thus, flexibility is currently agreed upon in more and more contracts. This might secure jobs or else help create new ones in the long run. Since flexibility does not mean reduction in total working time agreed upon, but rather a flexible distribution over a given time period there are no financial losses for employees which might raise justice problems with the exception of overtime pay that would not be paid anymore.

6.4. Moderate Increases or Reduction in Wage Levels and Additional Wage Related Labor Costs

High labor costs may provoke rationalizations and replacement of labor by capital (i.e., machines) and, as a consequence, may increase unemployment (Siebert, 1994; McKee & Bell, 1986). Moderate labor costs may allow price reduction, thus, improving the chances of successful competition. It might also improve profits which would be available for new investments. To judge the social justice of this measure, it has to be considered how this saved money is used. If wage reductions are used to save jobs, it would actually be in the self-interest of employees to agree to wage reductions. If they are used to create new jobs, it could be justified as an act of solidarity by employees with the unemployed.

Usually, wage agreements negotiated between unions and employers contain linear wage increases over all wage levels. The fact is, that successive linear wage increases had the effect of spreading open income inequality significantly over the decades. Since this effect was not the explicit and justified consent in the wage contracts, it seems reasonable to reduce these accumulated inequalities compensatorily by reducing wages in a nonlinear manner. Again, however, we have to keep in mind that those who had the advantage of linear increases in the past will now claim the preservation of acquired entitlements. It might even be that a preservation of differential wages would be claimed.

6.5. Spread of Wages at the Lower End of the Income Scale

The relatively high proportion of the poorly qualified among the unemployed gives evidence to the view that the less demanding jobs are considered unproductive as long as wages are relatively too high and the jobs can easily be cancelled or replaced by machines (Siebert, 1994). What is most urgently needed are jobs for the poorly qualified: simple routine jobs in the industry, simple service jobs among others in personal services. Such jobs could be created if wages were lower (Franz, 1994; Klös, 1993).

The problem is the "working poor" effect which means that a full-time employment does not yield an income above the poverty level. To bypass this problem, several models of combining a market income with added welfare benefits are discussed to ensure a minimum income (Scharpf, 1993). The main problem here is to find a way to do it without wiping out the incentive to seek and accept a job. Layard (1994) demonstrated a functional relation between the duration of unemployment and the amount and the duration of granted unemployment benefits. His plea is a progressive reduction of benefits in order to further the incentive to seek and accept available jobs.

According to the German labor market laws no unemployed person can be expected to accept an offered job that is significantly below his or her former level of employment with respect to wage, kind of work, working hours, distance from home etc. Unemployment benefits cannot be shortened when offered jobs are refused which do not meet the standards of one's former employment.

The gap between a low working income and welfare benefits has to be significant in order to keep up the motivation to work: Employees should not judge their input for a work income inequitably high compared to the welfare benefits unemployed people receive.

6.6. Second Labor "Market"

In the majority of OECD countries, huge amounts in subsidies are spent to reduce unemployment. Free of charge retraining programs, wage subsidies, early retirement programs, financial support or tax privileges granted to specific branches or companies, takeover of insolvent companies by the state, and governmental expenditure programs to stimulate the economy are some of the measures used (Brinkmann & Buttler, 1994; Kühl, 1993; Blanpain & Sadowski, 1994). The slogan is "It is better to pay for labor than to pay for unemployment".

Compared with these measures, a "second labor market" would have a new quality. The idea is to establish publicly subsidized companies where jobless people find employment. The companies are expected to operate at a loss in the hope, that, over time, these losses will be gradually reduced by growing returns. To give an example: To buffer the consequences of the breakdown in East German industries, so-called "Beschäftigungsgesellschaften" (occupational corporations) were established, in the hope that they might have a chance to get orders for work and earn part of the costs created by them. The rate of these corporations that have achieved sustainable success and that are approaching financial independence, however, has turned out to be very low (Knuth, 1994). One of the many problems is that qualified and mobile employees rather seek their chances on the first labor market.

The structural problem with a second labor market is that it is not bound to the conditions and "economical laws" of a market (Franz, 1994; Siebert, 1994). Established to provide unemployed people with a meaningful task, dismissals because of poor business, lacking qualification, and motivation of employees are somewhat incompatible with the original purpose. The second labor market might turn more into "labor welfare" than to become a market. Consequently, essential effects of a successful participation in the first labor market might be lacking, such as self-esteem based on successful competition (Montada, 1994b). Moreover, social prestige should be expected to be low in case this second labor market is considered as an expensive rescue endeavor for losers and poorly qualified people. A transition into the first labor market will be the success criterion both for individuals and companies.

To belong to the second labor market over a prolonged period of time might well turn out to be discriminative. Therefore, the alternative to pay subsidies to the first labor market for creating jobs for the unemployed should be given preference (Scharpf, 1993). The counterargument, though, is hard to disprove: Employers will be tempted to misuse the subsidies by replacing regular positions with subsidized ones. Such a misuse would be hard to punish without jeopardizing jobs. A second justice-related counterargument is the following: Every subsidy is an intervention into the competitiveness of companies.

6.7. Promoting and Supporting New Ventures

Stable employment requires successful employers. Reduction of unemployment is not sustainably done by state support of dying industries. Instead, support of new ventures might be more successful even if many of them do not survive (Giersch, 1994). The ones that are successful are the fittest to provide employment. Within a market economy, long lasting state subsidies to poorly operating companies and branches are hard to justify. The basic economical tasks of a liberal state are to grant fair chances for all citizens by providing adequate education, to protect its citizens and industries against unfair exploitation, to protect the market by securing competition, and, above all, to help the national economy to be successful on an international market. Supporting individual companies can only be justified as a measure (1) to ensure competition and (2) to ensure the future. It is easier to justify a support of new ventures since they will stimulate competition. Supporting dying industries conveys wrong messages such as the following: The state is responsible for the survival of industries. Employees can count on the responsibility of the state instead of taking efforts to obtain better qualifications and to increase their mobility. Corporations can count on the state instead of taking efforts to maintain their ability to compete. Nevertheless, claims for state interventions to protect obsolete industries are quite common. Those who claim them have no doubts about their justice and their efficiency (Montada & Mohiyeddini, 1995).

6.8. Deregulation

The OECD (1994) as well as the EU (1994) claim a new evaluation of the many existing regulations in labor and business that were introduced for the protection of employees but bore the side effect of disadvantaging the unemployed. For illustrative purpose, I will mention one category of regulations. Protection against dismissals and severance pay, for instance, are in fact protecting the employees, yet, at the same time, they function as barriers against new employment (Bäcker, 1994; Walwei, 1993). Thus, they disadvantage the unemployed (Blanpain & Sadowski, 1984). The special German laws that protect elderly employees or the handicapped against dismissals do, in fact, protect the employed but significantly reduce the chances of the unemployed elderly or handicapped to find employment. Severence pay regulations operate in the same direction: Employers regularly prefer to pay for overtime done by their employees than to hire additional staff. The reason is that this way they avoid the risks the regulations are imposing in case of necessary dismissals. It is actually a case of insider protection at the expense of outsiders.

7. The Distribution of Costs

Occupational policies, as exemplified by this list of measures, have material and immaterial costs. The question is who should be charged with expenses and who should be burdened with immaterial costs; what would be just or unjust? When calculating the expenses for any measure, the expenses saved for welfare and unemployment benefits have to be subtracted. Furthermore, the expenses for long-term consequences of mass unemployment on the individual level (like, for instance, loss of human capital, health problems, drug abuse, delinquency, developmental disadvantages for children) as well as on the societal level (desintegration, growth of slums) may even by far surmount the costs that currently have to be paid.

Another question is the distribution of costs. In the public debate, biased proposals to defend own advantages are common practice. I am not in a position to suggest any specific reasonable distribution. Listening to the ongoing debate, however, I would like to raise some other questions:

1. Would it be inefficient and unjust to allocate costs in such a way that existing jobs were threatened by pressure to rationalize or that investments for creating new jobs became impossible?
2. Isn't it reasonable to distribute the costs not equally but proportionally to (the differences in) prosperity, because the utility of the same amount of money decreases with increasing wealth according to the law of marginal utility.
3. Is it just to insist on acquired entitlements (advantages) when, by keeping them, the undeserved disadvantages of others cannot be rectified? The youth, for instance, will have significantly lower chances on the labor market when the older generations defend their entitlements.

7.1. Is It Just to Defend Acquired Entitlements?

The typical pattern in every debate about occupational policies that aim at reducing unemployment is the defense of acquired entitlements, some of which were already mentioned above. It has to be noted that these entitlements were granted without considering their negative functions or side effects. The unions fought successfully for higher wages, for full payments during even prolonged periods of sick leave, for restrictions in working times etc., and they successfully negotiated contracts with the employers which turned out to be on the back of third parties: those who are laid off as a consequence of these contracts, those who cannot find an occupation including the youth (who is confronted with the fact that all positions are filled by the preceding generations who are protected by laws aginst lay off), and, last not least, the state or the society that has to pay a share of the unemployment benefits, pay for further consequences of unemployment and for welfare benefits.

While in the public debate terms like solidarity and social justice are frequently used, the defense of the parties' own advantages seems dominant in actual distributional conflicts. By looking at the results of several of our studies about how other peoples' disadvantaged life situation is perceived, this is somewhat surprising.

7.2. A Look at the Hidden Reservoir of Communitarian Attitudes and Feelings

Same as any other policy, the distribution of costs for occupational policies should be accepted by the public. Therefore, information about the distribution of views and attitudes in the public is important as long as it helps to identify gaps in knowledge, problematic attitudes, or incompatible justice conceptions and motivations. In this respect I will shortly review some lines of empirical results we obtained from some German studies.

These studies demonstrate that it is false to assume that attitudes and opinions about unemployment are predominantly egoistical. Existential guilt feelings about own advantages (advantages that are not justified by respondents as deserved) are not an exotic emotional response to unemployment but are normally distributed in various heterogeneous samples. Resentment about an unjust distribution of advantages and disadvantages are by no means restricted to the disadvantaged but were observed regularly in subpopulations that are well off economically, where everybody has a secure work position and where nobody fears being laid off. Insight into the causal relationships between ones' own economic situation and the less fortunate state of the unemployed have a similar normal distribution and are substantially correlated with judging unemployment as unjust, with existential guilt feelings, and with resentment about the injustice of the distribution of advantages. There is a general readiness to support the unemployed and some readiness to make personal sacrifices (Montada & Schneider, 1989, 1990b).

This is not denying that the defense of acquired entitlements is not a powerful motive in the political arena; it is evident in every distributional conflict. Looking at our survey data, we doubt however, that these motives were assumed, postulated, and articulated by the respective advocates in the political arena. It might well be that by overgeneralizing egoistical motives these advocates in fact induce these motives (Miller in this volume). It could be influential if studies which demonstrate the existence of attitudes of solidarity were acknowledged by political actors. Again, the social construction of the reality depends on information.

In sum, as I read our data, there is a rather broad motivational basis which could well be counted on in structuring a more communitarian policy. Looking at the literature regarding prosocial behavior and social support (Montada & Bierhoff, 1991) it becomes obvious, however, that the readiness to continued social support depends on its efficiency more than anything else (Rabinowitz, Karuza & Zevon 1986). Therefore, the policies applied may be costly - data from various polls prove that majorities in European countries are ready to reduce their own income if new jobs are created - but they have to be successful insofar that a significant number of people will be employed again and the rate of unemployment will go down drastically.

References

Ambos, I., Gertner, S. & Schiersmann, C. (1989). Zur Situation von Berufsrück-kehrerinnen. Frauenforschung, I/2, 5-26.

Bäcker, G. & Stolz-Willig, B. (1994). Mehr Teilzeit - aber wie? Zur Diskussion über Förderung und soziale Absicherung optionaler Arbeitszeiten. Wirtschafts- und Sozialwissenschaftliches Institut des DGB. WSI-Diskussionspapier Nr. 20.

Bäcker, G. (1994). Ältere Arbeitnehmer zwischen Dauerarbeitslosigkeit und demographischem Umbruch. In L. Montada (Ed.), Arbeitslosigkeit und soziale Gerechtigkeit (pp. 131-149). Frankfurt/M.: Campupp.

Banks, M. H. & Jackson, P. R. (1983). Unemployment and risk of minor psychiatric disorder in young people: Cross-sectional and longitudinal evidence. Psychological Medicine, 12, 789-798.

Blanpain, R. & Sadowski, D. (1994). Habe ich morgen noch einen Job? Die Zukunft der Arbeit in Europa. München: Verlag C. H. Beck.

Brinkmann, C. (1984). Die individuellen Folgen langfristiger Arbeitslosigkeit. Ergebnisse einer repräsentativen Längsschnittuntersuchung. Mitteilungen aus Arbeitsmarkt- und Berufsforschung, 17(4), 454-473.

Brinkmann, C. (1989). Ursachen und Auswirkungen von Langzeitarbeitslosigkeit. Gefährdetenhilfe, 4, 117-124.

Brinkmann, C. & Buttler, F. (1994). Weiterentwicklung der Arbeitsplatzförderung und mehr Selektivität. In L. Montada (Ed.), Arbeitslosigkeit und soziale Gerechtigkeit (pp. 312-321). Frankfurt/M.: Campus.

Brinkmann, C. & Wiedemann, E. (1994). Individuelle und gesellschaftliche Folgen von Erwerbslosigkeit in Ost und West. In L. Montada (Ed.), Arbeitslosigkeit und soziale Gerechtigkeit (pp. 175-192). Frankfurt/M.: Campus.

Brockner, (1990). Scope of justice in the workplace: How survivors react to co-workers layoffs. Journal of Social Issues, 46, 95-106.

Bundesministerium für Arbeit und Sozialordnung (Ed.) (1994). Teilzeit hilft. Teilzeit Arbeit. Ein Leitfaden für Arbeitnehmer und Arbeitgeber. Bonn: Bundesdruckerei.

Deutsches Institut für Wirtschaftsforschung (1992). Wochenbericht 33. Berlin: DIW.

Buttler, F. & Cramer, U. (1991). Entwicklungen und Ursachen von mis-match Arbeitslosigkeit in Westdeutschland. Mitteilungen aus der Arbeitsmarkt- und Berufsforschung, 3, 483-500.

Franz, W. (1994). Säkulare Unterbeschäftigung: Ist die Zwei-Drittel-Gesellschaft noch zu vermeiden? In Alfred Herrhausen Gesellschaft für internationalen Dialog (Ed.), Arbeit der Zukunft -Zukunft der Arbeit (pp. 57-78). Stuttgart: Schäffer-Poeschel.

Franz, W. & Profit, S. (1994). Wege aus der Unterbeschäftigung. In H. König (Ed.), Bringt die EU-Beschäftigungsoffensive den Aufschwung? Die deutsche Wirtschaftsforschung nimmt Stellung zum Delors-Weißbuch (Sonderband 1, 101-122). Baden-Baden: Nomos

Fryer, D. & Payne, R. L. (1984). Proactive behavior in unemployment: Findings and implications. Leisure Studies, 3, 273-295.

Fryer, D. (1988). The experience of unemployment in social context. In S. Fisher & J. Reason (Eds.), Handbook of life stress, cognition, and health (pp. 211-238). Chichester: Wiley.

Giersch, H. (1994). Die Industrie und das Beschäftigungssystem im weltweiten Strukturwandel. In Alfred Herrhausen Gesellschaft für internationalen Dialog (Ed.), Arbeit der Zukunft - Zukunft der Arbeit (pp. 151-178). Stuttgart: Schäffer-Poeschel.

Hayeck, F. A. von (1991). Die Verfassung der Freiheit. Tübingen: Mohr.

Hoffmann, L. & Scheremet, W. (1994). Wege zur Überwindung der Arbeitslosigkeit in Deutschland und Europa. Liberal, 36, 2.

Keynes, J. M. (1960). The general theory of employment interest and money. London: Macmillan.

Kieselbach, T. (1994). Arbeitslosigkeit als psychologisches Problem -auf individueller und gesellschaftlicher Ebene. In L. Montada (Ed.), Arbeitslosigkeit und soziale Gerechtigkeit (pp. 233-263). Frankfurt/M.: Campus.

Klös, H.-P. (1993). Investive Arbeitsmarktpolitik statt konsumptiver Lohnersatz. In Forschungsinstitut der Friedrich-Ebert-Stiftung, Ab. Arbeits- und Sozialforschung (Ed.), Neu Ansätze in der Arbeitsmarktpolitik. Ist ein Gesamtkonzept für die neuen und alten Bundesländer erforderlich? Gesprächskreis Arbeit und Soziales Nr. 18 (S. 73-102). Bonn.

Knuth, M. (1994). Zwei Jahre ABS-Gesellschaften in den neuen Bundesländern. Ergebnisse einer schriftlichen Befragung im November 1993. IAT -AM 09. Gelsenkirchen: Institut Arbeit und Technik.

Kohli, M. (1995). Erwerbsarbeit und ihre Alternativen. In M. Baltes & L. Montada (Eds.), Produktives Leben im Alter (pp. 154-175). Frankfurt/M.: Campus.

Kommission der Europäischen Gemeinschaften zu Wachstum, Wettbewerbsfähigkeit und Beschäftigung (1994). Weißbuch. Luxemburg: EU.

Kramer, H. (1994). Maßnahmen gegen die Arbeitslosigkeit und zum Erhalt von Beschäftigungsverhältnissen aus österreichischer Sicht. In L. Montada (Ed.), Arbeitslosigkeit und soziale Gerechtigkeit (pp. 292-301). Frankfurt/M.: Campus.

Kühl, J. (1993). Echte Beschäftigungspolitik und aktivere Arbeitsmarktpolitik für Ost- und Westdeutschland. In Forschungsinstitut der Friedrich-Ebert-Stiftung, Ab. Arbeits- und Sozialforschung (Ed.), Neu Ansätze in der Arbeitsmarktpolitik. Ist ein Gesamtkonzept für die neuen und alten Bundesländer erforderlich? Gesprächskreis Arbeit und Soziales Nr. 18 (S. 13-31). Bonn.

Lane, R. E. (1986). Market justice and political justice. American Political Science Review, 80, 383-402.

Layard, R. (1994). Vermeidung von Langzeit-Arbeitslosigkeit. In Alfred Herrhausen Gesellschaft für internationalen Dialog (Ed.), Arbeit der Zukunft -Zukunft der Arbeit (S. 135-150). Stuttgart: Schäffer-Poeschel.

Lepenies, W. (1994). "Wäre ich König, so wäre ich gerecht." Gerechtigkeit: Ein Schlüsselbegriff in den gesellschaftspolitischen Auseinandersetzungen der Gegenwart. In L. Montada (Ed.), Arbeitslosigkeit und soziale Gerechtigkeit (pp. 9-33). Frankfurt/M.: Campus.

Madge, N. (1983). Unemployment and ist effects on children. Journal of Child Psychology and Psychiatry, 24, 311-319.

McKee, L. & Bell, C. (1986). His unemployment, her problem: The domestic and marital consequences of male unemployment. In S. Allen, A. Watson, K. Purcell & S. Wood (Eds.), The experience of unemployment (pp. 134-149). Basingstoke: Macmillan.

Merklein, R. (1994). Kann Arbeitslosigkeit "ungerecht" seub? Die zentrale Rolle der Löhne. In L. Montada (Ed.), Arbeitslosigkeit und soziale Gerechtigkeit (pp. 282-291). Frankfurt/M.: Campus.

Montada, L. (1994a). Arbeitslosigkeit ein Gerechtigkeitsproblem? In L. Montada (Ed.), Arbeitslosigkeit und soziale Gerechtigkeit (pp. 53-86). Frankfurt/M.: Campus.

Montada, L. (1994b). Maßnahmen gegen Arbeitslosigkeit: Bewertungen unter Gerechtigkeitsaspekten. In L. Montada (Ed.), Arbeitslosigkeit und soziale Gerechtigkeit (pp. 264-281). Frankfurt/M.: Campus.

Montada, L. (1994c). Injustice in harm and loss. Social Justice Research, 7, 5-28.

Montada, L. & Bierhoff, H.W. (Eds.) (1991). Altruism in social systems. Lewiston, NY: Hogrefe & Huber Publishers.

Montada, L. & Mohiyeddini, C. (1995). Arbeitslosigkeit und Gerechtigkeit. (Berichte aus der Arbeitsgruppe "Verantwortung, Gerechtigkeit, Moral" Nr. 87). Trier: Universität Trier, Fb I - Psychologie.

Montada, L. & Schneider, A. (1990a). Justice and emotional reactions to the disadvantaged. Social Justice Research, 3, 313-344.

Montada. L. & Schneider, A. (1990b). Coping mit Problemen sozialer Schwacher: Annotierte Ergebnistabellen(Berichte aus der Arbeitsgruppe "Verantwortung, Gerechtigkeit, Moral" Nr. 52). Trier: Universität Trier, Fb I -Psychologie.

Nozick, R. (1974). Anarchy, state, and utopia. New York: Basic Books.

Nullmeier, F. & Vobruba, G. 81994). Gerechtigkeit im sozialpolitischen Diskurs. In D. Döring, F. Nullmeier, R. Pioch & G. Vorbruba (Eds.), Gerechtigkeit im Wohlfahrtsstaat (pp. 11-66). Marburg: Schüren Presseverlag GmbH.

Organisation für Wirtschaftliche Zusammenarbeit und Entwicklung (1994). OECD-Beschäftigungsstudie. Fakten - Analysen - Strategien. Paris: OECD-Publications.

Pioch, R. & Vobruba, G. (1994). Gerechtigkeitsvorstellungen im Wohlfahrtsstaat. Sekundäreanalysen empirischer Untersuchungen zur Akzeptanz wohlfahrtsstaatlicher Maßnahmen. In D. Döring, F. Nullmeier, R. Pioch & G. Vorbruba (Eds.), Gerechtigkeit im Wohlfahrtsstaat (pp. 114-166). Marburg: Schüren Presseverlag GmbH.

Rabinowitz, V., Karuza, J. & Zevon, M. A. (1986). Fairness and effectiveness in premediated helping. In J. M. Olson, C.P. Hermann & M. P. Zanna (Eds.), Relative deprivation and social comparison (pp. 63-92). Hillsdale, N.J.: Lawrence Erlbaum.

Reich, R. B. (1992). The work of nations. Preparing ourselves for 21st century capitalism. New York:

Scharpf, F. W. (1993). Von der Finanzierung der Arbeitslosigkeit zur Subventionirung niedriger Erwerbseinkommen. Gewerkschaftliche Monatshefte, 7, 433-443.

Schlecht, O. (1994). Die Idee der Sozialen Marktwirtschaft. In P. Bocklet, G. Fels & H. Löwe (Eds.), Der Gesellschaft verpflichtet (pp. 89-101). Köln: Deutscher Institutsverlag.

Schmal, A. (1993). Problemgruppen oder Resreven für den Arbeitsmarkt. Frankfurt/M.: Campus.

Schmal, A. (1995). Bereitschaft und Motive zur Präferenz von Teilzeitbeschäftigung. Unveröff. Manuskript, Universität Trier.

Shklar, J. (1990). The faces of justice. New Haven: Yale University Press.

Siebert, H. (1994). Geht den Deutschen die Arbeit aus? München: Bertelsmann.

Timmins, N. (1995). The five giants. The biography of the welfare state. London: Harper.

Vobruba, G. (1994). Die Faktizität der Geltung. Gerechtigkeit im sozialpolitischen Umbau Diskurs. Vortrag gehalten auf dem 27. Kongreß der Deutschen Gesellschaft für Soziologie in Halle.

Walwei, U. (1993). External effects of dismissal protection on unemployed outsiders. Paper presented at the EALE-Conference in Maastricht, September 30th - October 3rd, 1993.

Wegener, B. (1994). Die Vorstellungen von sozialer Gerechtigkeit in den neuen und alten Bundesländern: Normative und rationale Tendenzen in der Phase des Übergangs. In B. Wegener u.a. (Eds.), Die Wahrnehmung sozialer Gerechtigkeit in Deutschland im internationalen Vergleich. Abschlußbericht für den deutschen Teil des internationalen Social Justice Projects (pp. 237-268). Berlin: Humboldt Universität zu Berlin, Institut für Soziologie.

11

What Is Fair in the Environmental Debate?*

Susan Clayton

1. What Is Fair in the Environmental Debate?

Public debate over environmental issues has become a battle to define what is fair. For the most part, none of the competing positions claims to be ruled principally by self-interest. And, although the economic literature on methods for allocating natural resources is vast, considerations of productivity and efficiency do not seem to be foremost in reactions to environmental conflicts. It is increasingly difficult to escape a sense that environmental resources are not limitless and that some of them, in fact, are already in short supply. Since there are not enough resources for everyone to have as much as she or he wants, the situation is perceived to require some distributive tradeoffs. There is therefore a need to determine what distributive rule, and even what process for determining that distributive rule, will be most just (Lerner, 1981). There is evidence that perceptions of justice affect environmental attitudes and behavior. Kals (1993), for example, found that perceived justice of various policies was a significant predictor of attitudes toward various environmental policies in Germany. Opotow (1994) has shown that including the bombardier beetle in one's scope of justice was a

*Thanks are due to two anonymous reviewers for their comments on an earlier draft.

Susan Clayton • Department of Psychology, The College of Wooster, Wooster, Ohio 44691

Current Societal Concerns about Justice, edited by Leo Montada and Melvin J. Lerner. Plenum Press, New York, 1996.

significant mediator between attitudes about the beetle and support for providing environmental protection for the beetle. Finally, Axelrod (1994; Axelrod & Lehman, 1992) has found evidence that, at least for some people, "principled" outcomes—which certainly include outcomes that would be defined as just—have a greater impact on decisions in environmental conflicts than do economic or social consequences. But there is no standard, culturally-promulgated way of thinking about justice with regard to the environment. It is only recently that human interaction with the natural environment has widely been seen as involving ethical decisions and considerations of fairness (e.g., Heberlein, 1972). Thus there is perhaps a broader range of ways in which justice is embodied in the environmental debate than in regard to other social issues, and there is more of a contest to see which view will emerge as the dominant one in public policy.

Appeals to justice matter. Framing an issue in terms of justice may lead to a resistance to considering other aspects, such as technological or economic ones (Vaughan & Siefert, 1992). In the U.S., for example, there is controversy over the use of Superfund money to clean up locations contaminated by toxic waste. Some feel that the sites should be completely cleaned, regardless of the cost. Others argue that some cost-benefit analysis should be involved, and that the amount of money required to "completely" clean a site is out of proportion to the risk compared to a less thorough cleaning. If one is framing the issue in terms of people's rights not to be exposed to toxic chemicals, attaching a monetary value to the lives saved may seem offensive.

Framing an issue in terms of justice may also bestow an importance that would otherwise be lacking, perhaps by placing a somewhat minor event in a larger context. Protests against local pollution among African American communities seem to have increased since the rise in awareness of "environmental discrimination"—the fact that minority communities suffer disproportionately from pollution in this country (Vaughan & Siefert, 1992).

Finally, framing an issue in terms of justice has behavioral implications. "Defining a situation as unjust is more than an act of categorization; it implies a strategy for action" (Capek, 1993, p.7). Framing environmental issues in terms of justice prescribes one alternative outcome as the correct one and all others as mistaken or immoral (Lerner, 1987). Moreover, different definitions of justice carry different behavioral prescriptions. An argument based on procedural justice—perhaps that laws are not being enforced or that relevant voices are being excluded from decision making—merely suggests that existing procedures should be stringently monitored for fairness. An argument based on equality or a new definition of rights suggests that the entire system and the way we think about environmental issues needs to be revamped. Once an issue has been framed in terms of a particular definition of justice, one is obliged to act in accordance with that definition or feel the guilt that results from cognitive dissonance. It could be argued that, for this reason, individuals create definitions of justice that justify the course of behavior that they prefer; a given view of justice could be the effect rather than the cause. This still suggests that justice must be important to people if they need to feel that they are behaving in conformity with its dictates. In either case, it is useful to examine the ways in which justice is described with regard to environmental issues, as a way both to examine the courses of action that are being espoused and to analyze the way in which justice is operationalized with regard to a new and increasingly important social issue.

2. Justice Arguments

2.1. The Justice of the Marketplace

One way of framing the environmental conflicts with which society is currently faced is to translate them into the terms of the marketplace, suggesting that the fair way to deal with natural resources is to sell them. This can be said to incorporate an equity-based approach, with the focus on outcomes (environmental resources consumed) relative to inputs (money). The value of nature is discovered by finding out who is willing to pay for it, and how much. Fairness is ensured by having people pay for what they get. Economic analyses attempt to measure the value of environmental goods by asking people how much they would be willing to pay to preserve those goods—for example, how much they would pay to save 40,000 birds from an oil spill (Kahneman, Ritov, Jacowitz & Grant, 1993)—in part so that "fair" compensation for the use of those resources can be determined. Another aspect of this approach that increases its perceived fairness is the perception that people make decisions and trade-offs freely, rather than under the constraint of state regulation.

This approach is already implemented in a variety of ways. For example, the 1990 Clean Air Act in the U.S. allows industrial plants certain pollution levels; if they pollute below those levels they earn certain credits, which may be sold to other plants who exceed their own levels. Thus the dirtier plants are buying the ability to contaminate, and in that sense use, a certain amount of air. The Chicago Board of Trade now includes a market in these pollution credits (Power & Rauber, 1993).

On a more individual level, many cities now try to increase environmental conservation by chargingcitizens for the number of trash bags they put out to be collected, thus encouraging recycling, composting, and source reduction. Another proposal on the table is for those who use public lands in the U.S.—by hiking, boating, etc.—to pay "their fair share" for the privilege, which is now free (Rauber, 1993). A letter to the New York Times put it this way: "It's time for these freeloaders [the wilderness preservationists] to pony up a substantial ante to the Federal coffers if they want to use Federal lands" (Martin, 1993, p. A14). Environmental groups use the same language when they describe the problem as being due to unfair subsidies to timber, mining, and ranching groups and press for them to pay "fair market value" (Johnson, 1993, p.13).

The principal criticism of this approach is that environmental resources cannot really be allocated in the way that market goods can. In almost every case imaginable, the loss of these resources is felt by a wide community, which may not be the recipient of the payment for those resources and which almost certainly has not unanimously decided to sell them. If, for example, a citizen were to pay to hike in a national forest, who deserves to collect those fees? If, alternatively, a timber company buys the use of that forest, how are the people who will not have the chance to visit it—including future generations—to be compensated for that loss? In a more complicated example, if the general high level of consumption in a developed country leads to environmental degradation in a neighboring country (through air and water pollution, acid rain, etc.), will the inhabitants of the neighboring country be given the opportunity to agree to "sell" their environmental resources, and will compensation be given to each citizen?

A practical correlate of this difficulty in assessing and distributing fees is that the amount individuals are willing to pay for public goods does not seem to reflect the extent to which they value those goods, as shown by apparent paradoxes such as the fact that individuals indicate almost equivalent monetary willingness-to-pay for some lakes in Ontario or all lakes in Ontario (Kahneman, 1986). Kahneman and his colleagues (e.g., Kahneman et al., 1993) suggest that individuals assignvalue to environmental goods through a "contribution model": they determine how much they would be willing to give themselves based on an assumption that others would also contribute. The fact is that, since environmental resources are not designed to be appreciated or consumed by a single individual or even a single organizational entity, it is impossible to find a "fair" price for which to sell them to an individual or entity.

A more broad-based criticism attacks the principle of the market by stating that the enjoyment of environmental resources should not be limited to those who are financially well-off. Finally, there may be negative side effects of using economic incentives to motivate conservation behavior. Research on intrinsic and extrinsic motivation suggests, for example, that if people believe they are recycling only to avoid a fine they will be more likely to discontinue this behavior if the economic incentives are removed, that they will be less likely to generalize this to other conservation behaviors, and that they may be less likely to form pro-environmental attitudes (DeYoung, 1993). Perhaps for these reasons, Syme and his colleagues have consistently found that a market-driven process is not evaluated positively as a way to allocate scarce water resources (Syme & Fenton, 1993; Syme & Nancarrow, 1992).

2.2. Equality

The reliance on a theme of justice as equality in the environmental debate is represented by a concern with a state of imbalance: some people and countries consume far more of our environmental resources than others; some people and countries are affected by environmental pollution to a far greater extent than others. Currently, poor, rural, and black communities in the U.S. are disproportionately chosen as sites for the disposal of toxic waste because their lack of political power has made them less likely to mount effective resistance (Bullard, 1990; U.S. General Accounting Office, 1983). A similar logic led World Bank Chief Economist Lawrence Summers to suggest that toxic waste should be dumped in the "underpolluted" Third World (in Power & Rauber, 1993, p.89). A common use of the term "environmental justice" in current discourse implies the opposite of "environmental racism"—in other words, the struggle to ensure that no groups, particularly minority groups, suffer disproportionately from the effects of environmental degradation. Groups that call themselves "environmental justice" organizations are more likely than traditional environmental groups to focus on inequality (Gale, 1983). In the Spring of 1994, President Clinton signed an Executive Order (E.O. 12898) requiring federal agencies to "consider the issues of environmental justice in their decision-making" because of the fact that low-income and minority communities "have been asked to bear a disproportionate share" of the pollution resulting from modern technology (Browner, 1994). For many of those who espouse this argument, inequalities among people are the core problem to be addressed, and negative effects on the environment stemming from this inequality would resolve themselves if the underlying problem were addressed (Bookchin, 1990). It is worth noting, though, that equality is less likely to be used as a distribution principle when a resource is unpartitioned or uncountable (like air, or water; Messick, 1993). It may be easier to make sure that toxic dumps are not unequally allocated than to do the same with air pollution.

This focus on equality of outcomes relates very closely to a concern with equality of opportunity or participation; Environmental Protection Agency Administrator Carol Browner described the Executive Order 12898 as designed to "involve these communities in the decisionmaking of the government" (Browner, 1994). This can be described as a focus on procedural justice.

2.3. Procedural Issues

Procedural justice places the focus on the fairness of the process by which goods are allocated and decisions made; in particular, the opportunity for all interested parties to participate in the decision process is perceived as a cornerstone of procedural justice (Lind & Tyler, 1988). A common complaint from all parties is that environmental regulations are developed unfairly, without giving opposing sides the opportunity to participate. Recently, for example, timber companies have gone to court to argue that the Clinton administration's plan for protecting forests in the Pacific Northwest "was developed in violation of open meeting laws" (Cushman, 1994, p. A3).

The environmental movement has been criticized for violating procedural justice by taking an elitist position, wherein white, middle-class environmentalists from developed countries dictate the need for less privileged individuals and poorer nations to be environmentally aware (for an assessment of this criticism, see Morrison & Dunlap, 1986). This criticism is reflected in groups such as the Fairness to Landowners Committee in the U.S., which describes itself as representing "moms and pops, not oil companies and miners" (Schneider, 1992b, p. A4) against the efforts of radical environmentalists; a letter to the New York Times describing opponents to hard-rock mining as "a minority of ennui-motivated affluent urbanites, whose intellectual base is reminiscent of the 'Red' sympathizers of the 1920s" (Martin, 1993, p. A14); and a U.S. Senator who describes environmentalists as "trust-fund babies who come out to hike in thousand-dollar equipment" (Nighthorse Campbell, quoted in Johnson, 1993, p. 13). An example of how this elitism can have a negative effect is suggested by U.S. embargoes, intended to prohibit the import of tuna caught through fishing practices (drift nets) that kill dolphins, are said to be "impossibly high" standards for third world fishing fleets, leading to unemployment among tuna fishers and even economic depression in these countries (Brooke, 1992). A different version of the procedural critique of environmentalism focuses on the way in which governmental regulations can limit the ability of private individuals to make their own decisions: the chair of a national coalition of property owner groups complained that "the Government issues more and more regulations, and we're losing local control over our land" (Howard, quoted in Schneider, 1992a, p. A1).

The environmental movement, meanwhile, has procedural criticisms of its own to make. One is that the rules that are on the books are not being enforced (e.g., Egan, 1991). A second is that big companies exert disproportionate influence on policy-making. Thus Ralph Nader has stated that polluting corporations have an "unfounded legitimacy" that "destroys the most fundamental rights of people" and "block or manipulate existing laws" (1970, p. 15) . The procedural theme is pronounced in the fund-raising literature from environmental groups, which accuses the U.S. Forest Service of "defying the public trust" and the oil companies of "[creating] a giant loophole in the ... law", and talks of ensuring a "fair trial for the Arctic" and "the rights of citizens to have a day in court to protect our streams" (see Clayton, 1991). A suggestion of an unfair competition is also given by language such as "giant timber companies" against the "fragile wilderness", or the "corporate goliaths" against the ordinary citizen. As above, the opposing side is often demonized, referred to in fund-raising literature as "shameful, vicious, and greedy" or even "renegade, destructive, thoughtless, despicable, greedy, insidious, bloody, brutal" (Clayton, 1991). A third procedural criticism relates back to the idea of "environmental justice" and charges that various involved parties, usually those without much social power, have been excluded from participation in decisions about environmental matters that will affect them. Capek (1993) describes part of the environmental justice frame as "the right to democratic participation in deciding the future of the community" (p. 16).

There are drawbacks to resorting to simplistic good guy-bad guy discourse. When environmentalists do it, they run the risk of drawing absolute moral distinctions that may promote an us-them mentality and scare off potential supporters who are afraid they cannot live up to such a strict moral standard (Roszak, 1992). It also promotes a view of environmental degradation as the fault of someone else, and inhibits the acceptance of one's own contribution to the problem. For either side, the stress on group divisions and competitions is likely to make the achieve ment of a mutually acceptable resolution to environmental dilemmas more difficult. Finally, a focus on procedural complaints takes attention away from problems of resource distribution—which is really the bottom line in environmental concerns.

2.4. Rights

Many anti-environmental groups frame their opposition in terms of property rights. Rural landowners, along with timber and mining companies, have been filing lawsuits prompted by restrictions on the ways in which private property can be used, based on the need for environmental protection (one group is called the Fairness to Landowners Committee; Schneider, 1992b). The legal argument is that these restrictions constitute a "taking" of the land, and the landowners are thus entitled to "just" compensation from the government under the Fifth Amendment to the U.S. Constitution: "nor shall private property be taken for public use without just compensation" (e.g., *Lucas v. South Carolina Coastal Council*, 1992, in which the owner of waterfront land in South Carolina demanded compensation after being prevented from building on his land).

On the other hand, environmental organizations have also tried to expand the concept of rights. The United Nations is working to establish environmental protection as a basic human right (Parker, 1991). Another thread in the environmental groups' argument calls for rights to be allocated to entities that normally might not be considered to have rights: future generations, for example, or nonhuman entities (animals, species, ecosystems). Roderick Nash (1989) has drawn a parallel between the liberation of nature and the liberation of slaves, suggesting that the circle of entities to which we grant rights has tended to expand over time.

An argument based on rights has broad appeal (Clayton, 1994; Syme & Nancarrow, 1992). Cvetkovich and Earle (1994) found that property rights were frequently mentioned in a public hearing on a wildlife protection ordinance. Unfortunately, agreeing that rights are important does not imply much in the way of common ground, since it remains to be determined who will have rights and what those rights will include. Cvetkovich and Earle have also pointed out that rights arguments tend to be absolutist and do not lend themselves to compromise.

2.5. Responsibility

A final argument relating to themes of justice that is seen in the debate over environmental issues invokes responsibility, which

Schwartz (1975) has described as implicated in "the justice of need". Individuals are admonished to recognize the obligation to care for someone or something else. Most commonly, this argument is seen in the environmental literature, and particularly in the writings of Wendell Berry, who attempts what he calls "a Biblical argument for ecological and agricultural responsibility" (1981, p. 267). Berry takes seriously the idea that humans are meant to be stewards over the earth, and argues that this means taking care of natural resources rather than taking them for granted. The reference to responsibility is probably more compatible with the environmental movement since its prevailing ideology concerns the necessary changes in human behavior, and thus focuses on the consequences of this behavior. The preface to the Sierra Club handbook for environment activists states, "each person must become ecologically responsible—not only as a consumer of the planet's resources, but as a procreator of its most prolific species" (Mitchell & Stallings, 1970, p. 12). In contrast, a speaker at an anti-environmentalist conference stated "I do not support that damage to the earth is being done and that man is responsible" (Ray, quoted in Poole, 1992, p. 91). However, an argument based on responsibility may also be used to oppose environmental policies, when pointing out potential human costs—e.g., in jobs—of environmental protection and suggesting that those in power are obligated to protect their constituents. Members of anti-environmental organizations have also referred to "civic responsibility" as their reason for getting involved (Gottlieb, in Poole, 1992, p. 93). Schwartz describes perceived responsibility as resulting from several possible causes. One, a perception that one has caused the need, is probably most relevant to environmental arguments, which stress the detrimental effects of humans on the natural environment. People are less likely to feel that they are causally responsible for loggers having lost their jobs, so this is less relevant to anti-environmental arguments. However, responsibility may also be based on one's role or assigned in a particular situation; this is more likely to underly the responsibilities stressed by anti-environmentalists. This also seems to be the type of responsibility emphasized by Berry.

3. Relevance of Different Values to Appeal of Different Positions

Although some environmental organizations (e.g., the Environmental Defense Fund) support the free-market approach, the equity-based model of justice appears more congenial to those opposed to the environmental movement than to environmental advocates. Equality of suffering—in other words, the idea that nobody should bear a dispropor-tionate amount of the environmental burden—works better for environ-mentalists than for anti-environmentalists, but the reverse is true for the procedural argument, including equality of opportunity. As stated above, the rights argument seems to appeal to both sides, while a responsibil-ity-based appeal is preferred by environmentalists. In general, there is evidence that environmentalism is more associated with a concern for justice for the larger community, and thus responsibility and equal sacrifice, while anti-environmentalism is more individually focused, thus oriented toward a concern with procedural justice and equity (Clayton, 1991, 1994; Cvetkovich & Earle, 1994; Syme & Fenton, 1993; Syme & Nancarrow, 1992).

In several studies, I have tried to examine the relationship between an individual or group focus and type of justice appeal preferred with regard to environmental issues. In a first study (Clayton, 1991), fundrais-ing appeals for an environmental group and for the fight against lung disease were constructed either to focus on an individual or to make reference to wider, societal issues. The environmental appeal was rated as more effective in the societal format, and the illness appeal in the individual format. Though far from conclusive, this finding supports the hypothesis that the environmental cause lends itself to a communal-type argument. A second study (Clayton, 1994) compared environmental and anti-environmental appeals using parallel models of justice. For exam-ple, the environmental argument based on procedural justice focused on the greater power of timber and oil companies than average citizens in dictating America's energy policy; the antienvironmental appeal focused on the greater power of white, middle-class environmentalists than other (not so well-connected) citizens in influencing environmental policy in the U.S. The environmental appeals generated greater agreement than the anti-environmental appeals, and the procedural and rights-based appeals tended to receive greater agreement than appeals based on responsibility, equal access, or equal sacrifice. However, this was quali-fied by an interaction between type of justice appeal and position argued: as expected, the anti-environmental position received most agreement when argued on the basis of procedural justice, while the environmental position received equally high levels of agreement using an appeal based on responsibility or equal sacrifice.

In neither of the above studies was it possible to make the appeals completely comparable in both conditions, leading to the possibility that the results were due to some idiosyncratic qualities of the argument rather than the factor being manipulated. So, in a third study, two specific environmental conflicts were described either in general or as they affected specific (fictional) individuals. The first conflict had to do with access to national parks—whether the parks should be left in their natural state or made more accessible, with roads, rest areas, etc. In one condition, the conflict was described in general; in a second, it was described in terms of "Lucia, a paraplegic who has always wanted to see Mt. Everest". The second conflict concerned the ability of the government to prevent private landowners from developing their land: it was described either in general terms or in terms of "Ross Johnson, who bought land with the intent of building on it but was told he could not build because it would threaten the local ecosystem". After reading each conflict in one of the two conditions, subjects were asked to rate on seven-point scales the importance of eight considerations to resolving the conflict: responsibility to future generations, other species, or people currently alive; individual rights; ensuring a fair decision process, in which all concerned parties participate; equal allocation; allocation on the basis of merit; and allocation on the basis of need. Subjects were also asked to complete an Environmental Attitudes Scale (Thompson & Barton, 1992), which measures ecocentric attitudes (valuing nature for its own sake), anthropocentric attitudes (valuing nature for the ways in which it can benefit humanity), and environmental apathy.

Results showed that, overall, responsibility to other species and ensuring a fair decision process were rated as the most important considerations, followed in decreasing order of importance by responsibility to future generations and to people currently alive, individual rights, equal allocation, allocation on the basis of need, and allocation on the basis of merit. As expected, however, experimental condition affected the different principles in different ways. The biggest differences were for individual rights and ensuring a fair process, both of which were rated as significantly more important when the conflict was described in terms of individuals. There was a tendency for responsibility to other people currently alive to get higher ratings when the conflict was described generally. Other principles were more or less unaffected by experimental condition. The major findings from this study are, first, that responsibility to other species was rated fairly high—probably because of the environmental nature of the conflict—but that the importance people generally place on procedural justice was also confirmed; second, that the more individually-oriented types of justice were more important when the conflict was described at an individual level. This shows that, even within the environmental debate, discussion can be framed to make different models of justice more or less salient. It seems that preference for particular models of justice is not completely fixed across different contexts, but at least in part something that can be consciously manipulated by the people who describe a situation.

Individual differences also mattered: ecocentric attitudes were signficantly correlated with rated importance of responsibility to other species, while the reverse was true for environmental apathy; ecocentric attitudes were negatively correlated with rated importance of individual rights, and anthropocentric attitudes and environmental apathy were both positively correlated with this principle.

The demands of any model of justice, of course, will vary depending on who is included in one's moral community. Equal access to resources has very different implications if future generations are included than if they are not (Laslett & Fishkin, 1992). Responsibility to consider the welfare of others means one thing if only humans are included; another if animals or other living organisms are considered as well. It may be that standards for determining that a class of entities is worth of moral consideration are determined by one's values (Seligman, 1989). Several authors (e.g., Axelrod, 1994; Merchant, 1992; Stern & Dietz, 1994) have recently proposed similar schemes for value orientations toward the environment. Essentially, one's values can be described as egoistic, or self-centered; altruistic, or person-centered; and ecocentric, or environment-centered. (These value orientations in turn may be a product of one's stage of ego development; cf. Greenwald Robbins & Greenwald, 1994). It is possible for concern for the environment to be related to any of these sources of value—for example, one can try to reduce resource consumption because of a belief that it will be personally beneficial, because of a concern for other people, or because of a concern for the ecosystem (Stern & Dietz, 1994). However, the scope of justice and therefore the implications of a particular model of justice should vary according to one's value orientation. The study described above showed that, in a very limited way, the basis for one's attitudes toward nature predicted a preference for a particular type of justice argument. I would expect this also to be true of value orientation measured more broadly.

4. Implications for Environmental Justice

Beliefs about what is fair change as the prevailing social norms change (Hegtvedt & Flinn, 1993). A benefit to which one becomes accustomed is perceived as an entitlement, as has been the case for subsidized grazing fees for American ranchers and subsidized water for American farmers; conversely, a task to which one becomes accustomed is perceived as an obligation. As Robert Cooter (1993) has observed, a norm can change the "sign" associated with a behavior: if recycling is unusual, then the behavior of recycling is experienced as incurring a cost; if recycling is normal, than failure to recycle incurs a cost. This means that, even if pro-environmental behavior and regulations are perceived as onerous and unfair by some, they do not have to retain this characterization. The reference state can be changed.

Justice is not determined democratically. Rawls' concern with the "veil of ignorance" (1971) illustrates his belief that the perception of what is just and fair will be affected by the way in which one will be affected by a given definition of justice—we have the ability to make an imbalance in our own favor seem fair. Moreover, prevailing standards of justice tend to be disproportionately affected by the interests of those who have more power in the society and thus the time and resources to promote their own position. As illustrated by Opotow's discussion of moral exclusion (this issue; 1990) and by the phenomena of environmental racism, perceptions of fairness with regard to environmental issues are likely to be subjective and biased. Even equality can be determined in a way that benefits the one making the determinations (Messick, 1993). Thus the predominate model of environmental justice in a society may not be the one that will promote the general welfare (Hegtvedt & Flinn, 1993).

Support for established norms of justice can be altered by awareness that the resources being distributed are less abundant than they were previously or by a changed evaluation of those resources (and the former may well lead to the latter) (Jasso, 1983). When different notions of justice are in conflict, resolution of dilemmas should occur not through competing entitlements under a single principle of justice but through negotiation to develop a consensual principle (Hegtvedt & Flinn, 1993), or perhaps a compromise that is compatible with several principles (cf. Dudley, 1992). Thus the solution to current environmental debates that are couched in the language of justice may be to promote open discussion of fairness in which all relevant parties are represented (at least by proxy, as for animals and future generations) (Cvetkovich & Earle, 1994). If fairness is really the principal concern of those involved, then a greater level of agreement may be reached when different perspectives have been heard, and the way in which changing environmental conditions affect the collective welfare is apparent. Such open discussion of different rules seems to promote a greater concern with collective welfare (Kahn, Nelson, Gaeddert & Hearn, 1982), as do awareness of the way in which some group members may be suffering (O'Malley & Becker, 1984) and awareness of the diminishing availability of resources (Hegtvedt, 1987).

It would be overly optimistic to suggest that simple discussion would lead to unanimity about a principle of justice and that environmental dilemmas would be magically resolved through consensus. Even open discussion requires a preliminary decision about who should be represented at that discussion, and there is certainly no agreement on this issue. However, an awareness of the malleability of perceptions of fairness and the ways in which they can be affected can encourage us not to be too deferential to arguments based on justice. On the individual level, DeYoung (1991) suggests that pro-environmental behavior may be associated more with the intrinsic satisfaction derived thereof than with a focus on receiving fair compensation for lifestyle sacrifices. On the societal level, rather than implementing (or failing to implement) a policy merely because it is congruent with a statement of justice with which it is hard to disagree (e.g., the rights of property-owners to control their own land; the responsibility of government to look after its citizens), we should think through the effects of any policy and evaluate it from a number of different justice perspectives. Then we can make decisions that really will maximize the collective welfare rather than bowing to the tyranny represented by a single, absolute definition of what is fair.

References

Axelrod, L. (1994). Balancing personal needs with environmental preservation: Identifying the values that guide decisions in ecological dilemmas. Journal of Social Issues, 50 (3), 85-104.

Axelrod, L. & Lehman, D. (1992, August). The utility of outcome desires in predicting environmentally-concerned behavior: A multivariate analysis. Paper presented at the 100th convention of the American Psychological Association, Washington, DC.

Berry, W. (1981). The gift of good land. San Francisco: North Point Press.

Bookchin, M. (1990). Remaking society: Pathways to a green future. Boston: South End Press.

Brooke, J. (1992, May 3). America—environmental dictator? New York Times, p. F7.

Browner, C. (1994, February 11). Press briefing.

Bullard, R. (1990). Dumping in Dixie: Race, class. and environmental quality. Boulder, CO: Westview Press.

Capek, S. M. (1993). The "environmental justice" frame: A conceptual discussion and an application. Social Problems, (1), 5-24.

Clayton, S. (1991, August). Environmental justice. Paper presented at the annual meeting of the American Psychological Association, San Francisco, CA.

Clayton, S. (1994). Appeals to justice in the environmental debate. Journal of Social Issues, 50 (3), 13-27.

Cooter, R. (1993, July). Where do social norms come from? Decentralizing law. Paper presented at the Fourth International Conference on Social Justice, Trier, Germany.

Cushman, J. H., Jr. (1994, May 7). Owl case tests strategy to promote consensus. New York Times, p. A3.

Cvetkovich, G. & Earle, T. (1994). The construction of justice: A case study of public participation in land management. Journal of Social Issues, 50 (3), 161-178.

DeYoung, R. (1991). Some psychological aspects of living lightly: Desired lifestyle patterns and conservation behavior. Journal of Environmental Systems, 20, 215-227.

DeYoung, R. (1993). Changing behavior and making it stick: The conceptualization and management of conservation behavior. Environment and Behavior, 25, 485-505.

Dudley, N. J. (1992). Water allocation by markets, common property and capacity sharing: Companions or competitors? Natural Resources Journal, 32, 757-778.

Gale, R. (1983). The environmental movement and the left: Antagonists or allies? Sociological Inquiry, 53, 179-199.

Greenwald Robbins, J. & Greenwald, R. (1994). Environmental attitudes conceptualized through developmental theory: A qualitative analysis. Journal of Social Issues, 50 (3), 29-47.

Heberlein, T. A. (1972). The land ethic realized: Some social psychological explanations for changing environmental attitudes. Journal of Social Issues, 28(4), 79-87.

Hegtvedt, K. A. (1987). When rewards are scarce: Equal or equitable distributions? Social Forces, 66, 183-207.

Hegtvedt K. A. & Flinn, P. J. (1993). Intergenerational justice and the environment: Determining the fair use of Mono Basin water. Paper presented at the meetings of the International Institute of Sociology, Paris.

Johnson, D. (1993, April 4). West that is no more turns back land-use fees. New York Times, p. 13.

Kahn, A., Nelson, R. E., Gaeddert, W. & Hearn, J. L. (1982). The justice process: Deciding upon equity or equality. Social Psychology Quarterly, 45, 3-8.

Kahneman, D. (1986). Comments on the contingent valuation method. In P. G. Cummings, D. S. Brookshire & W. D. Schulze (Eds.), Valuing public goods: An assessment of the contingent valuation method (pp. 185-193). Totowa, NJ: Rowman & Allanheld.

Kahneman, D., Ritov, I., Jacowitz, K. & Grant, P. (1993). Stated willingness to pay for public goods: A psychological perspective. Psychological Science, 4, 310-315.

Kals, E. (1993). Pollution control, justice, and responsibility: Who is willing to engage in the protection of air quality? Paper presented at the Fourth International Conference on Social Justice, Trier, Germany.

Laslett, P. & Fishkin, J. S. (1992). Introduction: Processional justice. In P. Laslett & J. S.Fishkin (Eds.) Justice between age groups and generations (pp 1-23). New Haven: Yale University Press.

Lerner, M. J. (1987). Integrating societal and psychological rules of entitlement: The basic task of each social actor and fundamental problem for the social sciences. Social Justice Research, 1, 107-125.

Lerner, S. C. (1981). Adapting to scarcity and change (I): Stating the problem. In M. J.Lerner & S. C. Lerner (Eds.), The justice motive in social behavior (pp. 3-10). New York: Plenum.

Lind, E. A. & Tyler, T. R. (1988). The psychology of procedural justice. New York: Plenum.

Lucas v. South Carolina Coastal Council 112 S.Ct. 2886 (1992).

Martin, W. M. (1993, April 14). Letter to the editor. New York Times, p. A14.

Merchant, C. (1992). Radical ecology: The search for a livable world. New York:Routledge, Chapman, & Hall.

Messick, D. M. (1993). Equality as a decision heuristic. In B. A. Mellers & J. Baron (Eds.), Psychological perspectives on justice (pp. 11-31). Cambridge: Cambridge University Press.

Mitchell, J. G. & Stallings, C. L. (1970, Eds.). Ecotactics: The Sierra Club handbook for environment activists. New York: Simon & Schuster.

Morrison, D. E. & Dunlap, R. E. (1986). Environmentalism and elitism: A conceptual and empirical analysis. Environmental management, 10, 581-589.

Nader, R. (1970). Introduction. In J. G. Mitchell & C. L. Stallings (Eds.), Ecotactics: The Sierra Club handbook for environment activists. New York: Simon & Schuster.

Nash, R. F. (1989). The rights of nature: A history of environmental ethics. Madison, WI: University of Wisconsin Press.

O'Malley, M. N. & Becker, D. (1984). Removing egocentric bias: The relevance of distress cues to evaluation of fairness. Personality and Social Psychology Bulletin, 10, 235-242.

Opotow, S. (1990). Moral exclusion and injustice: An introduction. Journal of Social Issues, 46 (1), 1-20.

Opotow, S. (1994). Predicting protection: Scope of justice and the natural world. Journal of Social Issues, 50 (3), 49-63.

Parker, V. (1991, Spring). Legal defense fund mounts major international effort to link human and environmental rights. In Brief [newsletter of the Sierra Club Legal Defense Fund], pp. 1,7.

Poole, W. (1992). Neither wise nor well. Sierra, 77 (6), 59-61, 88-93.

Power, T. M. & Rauber, P. (1993). The price of everything. Sierra, 78 (6), 87-96.

Rauber, P. (1993). What price a walk in the woods? Sierra, 78 (3), 46-49.

Rawls, J. (1971). A theory of justice. Cambridge: Harvard University Press.

Roszak, T. (1992, June 9). Green guilt and ecological overload. New York Times, p. A27.

Schneider, K. (1992a, January 20). Environment laws face a stiff test from landowners. New York Times, pp. A1, A15.

Schneider, K. (1992b, February 16). When the bad guy is seen as the one in the green hat. New York Times, p. A4.

Schwartz, S. (1975). The justice of need and the activation of humanitarian norms. Journal of Social Issues, 31 (3), 11-136.

Seligman, C. (1989). Environmental ethics. Journal of Social Issues, 45 (1), 169-184.

Stern, P. & Dietz, T. (1994). The value basis of environmental concern. Journal of Social Issues, 50 (3), 65-84.

Syme, G. & Fenton, D. (1993). Perceptions of equity and procedural preferences for water allocation decisions. Society and Natural Resources, 6, 347-360.

Syme, G. & Nancarrow, B. (1992). Perceptions of fairness and social justice in the allocation of water resources in Australia (CSIRO Consultancy Report No. 92/38). Perth, Australia: CSIRO.

Thompson, S. & Barton, M. (1992, August). Ecocentric and anthropocentric attitudes toward the environment. Paper presented at the annual meeting of the American Psychological Association, Washington, DC.

U.S. General Accounting Office. (1983). Siting of hazardous waste landfills and their correlation with racial and economic status of surrounding communities. Washington, DC: Government Printing Office.

Vaughan, E. & Siefert, M. (1992). Variability in the framing of risk issues. Journal of Social Issues, 48 (4), 119-135.

12

Is Justice Finite? The Case of Environmental Inclusion

Susan Opotow

Over the past 25 years, the environmental movement has argued for an increasingly wider consideration in our thinking about the natural world. It has argued, first, that a broader constituency is entitled to natural resources and, second, that a broader range of societal arrangements affect the natural world. Both inclusionary trends offer the opportunity to examine the social and psychological factors that widen a society's "scope of justice," the psychological boundary for extending considerations of fairness toward others. Tracing successively broader ecophilosophies over the past quarter century and describing typologies of values and research on the scope of justice, this chapter examines social psychological factors that can widen and constrict the scope of justice. Looking at this increasingly inclusionary environmental trend raises the question, "Does inclusion have limits?" The next section describes the scope of justice and its relevance to environmental attitudes and behavior.

1. The Scope of Justice

Our *scope of justice* is a fundamental psychological orientation and a key determinant of attitudes, social judgments, and behavior toward

Susan Opotow • Graduate Program in Dispute Resolution, University of Massachusetts–Boston, Boston, Massachusetts 02125-3393

Current Societal Concerns about Justice, edited by Leo Montada and Melvin J. Lerner. Plenum Press, New York, 1996.

others. The scope of justice consists of three attitudes: (1) believing that considerations of fairness apply to another; (2) willingness to make sacrifices to foster another's well-being; and (3) willingness to allocate a share of community resources to another (Opotow, 1987, 1993). For social categories inside our scope of justice, concerns about deserving and fair treatment are salient (Deutsch, 1974; Lerner, 1975). Moral exclusion occurs when we exclude groups or individuals from the scope of justice (Opotow, 1990c). Throughout human history, exclusion from the scope of justice has been justified by virtually any characteristic capable of differentiating people (cf., Archer, 1985; Tajfel, 1978), including gender, age, skin color, ethnicity, religious beliefs, class status, and species membership. For social categories outside the scope of justice, the concepts, "deserving" and "fairness," do not apply and can even seem irrelevant. We perceive those outsiders as nonentities, undeserving, or expendable. Harm that befalls them does not prompt the concern, remorse, anguish, or outrage that occurs when those inside the scope of justice are harmed (Staub, 1990). As a consequence of exclusion, moral values and rules that apply in relations with insiders do not apply to those outside the scope of justice, licensing moral justifications—even jubilation—for harm inflicted on outsiders (Opotow, 1995).

Social conventions shape our perception about the kinds of social categories are inside the scope of justice and are entitled to considerations of justice and to allocations of help and resources. Although the scope of justice is a dynamic construct that undergoes considerable change over time, we tend to view current, conventional boundaries - the status quo - as "correct" and immutable.

1.1. The Scope of Justice and the Natural World

The degree to which non-human animate and inanimate aspects of the natural world are included in the scope of justice has varied considerably over time and between cultures and religious and philosophical traditions. Conventional western philosophical tradition depicts humankind as the pinnacle of the evolutionary ladder, superior to everything else on Earth, justifying the power and rights people exert over everything else (Eliade, 1978/1982; Passmore, 1975, 1980). Genesis I 26-29 affirmed the dominion of humankind over the earth. "Rough" places, such as forests, marshes, were considered God's unfinished work in need of the civilizing, human touch (Simmons, 1993). While North American colonists viewed the "New World" as a threatening, untrodden land infested with wild animals and "savages," native North American people viewed the natural environment as a bountiful place that conferred benefits on people and venerated animate and inanimate aspects of nature as well as the Earth itself as the sacred mother of all life (Merchant, 1989; Stevens, 1994).

1.2. Broadening the Environmental Constituency

Changing over the centuries, the traditional Western view of the natural world has undergone rapid change in the past 25 years. There has been a gradual evolution away from a present- and human-centered view, and greater emphasis on the effect of resource depletion and waste disposal (e.g., the shrinking ozone layer) on distant and future generations of people and non- human environmental features. Moral philosophers have argued for various boundaries of the "moral community" or scope of justice including sentient animals (Regan, 1983; Singer, 1975), all living creatures (Schweitzer, 1961), and - consistent with the Gaia hypothesis that the entire the natural world comprises a single, interconnected system (Lovelock, 1979) - inanimate, natural environmental features such as soils, water, and plants (Leopold, 1949; Stone, 1988).

As moral philosophers have debated appropriate boundaries of the scope of justice, environmental activists have also identified a broad range of societal arrangements that influence human behavior toward the natural world. The next section describes challenges to conventional view of the natural world that have occurred over the past 25 years.

2. The Environmental Movement: Enlarging the Scope of Justice

2.1. Background

After growing slowly in fits and starts over the past century, the environmental movement in North America gained considerable momentum by Earth Day in 1970 (List, 1993). Yet, in spite of a spate of legislated environmental protections that followed the first Earth Day and a United Nations-sponsored World Summit on the Environment in Stockholm in 1972, the world saw little abatement in acute environment crises more than two decades later. Discharges of toxic chemical, air and water pollution, and land degradation remained major, world-wide problems, while stratospheric ozone depletion, loss of biodiversity, and climate change emerged as new world-wide concerns (Tolba & El-Kholy, 1992). The quickening pace of environmental degradation, intensified consumption levels, and the belief that ground continued to be lost in the battle to keep humans in balance with nature led to increasing calls and support for militant environmentalism (List, 1993).

2.2. Societal Arrangements that Influence Environmental Behavior

Our view of natural environment is a dynamic social construction that influences how we perceive and interact with the natural world in everyday life, how we make land-use decisions, and how we view the link between society and nature (Katz & Kirby, 1991; Simmons, 1993). Traditional, anthropocentric ecological views, such as those of the "Wise Use" movement that view Earth as a set of natural resources for humankind to manage wisely, have been increasingly challenged by more radical "ecocentric" philosophies, such as those of militant groups, Earth First! and the Monkey Wrench Gang, that view all aspects of the natural environment -whether alive or not - as ends in their own right (Clayton, 1994; Hargrove, 1989; List, 1993; Nash, 1989). These emerging radical, ecocentric philosophies championed awareness of other species, the unity of all things, adaptation to cosmic rhythms, and low environmental impact activities. They found support in Eastern philosophical traditions, such as Buddhism, the Zen tradition, Taoism, Hinduism (Callicott & Ames, 1989), and in traditions of aboriginal people. The next sections describe four prominent ecophilosophies: deep ecology, ecofeminism, social ecology, and environmental justice.

2.2.1. Deep Ecology

"Deep ecology" (Naess, 1973) focused on protecting natural aspects of the Earth because of their intrinsic value and on widening the scope of environmental inclusion by valuing all environmental objects regardless of their utility for human life. Deep ecologists called for human identification with the nonhuman world and rejected the view that humans are the master of other species. It pointedly distinguished itself from "shallower" (p. 95) ecological thinking, characterized by utilitarian concerns about benefiting present or future humans. The deep ecology ecophilosophy drew wider justice boundaries that extended environmental concern beyond humankind and economic considerations to advocate "ecological egalitarianism" (p. 96) and advocated militant protection of nonhuman ecological entities such as forests and baby seals. While still controversial, radical environmental activism spurred by the deep ecology ecophilosophy has increasingly gained public sympathy and has become an increasingly influential force in the environment movement (List, 1993).

At the same time, subsequent ecophilosophies, particularly ecofeminism, social ecology, and environmental justice, have criticized the deep ecology ecophilosophy for neglecting more fundamental social arrangement that cause ecological degradation.

2.2.2. Ecofeminism

Ecofeminists asserted that deep ecology misrepresented "human" relations with the natural world because it is based only on the perspectives and actions of men (d'Eaubonne, 1980; Merchant, 1979). Ecofeminists assert that the natural world and women are both victims of male oppression, exploitation, and harm doing: "The twin dominations of women and nature are social problems rooted both in very concrete, historical, socioeconomic circumstances and in oppressive patriarchal conceptual frameworks, which maintain and sanction these circumstances" (Warren, 1993, p. 85). Ecofeminists argue that an understanding of these root causes of environmental degradation and recognizing the deep interconnections between people and the natural world is a crucial first step in identifying innovative ways that humans can live in harmony with nature.

2.2.3. Social Ecology

The social ecology movement argued that a broader consideration of social domination was needed that went beyond gender issues. Bookchin (1982) argued that domination by and within human hierarchies is played out in the natural landscape as well as in our psychological orientation toward the natural world (Bookchin, 1982). The pyramid of dominance - with nature at the bottom of the hierarchy - negates much potential for liberty, freedom, and a sense of community. Instead society strives to satisfy the demand for consumer goods at a vast human and environmental cost (Simmons, 1993). In contrast to viewing nature as a commodity, social ecologists describe nature as a participatory realm of life- forms that interact and are complementary, offering humankind a model of interdependencies based on freedom rather than on domination (Bookchin, 1982).

2.2.4 Environmental Justice

The environmental justice (or "environmental racism" movement) linked environmental degradation with racism in galvanizing data indicating that "race is a major factor related to the presence of hazardous wastes in residential communities throughout the United States" (Commission for Racial Justice, 1987, p. x). The disproportionate siting of toxic dumps and locally-unwanted land uses ("LULUs") in communities of color has increasingly activated protest in those communities and has prompted awareness of the exclusion of people of color from the environmental decisions that affect them and from the environmental movement. Environmental justice critiques of dominant ecophilosophies argue that they focus more on protecting the environment from people than on protecting some groups of people from the environment - particularly from man-made environmental stressors such as pollution discharges in air and water, noise, vibrations, and aesthetic problems (Bullard, 1994).

In sum, critical analyses of the societal arrangements and alarm over the pace of ecological degradation have provoked a rethinking of scope of justice. During the past 25 years an increasingly inclusive environmental ethic has critiqued societal arrangements, particularly sexism, social hierarchies, and racism, as fostering environmental degradation. As environmental degradation moved environmental concerns from background to foreground, economic utilization of environmental resources was no longer acceptable as the sole consideration. Instead, awareness of the interdependence between humans (in diverse social circumstances) and many kinds of environmental entities has prompted more complex analyses that have included resource allocation to social categories that were previously outside the scope of justice (Opotow, 1994). As a consequence, justice concerns are increasingly relevant in our thinking about the natural world (Clayton & Opotow, 1994; Opotow & Clayton, 1994).

As the environmental movement has gained momentum, individuals and communities have invested time, effort, and resources in grassroots conservation efforts that have included recycling; substituting grain- and legume-based diets for animal-based diets; composting organic waste; installing bluebird, owl, and bat nesting boxes; landscaping to encourage species diversity; adopting energy and water conservation measures; promoting Green candidates for public office; and lobbying for local and environmental issues. Worldwide, people have shown themselves increasingly willing to spend more as "green consumers" (Tolba & El-Kholy, 1992).

While more inclusive environmental views that emphasize human relatedness with the natural world intuitively seem more authentic, it is important to note that exclusion, too, gains public acceptance in similar ways. While it is beyond the scope of this paper to examine its trajectory, arguments that advocate increasingly exclusionary social arrangements also have a decidedly moral gloss and are cast as advances promoting the betterment of society, however exclusively that society is defined (e.g., the Third Reich) (see Opotow, 1990a; Opotow, 1990b). The point here is that seemingly- moral statements and transcendent ideologies can be employed for both inclusionary and exclusionary purposes.

The next section describes several tripartite typologies that categorize different justice boundaries toward the natural environment.

3. Typologies of Environmental Inclusion

Values, considered deeper than beliefs, determine attitudes and predict behaviors (Axelrod, 1994; Stern & Dietz, 1994). Values make an important contribution to our sense of justice because they identify the factors and constituencies to consider for decisions to be viewed as fair (Opotow & Clayton, 1994). Several recent theories have proposed a similar, tripartite typology of environmental values: oneself, humankind, and the Earth (Axelrod, 1994; Greenwald & Greenwald, 1994; Merchant, 1992; Stern & Dietz, 1994). These typologies order the arguments among moral philosophers concerning the moral community and those of ecophilosophers, moving from a narrower moral community and "shallow" ecological thinking to a broader moral community and "deep" ecological thinking.

3.1. Self-Centered Environmental Values

The first category of environmental values is a self-centered orientation. Stern & Dietz (1994) identify "egoistic" environmental values that occur when people approve protection of aspects of the environment that affect them personally and disapprove of those that incur personal costs. Merchant (1992) identifies "egocentric" environmental ethics as maximizing self-interest and believing that what is good for the individual will be good for the society as a whole. Greenwald & Greenwald (1994) identify women at Kegan's (1982) "imperial self" stage as only expressing concern about environmental issues that have an immediate and direct impact on their own well-being. Axelrod (1994) identifies an "economic" domain that is concerned with security, achievement, material rewards and avoidance of costs. People in this domain would oppose environmental protections that result in higher taxes or other personal costs.

3.2. Human-Centered Environmental Values

The second category of environmental values is an anthropocentric, human-centered of the natural world in which the utility of the environment to meet human needs is relevant (cf., Cooter, 1987). Stern & Dietz identify "altruistic" environmental values as a moral obligation to act when adverse consequences would be likely to occur to others (cf., Schwartz, 1977) and to act in accordance with the Golden Rule, "Do unto others as you would have others do unto you." Merchant identifies a "utilitarian" basis for environmental ethics as doing the most good for the greatest number of people. Greenwald & Greenwald identify woman at Kegan's "interpersonal self" stage as concerned about care and caretaking for those close to them, particularly their family and community; as comfortable conforming with conventional mainstream rules and values; and as having difficulty handling "difference." For example, using consumer-provided cloth bags for groceries at the supermarket would be embarrassing unless it conformed to store policy and everyone else were doing it. Axelrod identifies a "social" domain as concern with the social consequences of one's actions, with the desire to conform and belong, and with pursuing actions that affect the welfare of close others. People in this domain will engage in environmentally-protective behavior when it will minimize the plight of other people.

3.3. Planet-Centered Environmental Values

The third category of environmental values is a planet-centered orientation that stresses interdependence between the natural and the human world. Stern & Deitz identify "biospheric" values as judging human behavior on the basis of its costs and benefits to the biosphere, a view consistent with Dunlap & Van Liere's (1978) "New Environmental Paradigm." Merchant identifies "ecocentric" environmental ethics as based on laws of ecology, diversity, and harmony. Greenwald & Greenwald identify woman at Kegan's "institutional self" stage as capable of constructing their own world-view, as willing to take personal responsibility for them, and as acting on the basis of their personal beliefs. They were willing to work for social change, such as keeping the environment healthy, and believe that individual effort can have a societal impact.

Axelrod also identifies a "universal" domain in which self-respect results from making a contribution to improve the world and valuing equality and environmental preservation, even when these goals incur social or economic costs.

This progression of environmental values is similar to the progression of moral judgments and social cognitions described in the developmental literature as children mature and progress from simple sensory-motor, physical, egoistic responses to more complex, symbolic, inferential, mutualistic responses (e.g., Kohlberg, 1981; Piaget, 1937/1954; Turiel, 1983). Critics of stage theory argue that higher levels of socio-cognitive or moral functioning do not depend only on maturation level, but also depend on situational factors; people at higher socio-cognitive and moral developmental levels can also behave at more primitive levels (Bandura, 1986; Montada, 1980).

Similarly, environmental value typologies propose an analogous developmental progression in adults from concrete to more abstract relationships, and from a less to a more inclusive environmental orientation. Yet, environmental inclusiveness, grounded in experience and knowledge (Finger, 1990), may also not be an invariant, unidirectional intellectual progression, but instead may be sensitive to situational factors that prompt particular environmental values to become salient (cf., Stern & Dietz, 1994). The environmental value typologies prompt two intriguing questions about expanding the scope of justice. First, what situational factors spur environmental values and foster environmental inclusion? Second, although expanding the scope of justice appears to be something that is desirable and good, are there practical difficulties with a wider scope of justice? The next section examines situational factors and perceptual biases that influence shrinkage and expansion of the scope of justice.

4. Dynamics of Inclusion

4.1. Limits to Environmental Inclusion

4.1.1. Situational Limits of Inclusion

I conducted research (Opotow, 1987, 1993) that examined the psychological influences on the scope of justice. The findings indicated that perceived utility of the target and perceived conflict severity modified the scope of justice. When the target of the study, a beetle, was described as beneficial it was more likely to be included in the scope of justice than when it was described as harmful. And, consistent with findings that concerns with justice shrink during conflict (Calabresi & Bobbitt, 1978; Greenberg, 1981; Leventhal, 1979), the beetle was more likely to be inside the scope of justice when conflict between people and the beetle for a resource (a parcel of land) was described as low rather than when it was described as high.

These findings suggests that when people are experiencing chronic or acute conflict or stress in their lives, abstract or distant environmental issues will be less salient; instead people will be more concerned with immediate, concrete issues and with securing their own well-being. The findings also suggest that people's response to environmental situations will reflect their perceptions of the utility of the environmental object. Thus, people who are intellectually capable of planetary-centered environmental values might respond to some situations with less inclusive environmental values as a result of their perceptions of the situation. When people believe that an environmental entity is harmful or that their well-being would be adversely affected by protecting a particular environmental entity, such as forests, wolves, or rattlesnakes, they might adopt a more self- or human- centered orientation than a planetary-centered one (cf., Brooke, 1985; Meier, 1992; Nash, 1993).

4.1.2. Perceptual Biases: The Illusion of Inclusiveness

As successive ecophilosophies identified societal arrangements that influence human behavior toward the natural world, they identified omissions of then-prevailing ecophilosophies. Each laid claim to a more inclusive, authentic ideology that identified societal impediments of ecological protection (cf., List, 1993). This is consistent with perceptions that the prevailing social conventions - those of the present and those of our own subgroup - are more inclusive and just than previous social conventions and those of others (cf., LeVine & Campbell, 1972). Just as psychological, physical, and temporal distance renders exclusionary attitudes easier to detect, ecophilosophies of other subgroups, other cultures, and from the past appear to be less inclusive and less fair than our own.

It is difficult, therefore, to recognize the limits to our own liberalism. Injustice based on shared social perceptions that are "institutionalized, invisible, and accepted as if inevitable" (Fine, 1990, p. 9) are ignored or legitimized. This illusion of moral inclusiveness is a self-serving and self-protective bias. Just to consider justice has a cost in energy and resources, and this cost is likely to rise when conflict escalates and resource scarcity increases (cf., Lerner, 1981). Exclusion can be an adaptive defense because it can simplify our lives and can conserve time, energy, and resources during one of the inevitable challenges that life offers. Thus, even the most inclusionary ecophilosophies of the present are likely to be supplanted by yet more inclusive ideologies that identify currently-neglected social issues that influence environmental degradation.

4.2. Expanding Environmental Inclusion

Even if inclusiveness is inescapably limited, research on the social psychological conditions that can widen the applicability of justice have identified helping behavior and a pluralistic orientation as capable of fostering inclusion.

4.2.1. Helping

"Willingness to help" is one factor that can differentiate inclusion from exclusion. I (Opotow, 1990c) examined three indicators of inclusion - believing that considerations of fairness apply to an opponent, willingness to help an opponent, and willingness to allocate money to an opponent - in research on the scope of justice in adolescents' interpersonal conflicts with peers. Participants' inclusiveness of an adversary could be categorized three ways: In addition to the two "absolute" and expected categories, inclusion and exclusion, a third, "conditional" category emerged in the data. In this category, willingness to help was a transitional phase between inclusion and exclusion. In the conditional category, participants "did not care" if their opponent were treated unfairly, "would not loan money" to their opponent, but they *were willing to help* an opponent (Opotow, 1990c, p. 5). Help asked for or given appeared to deter full-blown exclusion and served as an important bridge to reconciliation in interpersonal conflict.

This finding is consistent with research on prosocial behavior, which found that even small acts of help can foster a more positive evaluation of others, greater concern for others' welfare, and to the perception of oneself as the kind of person who will make sacrifices for others (Staub, 1979, 1990). In contrast, unwillingness to help leads to victim derogation and devaluation, and it reduces the applicability of justice (Lerner & Whitehead, 1980). Willingness to help may foster prosocial behavior and deter harm doing because it is able to check exclusion from the scope of justice.

4.2.2. Pluralism

Another way to widen the applicability of justice is to define distinct social categories as parts of a larger social entity in which justice rules are applicable (Tyler & Lind, 1990). This "pluralistic" orientation opposes uniformity (Ehrlich, 1982) and emphasizes that diverse attitudes and constituencies that must be considered for decisions to be viewed as fair.

Greenwald & Greenwald (1994) emphasize the importance of understanding how different people construct their attitudes if environmentalists wish to have an impact on the public. Their work on developmental stages of environmental values emphasizes that disagreement between people at different developmental stages may not result from a rejection of another's perspective but instead may result from individuals approaching environmental issues from different developmental positions, from different notions about what negotiation means, and what a just outcome would entail. Cvetkovich and Earle (1994) maintain that environmental protection might be better accomplished through inclusive, cooperative procedures that provide an opportunity for stakeholders to identify compatible environmental values for environmental decisions that their communities face than through adversarial, rights-oriented approaches.

While a pluralistic orientation can lead to agreement on fair procedures to distribute community resources and promote constructive conflict outcomes, pluralism is not easy: "True tolerance means looking difference squarely in the eye and admitting the appalling fact that when other people seem to differ from us, this is because they actually believe their view of the world to be true" (Kristol, 1989, p. A19). Research on attributive projection and false consensus counsels that we perceive others' beliefs and perceptions as more similar to our own than they actually are (Holmes, 1968; Ross, Greene & House, 1977). Imagining that others' views are indistinguishable from our own protects us from the intrusion of others' perspectives, supports the belief that our own social reality is correct, and avoids the tension that results from realizing that others' beliefs may be in opposition to our own (Higgins, 1981; Ross & Fletcher, 1985).

Pluralism may be able to widen the scope of justice because acknowledging another's viewpoint implies limits our own entitlements and places another's needs and entitlements in a position to be considered. In so doing, pluralism can reshape zero-sum, antagonistic environmental conflicts into creative, cooperative efforts to integrate diverse interests and it can combat the view that others are nonentities expendable, undeserving, and as outside the community in which moral rules, values, and considerations of fairness apply.

5. Summary: Challenges of Environmental Inclusion

Over the past 25 years, the environment has changed mainstream thinking by challenging societal conventions about the categories that belong inside the scope of justice. These challenges have urged the applicability of justice to nonhuman animals, plants, and to inanimate features of the natural world.

The answer to the question -"Is the scope of justice finite?" - posed in the beginning of the chapter, is both yes and no. The scope of justice is limited by situational constraints and by self-serving biases that obscure socially-acceptable exclusions from the scope of justice. Consequently, we perceive our scope of justice as inclusive when it is not and just while current injustices remain undetected.

As ecophilosophies have identified previously-ignored constituencies and short-sighted resource allocations that have resulted in environmental degradation and species extinctions, they have urged an expansion of our scope of justice that has influenced the way people think about the environment and has spurred grassroots conservation activities. Increasing inclusion, however, brings with it added responsibilities, attunement to the needs and claims of other environmental stakeholders, and the need to balance different points of view. It is not always possible to accommodate an expanding the scope of justice (Crosby & Lubin, 1990). Increasing an environmental scope of justice means acknowledging the needs and entitlements of presently-excluded human groups, animals, plants, future life on the planet, and the inanimate natural environment. Recognizing a broader environmental constituency also means recognizing wider claims on finite resources and more difficult allocation decisions. Current environmental analyses indicate that poverty, inequality, and ecological degradation are linked and that the challenge of achieving social policies that are people-centered and conservation-based remain (Tolba & El-Kholy, 1992). This challenge is even greater when social policies are not people-centered but instead view non-human and inanimate natural features as *bona fide* stakeholders in the natural world.

Conflict and stress generated by economic recession and by resource shortages, such as conflicts that pit jobs against habitat preservation for nonhuman environmental entities, can shrink the scope of justice. At the same time, prominent and frightening man-made environmental disasters, such as oil spills and toxin-laced land, while also conflictual and stressful can motivate environmental protection by emphasizing that the well-being of people and non- human aspects of the natural environment are linked. People who perceive their lives as affected by environmental degradation, such as polluted air and water, can view the broader environmental constituency as within the scope of justice because maintaining environmental health coincides with their own well-being (Stevens, 1993). Thus, planetary-centered environmental values might expand the scope of justice when they coincide with self- and human-centered values.

Just as the scope of environmental justice has been challenged and expanded in recent history, it is likely to continue to evolve. It is impossible to know how socioeconomic circumstances, societal arrangements, and natural events will shape the scope of justice of the future. As our conceptualization of the "correct" environmental constituency continues to evolve, the nature of our lives will also change. Indeed, many environmentalists agree, making changes in humankind's lifestyles and rethinking distributions of the limited planetary resources so that our behavior fosters the well-being of all environmental entities is our best hope for the planet's future.

References

Archer, D. (1985). Social deviance. In G. Lindzey & E. Aronson (Eds.), The handbook of social psychology (3rd ed., Vol.2, pp. 743-804). New York: Random House.

Axelrod, L. J. (1994). Balancing personal needs with environmental preservation: Identifying the values that guide decisions in ecological dilemmas. Journal of Social Issues, 50(2), 85-104.

Bandura, A. (1986). Social foundations of thought and action: A social cognitive theory. Englewood Cliffs, NJ: Prentice-Hall.

Bookchin, M. (1982). The ecology of freedom: The emergence and dissolution of hierarchy. Palo Alto: Cheshire Books.

Brooke, J. (1985, July 17). Fight in a Hartford suburb: Residents vs. rattlesnakes. The New York Times, B1, B2.

Bullard, R. D. (1994). Dumping in Dixie: Race, class, and environmental quality (2nd ed.). Boulder, CO: Westview.

Calabresi, G. & Bobbitt, P. (1978). Tragic choices. New York: W.W. Norton.

Callicott, J. B. & Ames, R. T. (1989). Nature in Asian traditions and thought. Albany, NY: SUNY Press.

Clayton, S. (1994). Appeals to justice in the environmental debate. Journal of Social Issues, 50(2), 13-27.

Clayton, S. & Opotow, S. (Eds.). (1994). Green justice: Conceptions of fairness and the natural world [Special issue]. Journal of Social Issues, 50(2).

Commission for Racial Justice. (1987). Toxic wastes and race: A national report on the racial and socioeconomic characteristics of communities with hazardous waste sites. New York: United Church of Christ.

Cooter, R. (1987). Justice at the confluence of law and economics. Social Justice Research, 1(1), 67-81.

Crosby, F. J. & Lubin, E. P. (1990). Extending the moral community: Logical and psychological dilemmas. Journal of Social Issues, 46(1), 163-172.

Cvetkovich, G. & Earle, T. C. (1994). The construction of justice: A case study of public participation in land management. Journal of Social Issues, 50(2), 161-178.

d'Eaubonne, F. (1980). Feminism or death. In E. Marks & I. de Courtivron (Eds.), New French feminism: An anthology. Amherst, MA: University of Massachusetts Press.

Deutsch, M. (1974). Awakening the sense of injustice. In M. J. Lerner & M. Ross (Eds.), The quest for justice: Myth, reality, ideal (pp. 19-42). Toronto: Holt, Rinehart and Winston.

Dunlap, R. E. & Van Liere, K. D. (1978). The new environmental paradigm: A proposed measuring instrument and preliminary results. Journal of Environmental Education, 9, 10-19.

Ehrlich, S. (1982). Pluralism on and off course. Oxford: Pergamon Press.

Eliade, M. (1978/1982). A history of religious ideas (Vol. 2) (W.R. Trask, Trans.). From Gautama Buddha to the Triumph of Christianity. Chicago: University of Chicago Press. (Original work published 1978).

Fine, M. (1990). "The public" in public schools: The social construction/constriction of moral communities. Journal of Social Issues, 46(1), 107-119.

Finger, M. (1990). From knowledge to action? Exploring the relationships between environmental experiences, learning, and behavior. Journal of Social Issues, 50(2), 141-160.

Greenberg, J. (1981). The justice of distributing scarce and abundant resources. In M. J. Lerner & S. C. Lerner (Eds.), The justice motive in social behavior: Adapting to times of scarcity and change (pp. 289-316. New York: Plenum.

Greenwald, J. M. & Greenwald, R. (1994). Environmental attitudes conceptualized through developmental theory: A qualitative analysis. Journal of Social Issues, 50(2), 29-47.

Hargrove, E. C. (1989). Foundations of environmental ethics. Englewood Cliffs, NY: Prentice Hall.

Higgins, E. T. (1981). Role-taking and social judgment: Alternative developmental perspectives and processes. In V. H. Flavell & L. Ross (Eds.), New directions in the study of social-cognitive development. Cambridge: Cambridge University Press.

Holmes, D. S. (1968). Dimensions of projection. Psychological Bulletin, 69, 248-268.

Katz, C. & Kirby, A. (1991). In the nature of things: The environment and everyday life. Transactions of the Institute for British Geography, 16, 259-271.

Kegan, R. (1982). The evolving self. Cambridge, MA: Harvard University Press. Francisco, CA: Harper and Row.

Kohlberg, L. (1981). The philosophy of moral development: Moral stages and the idea of justice. Vol 1. of Essays on moral development. San Francisco: Harper & Row.

Kristol. E. (1989, September 25). False tolerance, false unity. New York Times, A19.

Leopold, A. (1949). A Sand County almanac. New York: Oxford University Press.

Lerner, M. J. (1975). The justice motive in social behavior: Introduction. Journal of Social Issues, 31(3), 1-19.

Lerner, M. J. (1981). The justice motive in human relations: Some thoughts on what we know and need to know about justice. In M. J. Lerner & S. C. Lerner (Eds.), The justice motive in social behavior: Adapting to times of scarcity and change (pp. 11-35). New York: Plenum.

Lerner, M. J. & Whitehead, L. A. (1980). Procedural justice viewed in the context of justice motive theory. In G. Mikula (Ed.), Justice and social interaction (pp. 219-256). New York: Springer-Verlag.

Leventhal, G. S. (1972). Effects of external conflict on resource allocation and fairness within groups and organizations. In W. G. Austin & S. LeVine, R. A., & Campbell, D. T. (1972). Ethnocentrism: Theories of conflict, ethnic attitude, and group behavior. New York: John Wiley & Sons.

List, P. C. (1993). Radical environmentalism: Philosophy and Tactics. Belmont, CA: Wadsworth.

Lovelock, J. E. (1979). The Gaia Hypothesis: A new look of life on Earth. Oxford: Oxford University Press.

Meier, B. (1992, Aug. 10). Wolves return to Montana and the greetings are mixed. The New York Times, A1, A12.

Merchant, C. (1979). The death of nature: Women, ecology and the scientific revolution. New York: Harper and Row.

Merchant, C. (1989), Ecological revolutions, nature, gender, and science in New England. Chapel Hill, NC: University of North Carolina Press.

Merchant, C. (1992). Radical ecology: The search for a livable world. New York: Routledge.

Montada, L. (1980). Developmental changes in concepts of justice. In G. Mikula (Ed.), Justice and social interaction (pp. 257-284). New York: Springer.

Naess, A. (1973, Spring). The shallow and the deep, long-range ecology movements: A summary. Inquiry, 16, 95-100.

Nash, N. C. (1993, June 21) Bolivia's rain forest falls to relentless exploiters. The New York Times, A1, A8.

Nash, R. F. (1989). The rights of nature. Madison, WI: University of Wisconsin Press.

Opotow, S. V. (1987). Limits of fairness: An experimental examination of antecedents of the scope of justice. Dissertation Abstracts International, 48 (08B), 2500. (University microfilms No. 87-24072)

Opotow, S. (1990a). Moral exclusion and injustice: An introduction. Journal of Social Issues, 46(1), 1-20.

Opotow, S. (1990b). Deterring moral exclusion. Journal of Social Issues, 46(1), 173-182.

Opotow, S. (1990c). Justice beliefs in adolescents' interpersonal conflicts with peers. Paper presented at the annual convention of the American Psychological Association, Boston, MA.

Opotow, S. (1993). Animals and the scope of justice. Journal of Social Issues, 49(1), 71-85.

Opotow, S. (1994). Predicting protection: Scope of justice and the natural world. Journal of Social Issues, 50(2), 49-63.

Opotow, S. (1995). Drawing the line: Social categorization and moral exclusion. In J. Z. Rubin and B. B. Bunker, (Eds.), Conflict, Cooperation, and Justice (pp. 347-369). San Francisco: Jossey-Bass.

Opotow, S. & Clayton, S. (1994). Green justice: Conceptions of fairness and the natural world. Journal of Social Issues, 50(2), 1-11.

Passmore, J. (1975). Attitudes toward nature. In R.S. Peters (Eds.), Nature and conduct (pp. 251-264). London: Macmillan.

Passmore, J. (1980). Man's responsibility for nature (2nd ed.). London: Duckworth.

Piaget, J. (1954). The construction of reality in the child. New York: Basic Books. (Original work published 1937)

Regan, T. (1983). The case for animal rights. Berkeley, CA: University of California Press.

Ross, M., Greene, D. & House, P. (1977). The "false consensus effect": An egocentric bias in social perception and attribution processes. Journal of Experimental Social Psychology, 13, 279-301.

Ross, M. & Fletcher, G. J. O. (1985). Attribution and social perception. In G. Lindzey and E. Aronson (Eds.), The handbook of social psychology (3rd ed., Vol. 2, pp. 73-122). New York: Random House.

Schweitzer, A. (1961). Out of my life and thought: An autobiography. New York: Holt, Rinehart, and Winston.

Schwartz, S. H. (1977). Normative influences on altruism. In L. Berkowitz (Ed.), Advances in experimental social psychology (Vol. 10, pp. 221-279). New York: Academic Press.

Simmons, I. G. (1993). Interpreting nature: Cultural constructions of the environment. London: Routledge.

Singer, P. (1975). Animal liberation: A new ethics for our treatment of animals. New York: Avon Books.

Staub, E. (1979). Positive social behavior and morality: Socialization and development (Vol 2). New York: Academic Press.

Staub, E. (1990). Moral exclusion, personal goal theory, and extreme destructiveness. Journal of Social Issues, 46(1), 47-64.

Stern, P. C. & Dietz, T. (1994). The value basis of environmental concern. Journal of Social Issues, 50(2), 65-84.

Stevens, M. (1994, Aug. 8). Chief Joseph's revenge. The New Yorker, pp. 26-33.

Stevens, W. K. (1993, Jan 26). River life through U.S. broadly degraded. The New York Times, p. C1, C7.

Stone, C. (1988). Should trees have standing? Toward legal rights for natural objects. (2nd ed.). Portola Valley, CA: Tioga Publishing.

Tajfel, H. (1978). Differentiation between social groups: Studies in the social psychology of intergroup relations (European Monograph in Social Psychology, No. 14). London: Academic Press.

Turiel, E. (1983). The development of social knowledge: Morality and convention. New York: Cambridge University Press.

Tolba, M. K. & El-Kholy, O. A., (Eds.). (1992). The world environment 1972-1992. London: Chapman & Hall.

Tyler, T. R. & Lind, E. A. (1990). Intrinsic versus community-based justice models: When does group membership matter? Journal of Social Issues, 46, (1), 83-94.

Warren, K. (1993). Power and promise of ecological feminism. Environmental Ethics, 12, 125-145.

13

Are Proenvironmental Commitments Motivated by Health Concerns or by Perceived Justice?

Elisabeth Kals

1. Research in the Context of "Socioecological Justice"

Environmental Psychology is a relatively young discipline. Within this discipline, new approaches to handling justice relevant questions on preserving the natural environment were developed ("questions of socioecological justice"). As an introduction to this research field, its premises are discussed first. Subsequently, an overview of environmentally oriented justice relevant research questions is provided.

1.1. Basic Appraisals of the Extent, the Causes, and the Reduction of Environmental Problems

Significant destruction and pollution of the ecological environment* can be regarded as one of the major negative effects of the high standard of living in modern society. Most ecological problems produce numerous financial and nonmaterial costs to people and their environ-

---

*Ecological environment is defined as the entirety of the natural base of human beings with its various components (like air, water, soil).

Elisabeth Kals • Fachbereich I -Psychologie, Universität Trier, D - 54286 Trier, Germany

Current Societal Concerns about Justice, edited by Leo Montada and Melvin J. Lerner. Plenum Press, New York, 1996.

ment, like psychical and physical impairments and diseases, damages to the flora and fauna, and destruction of buildings. There is a long tradition of attempts to reduce the threats of these ecological damages. Some minor, mostly local ecological problems could successfully be controlled (examples: cf., Umweltbundesamt, 1988), however, more severe mainly global ecological problems and their long-term effects are still not under control, but are continually getting worse. This is the case in Germany (Umweltbundesamt, 1994), in other European countries, as well as in the United States (Conference of European Statisticians, 1987; Darnay, 1992).

The various forms of the more severe global destruction of the natural environment cover a wide range of ecological aspects and include (1) the excessive use of resources which are on principle renewable (e.g., deforestation), (2) the excessive use of nonrenewable resources (e.g., use of fossil fuels), and (3) the impairment or destruction of ecosystems due to toxic agents (e.g., the alteration of the atmosphere or the pollution of water; Bossel, 1990).

The range of these global and more severe ecological problems can be illustrated by some examples of world-wide undesirable ecological developments (cf., Bossel, 1990; Umweltbundesamt, 1994):

- The industrial nations embrace a fourth of the world population, but use up to 5/6 of the whole energy consumption. Correspondingly, the consumption of energy and raw materials per person in the industrial nations is approximately 30 to 50 times higher than in the developing countries.
- The world-wide consumption of fossil fuels doubles nearly every 35 years.
- The level of carbon dioxide in the atmosphere increased about 25 percent during the last hundred years.
- The decrease of ozone is accelerated, not only in the Antarctic and the Arctic circle but also above latitude 50o N. (the approximate location of, for example, Frankfut /Main, Prague, and Vancouver). At this latitude the ozone decreases about 4.7 percent every year.
- World-wide, a wooded area of approximately the size of the Federal Republic of Germany is destroyed every year.
- Deserts spread as a result of manifold dysfunctioning of various ecosystems. Consequently, land used for agriculture is lost. The corresponding world-wide loss again covers the size of the Federal Republic of Germany.

The list of global ecological problems could easily be enlarged and could be supplemented by further local ecological problems of individual countries, regions, or cities.

On a specific level, these ecological problems appear to be heterogeneous, and their causes can be attributed to different sources. On a more global level, all ecological problems endanger the quality of the natural environment, and their causes can be attributed to human behavior (e.g., the effects of production or consumption). Along this line, Maloney and Ward called the ecological crisis a "crisis of maladaptive behavior" (Maloney & Ward, 1973, p. 583).

Following this approach, it can be presumed that effective pollution control cannot be guaranteed by industrial approaches and technological solutions only, but has to be complemented by individual acts of voluntary sacrifices. For example, past developments have shown that technological approaches to reduce the toxic effects of traffic density (e.g., the development and promotion of vehicles with less exhaust fumes) are not successful enough to reduce the negative effects of the increased traffic; this would require a lowered use of vehicles.

The central premises of research in the field of environmental psychology can be summarized as follows: There are serious impairments of the natural environment which are caused by human behavior. Without diminishing the significance of supplemental approaches (like technological attempts), the ecological crisis must be reduced by changes in the relevant ecological behavior. The discipline of environmental psychology can contribute to the explanation and promotion of these proenvironmental commitments and sacrifices.

There are different perspectives within environmental psychology which provide a better understanding of proenvironmental appraisals and commitments. One perspective is espoused by the field of socioecological justice which is described below.

1.2. The Field of Socioecological Justice

The majority of proenvironmental behavior is linked with material and nonmaterial costs. Not littering the environment, for example, implies the inconvenience of taking garbage to the next garbage can or even back home; to take the bus or train instead of one's own car means a loss of convenience and time; to economize energy in one's household can cause inconveniences and can also cost money (if, for example, new technical equipment is expensive and will not help to save money in the long run); to support a conservation group that tries to increase pollution control may mean sacrifices in time and money.

On the other hand, it can well be assumed that frequent active pollutive behavior implies advantages for the agent: Normally, the agent does not intend to pollute the natural environment as such but rather pursues personal aims which interfere with ecological interests. If people are, for example, active members of motor sport clubs that organize races or other motor sport activities, the personal motives for these memberships will vary, but they will all aim at personal benefits (like the intention to enjoy races or, as a more general motive, to establish social contacts). The pollution of air and soil by motor sport activities is more or less consciously accepted as a side effect of these activities.

In most cases, people who profit from behavior which pollutes the environment are not identical to those who will be affected by pollution later on. Instead, there is a spatial and temporal shift between the causation of pollution and the observable negative effects from it.

In the same way, people who take sacrifices for the sake of nature will usually not enjoy direct benefits in their own living space in form of a better environment: Ecological benefit can only be expected in the long run and by accumulated effects of numerous sacrifices.

Taken together, acting proenvironmentally normally causes personal costs which are not compensated by personal experiences of a better environment whereas pollutive behavior often implies personal benefits without causing the agent to experience or bear the costs of the ecological side effects of such behavior.*

These conflicts are the basis of the so-called "social trap" (Hardin, 1968; Platt, 1973): One conflict might exist between the interests of the individual versus the interests of the social community, the other between short-term versus long-term effects (cf., Ernst & Spada, 1993; Spada & Opwis, 1985; Stern & Gardener, 1981).

Under the perspective of socioecological justice, these conflicts pose serious justice problems, such as:

- Are personal sacrifices for the sake of the natural environment really necessary and sufficiently well-founded? For example, is there a basic claim to live within an unpolluted nature which has to be satisfied?

---

*With some categories of behavior, the agent experiences the ecological consequences of his behavior directly (e.g., when the ecological effects are mainly limited to one's own property or estate). However, this kind of behavior contains other justice relevant significance and is therefore neglected in this chapter.

- Provided the need for sacrifices is sufficiently substantiated, how should costs and benefits be distributed? Is it necessary that costs and benefits are equally distributed, or can it be justified by specific circumstances that some people profit by polluting nature more than others?
- Under what maxim or justice principle should restrictions and rules to control the utilization of nature be issued? And what is an adequate and just way to control the compliance of these measures or to punish their violations?

Some of these questions are already discussed in the literature, whereas others are mainly left out, as will be demonstrated by the following overview.

1.3 Overview of Empirical Justice Relevant Psychological Contributions to the Promotion of Proenvironmental Behavior

The beginning of systematic research in environmental psychology dates back to the late seventies.* During the first research period, the understanding and promotion of proenvironmental behavior was derived from the perspective of socioecological justice. The first empirical studies in the field of environmental psychology were triggered by the necessity of energy conservation during the energy crisis of the 1970s (Kushler, 1989). These first studies included questions in the context of socioecological justice, like attributions of blame for the energy crisis (e.g., blaming the citizens versus blaming the state or oil companies) or justice considerations about the just distribution of the sacrifices which were necessary to overcome the energy crisis (like the perceived justice of sacrifices in private households to reduce energy consumption; e.g., Becker, Seligman, Fazio & Darley, 1981; Hummel, Levit & Loomis, 1978; Tyler, Orwin & Schurer, 1982).

Presumably due to the diminishing presence of the actual ecological crisis, questions on justice were less focused on in the environmental research that followed. Research tasks other than the examination of justice relevant questions crystallized (e.g., developing standardized scales to measure ecologically relevant appraisals and behavior; formulating theoretical models for the explanation of proenvironmental behavior; predicting proenvironmental behavior from perspectives other than justice research, such as the influence of social groups).

---

*Research in environmental psychology was first advanced in the English-speaking world. German research followed approximately five years later (cf., Kruse & Arlt, 1984).

Meanwhile, there is an increase in investigations dealing with the antecedents and explanations of people's proenvironmental behavior. This can be demonstrated by international bibliographies (e.g., Kruse & Arlt, 1984), by surveys of research topics (cf., Craik, 1973; Kaminski, 1988), by meta-analyses (e.g., Hines, Hungerford & Tomera, 1986/87), and by especially interesting investigations dealing with specific ecological problems (e.g., Löfstedt, 1992, 1993; Syme, Beven & Sumner, 1993). But in the current literature the perspective of socioecological justice is only occasionally presented (Clayton, 1994; Horwitz, 1994; Renn, Webler & Kastenholz, 1994; Sitter, 1987). Significant discussion can only be found for some selective justice issues, like for example the moral basis upon which people's readiness to pay for environmental improvements is founded (Mitchell & Carson, 1989).

There are different explanations for this shift away from an emphasis on justice research. The first systematic research was triggered by the necessity of rapid private and industrial sacrifices to cope with the energy crisis. It is possible that this specific and time-limited crisis appeared to be less complex and easier to understand than, for instance, the above mentioned global ecological problems. Additionally, the energy crisis had direct implications for the citizens, such as the significant increase in fuel prices. This should have promoted dissatisfaction and the motivation to change the energy crisis by specific measures. The selection and the evaluation of specific measures to reduce the energy crisis could have provoked justice relevant questions (e.g., about the just energy conservation measures).

In sum, there is no continuous tradition of empirical research within the field of socioecological justice. Therefore, the following new structural model was developed to serve as a frame for gaining more empirical evidence.

2. A Structural Model to Explain Proenvironmental Behavior

It is presumed that the more the burdens of proenvironmental behavior are regarded as just, the more the behavior will be promoted. The point in question is: Under what conditions is it likely that the corresponding personal costs associated with protecting the natural environment will be accepted as just respectively will be denied due to their perceived injustice?

Two successive studies were conducted to answer this question empirically (cf., Kals, 1994; Kals & Montada, 1994). Their underlying structural model to explain proenvironmental behavior and commitments is given in Figure 1.

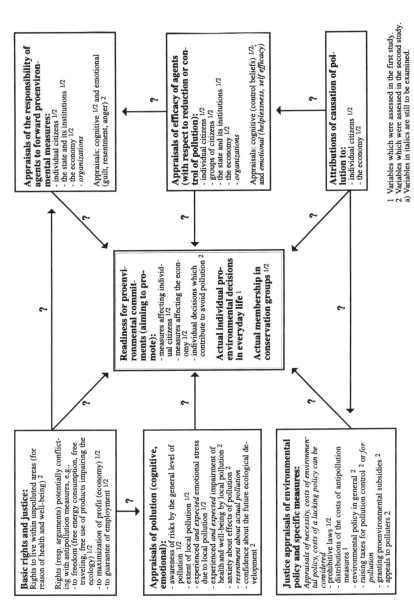

Figure 1. Structural Model of Proenvironmental Commitments[a]

As this model shows, six groups of predictor variables were considered to explain various forms of proenvironmental commitment (such as the acceptance of measures affecting individual citizens or economy) and manifest behavior (individual proenvironmental decisions in every day life and actual membership in conservation groups):

1. appraisals of basic rights and justice, meaning basic environmental rights and arguments (like job endangering) potentially in conflict with antipollution measures;
2. cognitive and emotional appraisals of pollution in general;
3. justice appraisals of environmental policy in general and of specific antipollution measures;
4. attributions of different causes for pollution;
5. appraisals of the efficacy of various agents (with respect to the reduction or control of pollution);
6. appraisals of the responsibility of various agents to promote proenvironmental measures.

The predictor variables refer to socioecological justice and can be differentiated into morally oriented predictors (e.g., the attribution of the responsibility to promote proenvironmental measures) and self-oriented predictors (e.g., experienced emotional stress due to local pollution).

Not all morally oriented predictors comprise justice considerations directly. This is only the case for the first and third group of predictor variables. The remaining four groups of predictor variables, however, can be interpreted in the light of justice considerations and should make independent contributions to the explanation of proenvironmental behavior. For purpose of illustration, the following corresponding hypotheses are exemplified for all groups of predictor variables:

Basic rights and justice, as the first group of predictor variables, refer to the problem of justice inherent to appraisals of proenvironmental sacrifices. There are several ways to deny the necessity and, subsequently, the justice of proenvironmental sacrifices in general: If no basic right to live within unpolluted areas is claimed, no efforts will be necessary to ensure an unpolluted natural environment. In addition, arguments can be formulated against all private measures of pollution control (e.g., unacceptable inconveniences associated with restricting the use of private cars). The underlying norms and aims (e.g., the claim to live a convenient life) have to be balanced with ecological norms. The more priority is given to conflicting norms, the more the corresponding arguments against proenvironmental measures should be accepted and the more the private proenvironmental measures should be rejected as unjust.

The second group of predictors, the appraisals of pollution, also concern the justice problem if proenvironmental sacrifices are sufficiently well-founded. The first predictor (awareness of risks by the general level of pollution) refers to a moral goal because the risks of pollution are judged with regard to all citizens. The remaining variables of this predictor category are self-oriented because the underlying ultimate goal should be the protection of one's own self and of one's own life quality. To exemplify one hypothesis: If actual or anticipated ecological problems are denied in general, there will be no need and no perceived justice for proenvironmental sacrifices.

The direct justice appraisals of environmental policy in general and appraisals of specific antipollution measures are the third category of predictor variables. All of these justice appraisals offer possibilities to reject personal proenvironmental sacrifices due to the problem of unjust distribution, unjust implementation, or unjust control of demanding measures. To illustrate: The acceptance of the justice principle that the costs of proenvironmental measures should be paid by those who actually caused the problems is one way to justify the distribution of proenvironmental costs. If the private contribution to the causation of environmental pollution is negligible and if industrial agents are regarded as the main source of pollution, it is very likely that readiness to personally pay for the costs will be quite low. The costs should mainly be paid by the external industrial agents who are judged to have caused the pollution.

The fourth category of predictor variables concerns the attributions of the causation of pollution: If the causation of pollution is attributed to the economy as an external agency and not to individual citizens, the proenvironmental measures should pursue the main goal to reduce or control industrial pollution. Likewise, private proenvironmental commitments and measures should not be regarded as necessary or just and should therefore not be supported.

Concerning the fifth variable group, the appraisals of the efficacy of agents to reduce or control pollution, the following central hypothesis can be exemplified: Only those ecological measures which are judged as effective for improving the ecological situation should be regarded as just. Often individual control is perceived as ineffective compared to the huge extent of environmental problems (cf., Borsutzky & Nöldner, 1989; Krämer, 1989; Preiser & Wannemacher, 1983). As a consequence, ineffective personal sacrifices should be rejected as unjust.

Appraisals of the responsibility of agents to promote proenvironmental measures, as the sixth category of predictor variables, should also have powerful effects on the acceptance versus rejection of proenvironmental measures. It is likely, for example, that personal costs are regarded as unjust, when ecological responsibility is attributed to others instead of to the citizens who should bear the costs, namely, to industry or to the state.

All these hypotheses refer to expected main effects of the predictor variables. In Figure 1 additional relationships between the predictor variables are marked. The examination of these interrelationships are beyond the scope of this chapter but are reported elsewhere (Montada & Kals, 1995).

The power of most of the predictor variables has already been empirically examined. In the first study an exploratory set of predictors to explain proenvironmental behavior was assessed. In the second study the predictor set was enlarged to cross-validate and to deepen specific research questions. Therefore, a great amount of overlap exists between the assessed variables of both studies. Some of the predictor variables, written in italics in Figure 1, were neither assessed in the first nor in the second study.

Subsequently, the empirical findings to explain the underlying motives of ecologically beneficial behavior are offered. On the basis of the empirical findings, the structural model will be changed into an empirical one.

3. First Study

The initial study attempted to examine the empirical significance of the justice relevant questions to explain proenvironmental commitments.

3.1 Research Questions

The underlying research question refers to the explanation and prediction of proenvironmental commitments and behavior in the context of air pollution.

Appraisals were restricted to the problem of air pollution because there is insufficient evidence to conclude that psychological research on one environmental problem can be generalized on others. Therefore, all variables assessed in this study refer to one specific environmental problem. Air pollution was chosen because it represents one of the most severe ecological problems which causes personal stress and which has numerous causes (like traffic, industrial production, energy production, consumption etc.).

Various forms of commitment and self-reported behavior in the context of air pollution were measured (cf., Figure 1):

(I) *the readiness to actively support proenvironmental measures* (by supporting conservation groups, by giving regular financial donations, by participating in demonstrations etc.) (a) affecting individual citizens (e.g., supporting efforts to restrict private traffic) and (b) affecting the economy (e.g., strengthening ecological changes in industrial enterprises, like the reduction of their energy consumption), and

(II) *the actual individual proenvironmental decisions in everyday life for the protection of air quality* (e.g., purchasing goods with regard to the protection of air quality, such as the purchase of emission control devices for cars).

(III) *Memberships in conservation groups* and *memberships in motor sport clubs* were measured as objective contrasting criteria.

Within the conservation groups a heightened consciousness for ecological problems should be likely. In contrast, it is assumed that a high and active support of motor sport interests might interfere with ecological aims. This could lead to a somewhat lower level of environmental sensitivity with the effect that cognitive dissonance is prevented.

For the prediction of these proenvironmental commitments and behaviors, a set of predictor variables was operationalized (cf., Figure 1). All predictor variables refer either to appraisals of the global air pollution or to appraisals of local air pollution in one's own living space. Both groups of predictor variables include cognitive as well as emotive appraisals.

The operationalized appraisals in the context of local air pollution can be regarded as self-oriented judgments. These are *the perceived extent of air pollution in one's own living space* (predictor (1)) and *the emotional stress which is caused by this local air pollution* (2).

All appraisals in the context of global air pollution embrace valuations which touch moral dimensions. In detail, these are *the acceptance of rights conflicting with private control measures* (3.1; e.g., right of freedom which might be endangered by further restrictions of private traffic) and *conflicting with industrial pollution control measures* (3.2; e.g., right to maximization of profit which might be endangered by further proenvironmental restrictions for industrial production), *appraisals concerning the just distribution of the costs to finance pollution control to those who actually caused the pollution* (4.1) versus *to the whole community* (4.2), *the awareness of risks by the general level of air pollution* (5), *attributions of the causation of pollution to private polluters* (6.1) and *to industrial polluters* (6.2), *appraisals of the efficacy of private agents* (7.1) and *of industrial agents* (7.2), and *appraisals of the responsibility of agents to promote proenvironmental measures of pri-*

vate agents (8.1), *of industrial agents* (8.2), and *of governmental agents* (8.3).*

Only the third and the fourth group of variables (predictor (3.1) to (3.2) and (4.1) to (4.2)) represent direct justice considerations.

3.2. Sample and Measurement Instruments

The sample consisted of 255 German subjects, including two criterion groups, in which the environmentally-relevant behavior was expected to be extreme. The one group consisted of 54 active members of various conservation groups (like Greenpeace), the other of 47 active members of motor sport clubs. The 101 participants of the criterion groups were contacted personally at regular club meetings of the corresponding groups. The remaining 154 subjects of the sample are representatives of the general population. The overall response rate of 86 percent illustrates that the respondents were relatively representative for the three basic samples.

Data was collected by a German questionnaire.† Like all psychological studies dealing with ecological topics, the study had to address problems of social desirability. Therefore, the tendency to give socially desirable answers was assessed using a scale developed by Lück and Timeaus (1969, based on the original scale of Crowne & Marlowe, 1960).

All other variables were assessed by several newly constructed six-point Likert-type items. Included in the development of the scales are suggestions taken from previous scales that addressed different ecological problems (cf., Amelang, Tepe, Vagt & Wendt, 1977; Kessel & Tischler, 1984; Kley & Fietkau, 1979; Maloney & Ward, 1973; Schahn & Holzer, 1990) and from literature applying to justice considerations in other social contexts (cf., Montada, Schmitt & Dalbert, 1986).

All scales were factoranalyzed by principal component analyses followed by a varimax rotation. The factor analyses confirmed the a priori dimensions of the scales. All current item statistics (like mean value, standard deviation, corrected item total correlation) were computed. The internal consistency (Cronbachs Alpha) and different split half reliabilities of the scales were thoroughly controlled. The scores confirmed sufficient reliability of the factors. The validity of the factors was successfully checked by group comparisons: For each criterion group (members of motor sport clubs and members of conservation

---

*The justice appraisals of prohibitive laws are not focused on in this chapter.
†The questionnaire used in the first and second study, including item statistics, can be sent to the interested reader.

groups) control groups having an equal number of subjects were selected by matching age, gender, and educational level. As expected, members of conservation groups showed a higher level of sensitivity for air pollution in general and expressed higher proenvironmental commitments than members of the control group. For members of the motor sport clubs the mean differences were reversed.

In accordance with the results of the factor analyses, all statistical findings reported below are based on composite scores (mean values across those items belonging to one factor) instead of factor scores. The range of the scores varied from 1 (high agreement with the respective content of the items) to 6 (low agreement).*

3.3. Summary of the Main Predictive Results

Multiple regression analyses were conducted to examine the main research question concerning the prediction and explanation of proenvironmental commitments and behavior. Without discussing the results of the first study in full, the main results can be summarized as follows:

1. The *justice appraisals of rights (like job security) potentially conflicting with antipollution measures for the citizens* (3.1) and *for the industry* (3.2) were two of the most powerful predictors for all criteria. The more the conflicting rights were rejected, the more proenvironmental commitments were expressed and various forms of manifest behavior performed. These basic justice appraisals explained up to a maximal amount of 51 percent of explained criterion variance (of the readiness for commitments aiming to promote proenvironmental measures).

2. The direct justice appraisals concerning the *just distribution of the costs of pollution control to those who actually caused the pollution* (4.1) versus *to the community* (4.2) were also stable predictors for all criteria but less powerful than the rights potentially conflicting with antipollution measures. The perceived justice of the distributions of the costs of antipollution measures explained up to a quarter of the variance of a criterion variable (again of the readiness for commitments aiming to promote proenvironmental measures). When only the predictors on cost distribution were included in stepwise multiple regression analyses, both predictor variables qualified in all regression

---

*Subsequently, all selected regression analyses were based on the total sample. The validity of these analyses within the subsamples of the criterion groups was successfully proven.

analyses and increased the probability of the performance of proenvironmental behavior. This demonstrates that the two justice principles were not working as competitive but as supplemental principles.

3. In correspondence with the first main result, the other morally relevant appraisals were also stable and powerful predictors. All variables touching a moral scope contributed positively and independently to the prediction of proenvironmental commitments and behavior: *a high consciousness for the extent and risks of the general level of pollution* (5), *a high attribution of the causation of air pollution* (6.1 and 6.2), *the perceived efficacy of various actions to control pollution* (7.1 and 7.2), and *a high attribution of the responsibility for the protection of air quality* (8.1 and 8.2). These morally relevant predictors together explained more than 60 percent of the variance of the proenvironmental commitments and behaviors. Again, the problem of air pollution seemed to be accepted as a morally relevant problem of the citizens.

4. The *self-oriented predictors concerning appraisals of local air pollution* (1 and 2) were not stable predictors for all proenvironmental criteria. In most regression analyses these appraisals of local air pollution did not qualify.

5. By including all predictor variables in full regression analyses (cf., Figure 1), a maximum of approximately 70 percent of the criterion variance could be explained.

6. *Commitments* were good predictors of the *self-reported actual behavior* as well as of the actual memberships in criterion groups.

7. For the prediction of all criteria the *tendency to give socially desirable answers* remained insignificant.

8. Most predictor patterns were stable. Hardly any sign of suppression effects could be found.

4. Second Study

On the basis of the aforementioned results, the second study was conducted (cf., Kals, 1994; Kals & Montada, 1994). The selection of the operationalized variables was improved.

4.1. Research Questions

The major aim of the second study was also devoted to the justice relevant explanation and prediction of proenvironmental behavior.

However, on the basis of the above summarized results, the research question was specified as follows: Are commitments for the protection of air quality a function of morally relevant justice considerations, or can individual pollution control be explained by personal stress and health concern due to air pollution?

In this second study, some changes in the criterion variable set were made in comparison to the first study. Instead of the self-reported actual individual proenvironmental decisions in everyday life (commitment (II)) the corresponding readiness to perform this behavior was assessed:

(IV) *the readiness for proenvironmental individual decisions in everyday life which contribute to preventing air pollution* (e.g., the readiness to take a quick shower instead of a long hot bath).

The other criterion variables remained the same (*the readiness to actively support proenvironmental measures* (I) and *memberships in conservation groups* and *in motor sport clubs* (III)). Accordingly, only commitments and the objective criteria of memberships were assessed (cf., Figure 1). This decision is in correspondence with the fifth main result of the first study (that self-reported actual behavior can precisely be predicted by the commitments).

The set of predictor variables was enlarged and specified as follows (cf., Figure 1): Self-oriented variables referring to local air pollution remained insignificant in the first study. In the second study these variables were measured more comprehensively to increase the possibility that they will become significant. Specifically, the following self-oriented predictors were supplemented to the eight predictor categories of the first study: *the experienced impairment of health and well-being by local air pollution* (9; e.g., personal physical stress attributed to air pollution), *anxiety about personal effects of air pollution* (10), and *confidence about future development with respect to air pollution* (11).

Morally oriented cognitive predictors were also more fully assessed. Primarily, the direct justice appraisals referring to the questions on the just distribution of the costs to finance pollution control were substituted by the following more detailed justice relevant variables: *the perceived justice of German eco-policy in general* (12), *appraisals of raising taxes for pollution control from the citizens* (13.1) and *from the industry* (13.2), *appraisals of granting subsidies for antipollution measures and encouraging voluntary sacrifices for the citizens* (14.1) and *for the industry* (14.2), *the perceived justice of merely appealing to polluters instead of fixing further restrictions, appealing to the citizens* (15.1) and *appealing to industry* (15.2), and *appraisals of basic rights and justice concerning the right to live within unpolluted areas* (16). The already measured rights potentially conflicting with antipollution measures were assessed again (cf., predictors (3.1) and (3.2) of the first study).

The morally oriented predictors were supplemented in the same way as the self-oriented predictors by emotional appraisals. The added morally relevant emotions were *guilt concerning one's own pollutive behavior* (17), *resentment about the pollutive behavior of others* (18), and *anger about too much pollution control and its side effects* (19).

The remaining predictor variables from the first study as well as *the tendency to give socially desirable answers* were assessed again.

4.2. Sample and Research Method

A total of 518 persons served as subjects of the second study. Again, the sample embraced two criterion groups, 85 active members of conservation groups and 97 active members of motor sport clubs.

The methodological design of the first study proved to be successful, therefore, the procedures in the second study were the same (e.g., concerning the measurement instruments, the control of socially desirable answers, of reliability and validity of the scales). The only important change was the revision of the scales in accordance with the empirical results (e.g., the omission or substitution of particular items in accordance with the item-total correlation coefficients or the rewording of items and instructions).

4.3. Results on the Predictive Power of Justice versus Health Relevant Predictors

Multiple regression analyses were used to examine the predictive power of justice versus health relevant predictors for various forms of commitments.

Stepwise regression analyses which included all predictor variables (predictors (1) to (3.2) and (5) to (19)) were conducted for the prediction of all criteria in first analysis steps. One exemplifying result is given in Table 1 for the prediction of the readiness to pursue proenvironmental measures affecting individual citizens.

As can be seen, seven predictor variables qualified which accounted for nearly 53 percent of the criterion variance. A high *readiness to pursue proenvironmental measures affecting individual citizens* (I.a) will be expected if *rights to freedom, to maximization of profit, or to guarantee of employment, all potentially conflicting with private antipollution measures,* are declined (3.1), if *various citizen's acts to control air*

Table 1: Stepwise Multiple Regression Analysis of the Readiness to Pursue Proenvironmental Measures Affecting Individual Citizens (Predictor Variables (1) - (3.2) and (5) - 19))[a]

	Predictor variable	R^2	r	b	beta
(3.1)	Acceptance of rights potentially conflicting with private antipollution measures	.35	−.59	−.28**	−.29
(7.1)	Valuation of the efficacy of various citizen's actions to control air pollution	.46	.53	.25**	.21
(18)	Resentment about pollutive behaviors of others	.50	.53	.26**	.21
(13.1)	Justice of taxes to finance pollution control for the citizens	.51	.49	.11**	.11
(8.1)	Attribution of responsibility for the protection of the air to the citizens	.52	.47	.10*	.09
(14.2)	Justice of encouragement of voluntary sacrifices of the industry	.52	.05	.06**	.07
(19)	Anger about too much pollution control (intercept)	.53	−.47	−.09* 2.28	−.09

$F_{total} = 78.47$; df = 7/490; p < .01.

*.01 < p < .05; **p < .01.
[a] All variables ranging from 1 (high agreement) to 6 (low agreement).

pollution are judged as effective (7.1), if *resentment about pollutive behavior of others* is stated (18), if *raising taxes for pollution control for the citizens are judged as just* (13.1), if the *responsibility for the protection of air quality is attributed to the citizens* (8.1), if *the encouragement of voluntary sacrifices of the industry to control air pollution is regarded as just* (14.2), and if *anger about too much pollution control* is declined (19).

This equation demonstrates that only morally relevant variables predicted *the readiness to pursue proenvironmental measures for the citizens.* These predictors contained cognitive as well as emotional appraisals. Only one predictor variable referred to the industry (predictor (14.2)). All other predictors affected the citizens (representing internal agency) who would also have to bear the costs of the proenvironmental measures of the criterion variable. The power of the morally relevant predictors stands in sharp contrast to the insignificance of variables representing personal afflictions (like *variables of personal exposure to local air pollution* or *anxiety about affects of pollution*). This finding proved to be stable when the predictor set was varied in different ways (e.g., more or less powerful predictors were included simultaneously in regression analyses, or predictor variables were expanded or split in accordance with the corresponding item statistics). The significance of this result was not diminished by effects of social desirability.

All significant predictors could be interpreted in the light of justice and rights. Four of the predictors indirectly referred to justice considerations. Three significant predictors directly referred to justice considerations (predictors (3.1), (13.1) and (14.2)). These direct justice considerations predicted the commitment independent of other cognitive or emotional appraisals.

Despite differences in the prediction of various forms of commitments, these main results were confirmed by the regression equations predicting other commitments. Five conclusions can be drawn (cf., Kals & Montada, 1994):

1. Morally relevant emotional and cognitive predictors were powerful distinctive valuations to explain the various proenvironmental commitments and decisions. In addition, if the citizens (versus the industry) have to bear the costs of the criterion commitments, the significant predictors concerning the appraisals of the ecological responsibility, of efficacy of measures to control the pollution, and of causation of pollution will, in the tendency, also refer to the citizens (versus to the industry).
2. Direct justice considerations were especially powerful predictors. At least two direct variables of justice or basic rights did qualify in all equations.
3. In most regression analyses self- and health oriented predictors remained insignificant (like *experienced impairment of health by local pollution* (9) or *anxiety about personal effects of pollution* (10)).
4. The significance of the predictor variables could be confirmed when the predictor set was varied. The variable of social desirability did not qualify.
5. Again, commitments were good predictors of the actual memberships in criterion groups.

Due to the second main result, the central variables, which directly concern the issue of perceived justice, were focused in additional analyses. For this purpose, only the predictors directly comprising justice considerations were included in the regression analyses (predictors (3.1) to (3.2) and (12) to (16)). The results should be demonstrated by *the readiness to pursue proenvironmental measures affecting individual citizens* as the same commitment criterion as in the first equation (cf., Table 2).

Table 2: Stepwise Multiple Regression Analysis of the Readiness to Pursue Proenvironmental Measures Affecting Individual Citizens (Predictor Variables (3.1) -(3.2) and (12) - (16))[a]

Predictor variable	R^2	r	b	beta
(13.1) Justice of taxes to finance pollution control for the citizens	.24	.49	.34**	.33
(16) Acceptance of basic rights to live within unpolluted areas	.29	.41	.41**	.22
(12) Justice of German eco-policy in general	.33	-.34	-.20**	-.20
(14.2) Justice of encouragement of voluntary sacrifices of the industry	.34	.035	.11**	.14
(15.1) Justice of appeals sto the citizens instead of forced restrictions (intercept)	.35	-.23	-.09** 2.10	-.11

$F_{total} = 53.74$; df = 5/498; p < .01.

*.01 < p < .05; **p < .01/
[a]All variables ranging from 1 (high agreement) to 6 (low agreement)

In addition to two predictors which already qualified in the full model (the rejection of rights potentially conflicting with private antipollution measures no longer qualified), three justice considerations became significant: *the acceptance of basic rights to live within unpolluted areas* (16) *the rejection of perceived justice of German eco-policy in general* (12), and *the rejection of perceived justice of appeals to the citizens instead of forced restrictions* (15.1). All predictors accounted for 35 percent of the criterion variance. The regression weights were in accordance with the first regression equation. Again, the variable of social desirability was a nonsignificant predictor.

In addition to the above mentioned five conclusions, three conclusions can be formulated which are not restricted to the presented regression equations but consider the predictive power of the direct justice considerations for all criteria:

6. When only direct justice predictors were included in regression analyses, more justice predictors qualified than in the simultaneous models which took all predictors into account. For most of the commitment criteria, these predictors accounted for nearly half of the criterion variance. It can be concluded that the other morally relevant predictors and the direct justice predictors explained similar criterion variance.*

*This suggests that other morally relevant predictors implicitly contain justice considerations, as previously discussed.

7. The most powerful and stable justice predictors for all commitment criteria were *the perceived justice of raising taxes for
pollution control* (13.1 and 13.2), *basic rights to live within
unpolluted areas* (16), and *a general sense of possible injustices
of the environmental policy* (12). These three predictors qualified
in all regression equations in one of the first four steps. This clear
prediction pattern indicates the importance of the justice appraisal of the financial cost distribution as well as the significance of a sense of fundamental socioecological justice
considerations.
8. Appraisals of appeals to polluters instead of forced restrictions
(15.1 and 15.2) and *the perceived justice of the eco-policy in
general* (12) were the only justice considerations which contributed negatively to the prediction of proenvironmental commitments. All other assessed justice variables were positive
predictors.

In other words, the answer to the research question posed at the
beginning can be formulated as follows: Various commitments and the
support of conservation groups were not a function of personal health,
concerns or other self-oriented appraisals. Instead, these criteria were
predicted by morally relevant cognitive and emotional appraisals. The
cognitive appraisals referred either indirectly to justice considerations
or embraced direct appraisals of basic rights, of environmental policy in
general, and of specific antipollutive measures. These ecological justice
considerations proved to be distinctive variables of all proenvironmental
commitments.

5. Summary and Discussion of the Results of Both Studies

The present studies demonstrate that proenvironmental commitments and behavior can be understood as a function of justice consideration and not as a function of health- and self-oriented considerations.
This main result was replicated by two samples using varied measurement instruments. The significant predictors are summarized in the
following figure (cf., Figure 2).

In this figure, the most powerful and stable predictors of all six
clusters of predictor variables from the theoretical model (cf., Figure 1)
are presented. Not all of these predictors emerge as significant predictors
in the two regression analyses because these equations only serve as
examples. But additional equations are published elsewhere (Kals &
Montada, 1994; Montada & Kals, 1995). As can be seen, only morally

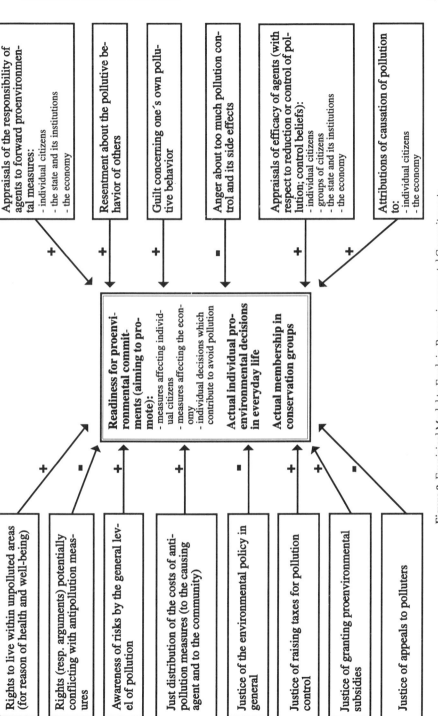

Figure 2. Empirical Model to Explain Proenvironmental Commitments.

relevant variables proved to be stable predictors. The significant predictors either refer indirectly to justice considerations or reflect direct justice considerations. The variables which refer indirectly to justice considerations include the following appraisals: *awareness of risks by the general* (not by the local) *level of pollution, the attribution of the causation of pollution, the perceived efficacy of various measures to reduce or control air pollution, the attribution of the responsibility of agents to promote proenvironmental measures, the expression of resentment about pollutive behavior of others, the expression of guilt concerning one's own pollutive behavior, and the lack of anger about too much pollution control.* The significant direct justice considerations are *the acceptance of basic ecological rights to live within unpolluted areas, the rejection of rights and arguments conflicting with antipollution measures, the just distribution of the costs of antipollution measures (on the causing agent and on the community), the perceived justice of raising taxes for pollution control and of granting subsidies for antipollution measures.* The only justice considerations which contributed negatively to the prediction of *proenvironmental commitments and behaviors* are the *perceived justice of the environmental policy in general and of appeals to polluters instead of forced restrictions.*

The negative contributions are interesting and need to be explained. The negative effect of the justice appraisal of the eco-policy overall demonstrates that a general sense of injustice in the decision making and enacting of the eco-policy represents a good precondition for the advancement of personal sacrifices. The negative contribution of the appraisals of appeals to polluters instead of forced restrictions indicates that the appraisals of proenvironmental appeals are not representing the same psychological dimension as, for example, the perceived justice of raising taxes to realize pollution control. This finding stands in contrast to justice theory stating that activities which are done by free will are per se just (Nozick, 1974). The empirical finding can be explained in two alternative ways (cf., Montada & Kals, 1995): First, appeals do not restrict freedom of decisions but they can be regarded as having either no effects on the self-reported actual behavior (e.g., due to the missing expectation of negative rewards when the appeals are ignored) or even negative effects (e.g., due to effects of reactance). Inefficient measures can be rejected as unjust (cf., the corresponding above mentioned hypothesis). Second, the perceived injustice of mere appeals can be based upon the perception of unequal distributions of the financial and nonmaterial costs: Some people will probably ignore the appeals, whereas others will contribute to the avoidance of pollution for the benefit of all, including the benefit of those who ignore the appeals.

The finding that self-oriented variables showed no significant effect is discussed next. All assessed proenvironmental commitments and behaviors serve as general preventive acts for the sake of the community and not primarily for the protection of oneself. The personal sacrifices cannot be regarded as worthwhile for one's own protection, because the sacrifices only contribute to the protection of the natural environment in general. In contrast, polluting behavior is often linked with personal short-term profits and long-term detriments for the social community, as described at the beginning of this chapter.

In this respect, long-term negative effects for the ecological environment have to be anticipated, and the corresponding moral ecological responsibility has to be accepted to get motivated for general preventive proenvironmental behavior because a personal profit normally cannot be expected. Therefore, only the morally oriented but not the self-oriented predictors refer to the same moral dimension as the criterion commitments and behaviors.

The finding that personal burdens caused by air pollution are of no relevance for proenvironmental commitments whereas global appraisals of air quality proved to be important is also in line with other empirical justice relevant findings. These findings are discussed as "phenomenon of the denial of personal disadvantage" (Crosby, Cordova & Jaskar, 1993, p. 88). The phenomenon is based on empirical research suggesting that people are more likely to deny personal disadvantages, such as social discrimination, than disadvantages at the societal level (cf., Crosby, Cordova & Jaskar, 1993; Nagata & Crosby, 1991). It can be assumed that the perception of personal disadvantages via discrimination or via suffering from a polluted local environment evokes considerable psychological hardships (such as endangering self-esteem or personal health) which can be prevented by denying personal suffering. In contrast, the perception of discrimination or pollution at a global societal level should be less threatening and could lead to active coping strategies more easily (such as developing commitments to take remedial measures).

Taken together, the results of the studies supported the theoretical model presented at the beginning of this chapter on the justice relevant explanation of proenvironmental behavior. A sense of socioecological justice, expressed in various justice considerations, seems as a meaningful precondition for the development of the necessary moral responsibility underlying ecologically beneficial behavior.

6. Outlook on Future Research

The above summarized results contribute to our knowledge of people's proenvironmental motivations from the perspective of justice considerations. However, with these results new questions arise:

The first issue refers to the generalizability of the previously discussed predictive results to proenvironmental commitments and behaviors in the context of environmental problems other than air pollution (such as water pollution, decrease of ozone, deforestation, alteration of the atmosphere etc.).

The second issue refers to the unexplained variance of the commitment criteria. There are two ways to consider the predictive power of the assessed variables. One way is to focus on the explained variance which in this study was more than 60 percent of the criterion variance. The other perspective is to focus on the unexplained variance. For the remaining unexplained 40 percent of the criterion variance additional cognitive and emotional appraisals have to be taken into consideration. As seen in Figure 1, these variables include expected instead of experienced emotional stress due to local pollution, expected instead of experienced impairment of health and well-being by pollution, resentment about actual pollution, the perceived justice of raising taxes for pollution instead for pollution control, additional forms of appraisals of environmental policy in general and of specific antipollutive measures (appraisals of necessity, of efficacy, and of costs), appraisals of the efficacy and of the ecological responsibility of organizations, and emotional valuations in the context of control beliefs (experienced helplessness, self efficacy).

The third issue expands the empirical model (cf., Figure 2) to determine whether proenvironmental behavior exists which cannot be explained by morally relevant appraisals and is, consequently, beyond the scope of this explanatory model.

If the variables do not refer to global ecological problems (like air pollution) but to local ecological problems, it is likely that proenvironmental behavior will not be morally oriented but self-oriented (e.g., motivation to protect one's own health or to assure the ecological quality in one's own living space). For example, the readiness to support measures to prevent the building of a waste incinerator plant in one's own neighborhood should have more self-oriented motivations than the readiness to prevent the same building of the industrial plant somewhere in the country where no personal affliction is expected. In the case of local resistance, only the self-oriented but not the morally oriented predictors refer to the same psychological dimension as the criterion variables.

In line with this hypothesis, the actions of local citizens to reduce specific local environmental problems cease when the specific problem is solved or when it seems to be unalterable. Alternatively, other ecologically beneficial projects which do not necessarily improve the quality of the local environment could be supported by those citizens.

The final issue considers the practical implications of developing programs to increase ecologically beneficial commitments and behaviors. The primary focus should be the promotion of specific morally relevant value judgments and the beliefs that personal financial and nonmaterial burdens are just. Awareness of personal afflictions and threats by ecological problems should not be emphasized. For the promotion of proenvironmental behavior, pollution control has to be accepted as a duty of the citizens, independent of individual emotional and physical affliction caused by local pollution.

Specifically, the following justice relevant appraisals should be promoted: The raising of taxes for pollution control for the citizens and for industry should be regarded as just. The perception of possible injustices in environmental policy in general should be promoted. Priority should be given to basic rights of the citizens to live within unpolluted areas, but not to rights to freedom, to maximization of profit, or to guarantee employment which might conflict with antipollution measures. In addition, the awareness of risks by the general level of pollution should be increased. The causation of air pollution should not only be attributed to external but also to private sources. The perceived efficacy of various agents (of the citizens, the state and industry) to control air pollution should be enlarged. The responsibility for the protection of air quality should not only be attributed to the state or to industry but also to individual citizens.

In the description of the studies and their results, information on the prediction of emotional appraisals by cognitive variables was excluded. According to this prediction, it is likely that changing these cognitive appraisals would result in changes to significant emotional appraisals: Resentment about the pollutive behavior of others and guilt concerning one's own pollutive behavior will probably increase. Anger about too much pollution control will probably decrease.

The data does not offer specific information on the decision of intervention strategies to change the cognitive appraisals in the intended direction. However, specific intervention knowledge to promote proenvironmental behavior does already exist (e.g., Borsutzky & Nöldner, 1989; De Young, 1985-1986; Sia, Hungerford & Tomera, 1986). Within social psychology there is a wide range of studies in other contexts offering information on the efficacy of different intervention strategies to develop practical intervention programs (cf., for example, Fiske & Taylor, 1984).

In summary, psychological perceptions of socioecological justice were studied at the beginning of systematic environmental research, but this justice focus showed no continuous research tradition. There are theoretical arguments that justice considerations are important to understand and to promote ecologically beneficial behavior. The two studies presented demonstrate that justice considerations are also represented in the structure of proenvironmental commitments and behaviors of the general population and of two criterion groups. These results indicate the necessity of further research in socioecological justice considerations with the aim of promoting proenvironmental behavior more effectively.

References

Amelang, M., Tepe, K., Vagt, G. & Wendt, W. (1977). Mitteilung über einige Schritte der Entwicklung einer Skala zum Umweltbewußtsein. Diagnostica, 23, 86-88.

Becker, L. J., Seligman, C., Fazio, R. H. & Darley, J. M. (1981). Relating attitudes to residential energy use. Environment and Behavior, 13, 590-609.

Borsutzky, D. & Nöldner, W. (1989). Psychosoziale Determinanten des Energiesparverhaltens. Theorie und Forschung (79): Psychologie (28). Regensburg: S. Roderer Verlag.

Bossel, H. (1990). Umweltwissen: Daten, Fakten, Zusammenhänge. Berlin: Springer.

Clayton, S. (1994). Appeals to justice in the environmental debate. Journal of Social Issues, 50, 13-27.

Conference of European Statisticians (ed.). (1987). Environment statistics in Europe and North America: An experimental compendium. New York: United Nations Publications.

Craik, K. H. (1973). Environmental psychology. Annual Review of Psychology, 24, 403-422.

Crosby, F., Cordova, D. & Jaskar, K. (1993). On the failure to see oneself as disadvantaged: Cognitive and emotional components. In M.A. Hogg & D. Abrams (eds.), Group motivation. Social psychological perspectives (pp. 87-104).

Crowne, D. P. & Marlowe, D. (1960). A new scale of social desirability independent of psychopathology. Journal of Consulting Psychology, 24, 349-354.

Darnay, A. J. (ed.). (1992). Statistical record of the environment. Detroit: Gale Research Company.

De Young, R. (1985-1986). Encouraging environmentally appropriate behavior: The role of intrinsic motivation. Journal of Environmental Systems, 15, 281-292.

Ernst, A. M. & Spada, H. (1993). Bis zum bitteren Ende? In J. Schahn & T. Giesinger (Hrsg.), Psychologie für den Umweltschutz (pp. 17-27). Weinheim: Psychologie Verlags Union.

Fiske, S.T. & Taylor, S. E. (1984). Social cognition. New York: McGraw-Hill.

Hardin, G. (1968). The tragedy of the commons. Science, 162, 1243-1248.

Hines, J. M., Hungerford, H. R. & Tomera, A. N. (1986/87). Analysis and synthesis of research on environmental behavior: A meta-analysis. Journal of Environmental Education, 18, 1-8.

Horwitz, W. A. (1994). Characteristics of environmental ethics: environmental activists' accounts. Ethics and Behavior, 4, 345-467.

Hummel, C. F., Levit, L., & Loomis, R. J. (1978). Perceptions of energy crisis. Who is blamed and how do citizens react to environment-lifestyle trade-offs? Environment and Behavior, 10, 37-88.

Kals, E. (1994). Straßenverkehr und Umweltschutz: Die ökologische Verantwortung des Bürgers. In A. Flade (Hrsg.), Mobilitätsverhalten (S. 255-266). Weinheim: Psychologie Verlags Union.

Kals, E. & Montada, L. (1994). Umweltschutz und die Verantwortung der Bürger. Zeitschrift für Sozialpsychologie, 25, 326-337.

Kaminski, G. (1988). Is the development of a psychological ecology useful and possible? (Bericht Nr. 28). Tübingen: Universität, Psychologisches Institut.

Kessel, H. & Tischler, W. (1984). Umweltbewußtsein. Ökologische Wertvorstellungen westlicher Industrienationen. Berlin: Edition Sigma Rainer Bohn Verlag.

Kley, J. & Fietkau, H.-J. (1979). Verhaltenswirksame Variablen des Umweltbewußtseins. Psychologie und Praxis, 1, 13-22.

Krämer, M. (1989). Problembewältigungsstrategien und politisches Engagement. PP-Aktuell, 8, 111-123.

Kruse, L. & Arlt, R. (1984). Environment and behavior. An international and multidisciplinary bibliography. 1970-1981. Vol. 1. Alphabetical listing by authors. Key word index. Vol. 2. Abstracts. München: K.G. Saur.

Kushler, M. G. (1989). Use of evaluation to improve energy conservation programs: A review and case study. Journal of Social Issues, 45, 153-168.

Löfstedt, R. E. (1992). Lay perspectives concerning climate change in Sweden. Energy and Environment, 3, 161-175.

Löfstedt, R. E. (1993). Lay perspectives concerning global climate change in Vienna, Austria. Energy and Environment, 4, 140-154.

Lück, H. E. & Timaeus, E. (1969). Skalen zur Messung Manifester Angst (MAS) und Sozialer Wünschbarkeit (SDS-E und SDS-CM). Diagnostica, 15, 134-141.

Maloney, M. P. & Ward, M. P. (1973). Ecology: Let's hear from the people. An objective scale for the measurement of ecological attitudes and knowledge. American Psychologist, 28, 583-586.

Mitchell, R. C. & Carson, R. T. (1989). Using surveys to value public goods: The contingent valuation method. Washington: Resources for the future.

Montada, L. & Kals, E. (1995). Perceived justice of ecological policy and proenvironmental commitments. Social Justice Research, 8, 305-327.

Montada, L., Schmitt, M. & Dalbert, C. (1986). Thinking about justice and dealing with one's own privileges: A study of existential guilt. In H.W. Bierhoff, R. Cohen & J. Greenberg (eds.), Justice in social relations (pp. 125-143). New York: Plenum Press.

Nagata, D. & Crosby, F. (1991). Comparisons, justice, and the internment of Japanese-Americans. In J. Suls & T.A. Wills (eds.), Social comparison: Contemporary theory and research (pp. 347-368). Hillsdale: Erlbaum.

Nozick, R. (1974), Anarchy, state and utopia. New York: Basic Books.

Platt, J. (1973). Social traps. American Psychologist, 28, 641-651.

Preiser, S. & Wannemacher, W. (1983). Kognitive Bedingungen sozialen und politischen Handelns. In S. Preiser (Hrsg.), Soziales und politisches Engagement (S. 108-167). Weinheim: Beltz.

Renn, O., Webler, T. & Kastenholz, H. (1994). Fairness and competence in siting a landfill: A case study from Switzerland. Laxenburg: Conference on Risk and Fairness. IIASA, Laxenburg, Austria (May 23-24, 1994).

Schahn, J. & Holzer, E. (1990). Konstruktion, Validierung und Anwendung von Skalen zur Erfassung des individuellen Umweltbewußtseins. Zeitschrift für Differentielle und Diagnostische Psychologie, 11, 185-204.

Sia, A. P., Hungerford, H. R. & Tomera, A.N. (1986). Selected predictors of responsible environmental behavior: An analysis. Journal of Environmental Education, 17, 31-40.

Sitter, B. (1987). Wie läßt sich ökologische Gerechtigkeit denken? Zeitschrift für ökologische Ethik, 31, 271-295.

Spada, H. & Opwis, K. (1985). Ökologisches Handeln im Konflikt: Die Allmende-Klemme. In P. Day, U. Fuhrer & U. Laucken (Hrsg.), Umwelt und Handeln (S. 63-85). Tübingen: Attempto.

Stern, P. C. & Gardener, G. T. (1981). The place of behavior change in the management of environmental problems. Zeitschrift für Umweltpolitik, 2, 213-239.

Syme, G. J., Beven, C. E., & Sumner, N. R. (1993). Motivation for reported involvement in local wetland preservation: The roles of knowledge, disposition, problem assessment, and arousal. Environment and Behavior, 25, 586-606.

Tyler, T. R., Orwin, R., & Schurer, L. (1982). Defensive denial and high cost prosocial behavior. Basic and Applied Social Psychology, 3, 267-281.

Umweltbundesamt (Hrsg.). (1988). Umweltpolitik. Vierter Immissionsschutzbericht der Bundesregierung. Bonn: Universitäts-Buchdruckerei.

Umweltbundesamt (Hrsg.). (1994). Daten zur Umwelt 1992/93. Berlin: Erich Schmidt Verlag.

14

Tradeoffs between Justice and Self-Interest

Leo Montada

In his introduction to this volume, Melvin Lerner refers to Russell Hardin's assertion (cf., Hardin's chapter in this volume) that in the view of scholars, when confronted with the demands of real world considerations, welfare and self-interest in the form of mutual benefit invariably trump justice. In the light of the contributions to this volume let us now consider the various implications of this observation. Both justice and welfare are multifaceted concepts which include a variety of criteria rendering different perspectives on social problems. When these criteria are conflicting, one of them may be given priority, even in circumstances where a tradeoff between different ones would offer the chance of a more adequate solution. Refering to the contributions to this volume I will comment on the multifaceted nature of these concepts, on the usefulness of differentiations both within and between the concepts, and various possibilities for reaching integrative solutions.

1. Justice or Justices?

When looking at the domain of distributive justice, for instance, we find a multiplicity of notions or criteria: equality, proportionality according to need, achievements, investments, memberships, seniority, age,

Leo Montada • Professor of Psychology, Fb I - Psychologie, Universitaet Trier, D-54286 Trier, Germany

Current Societal Concerns about Justice, edited by Leo Montada and Melvin J. Lerner. Plenum Press, New York, 1996.

social status, previous disadvantages, the preservation of acquired entitlements, and many more. Think, for instance, of the question of which
employees should be dismissed when business slows down: Every one
of the criteria mentioned is reasonable. As Walzer (1983) argued, not all
of the existing notions of justice are accepted as valid in all domains of
social and societal life - neither by moral philosophy nor by law nor by
culturally shaped common sense - but in most "spheres" (domains of
social life) and in most cases several principles of distribution are
considered legitimate and valid which do not converge on the same view
of what is or would be just or unjust.

Applying different notions results in diverging, even contradictory
judgements or solutions. Therefore, it would mean noursing an illusion
to speak of justice in the singular. Using the plural form "justices" would
imply the more adequate expectation that different notions of what is
just are legitimate and reasonable, that different people may favor
specific notions, and that it usually means onesidedness to consider one
single notion the truth about justice. This might have the taste of
relativism. Relativism is not contested, but it is not relativism in the
sense of "nothing is valid". Instead, as I would like to emphasize, it is a
positive relativism: In every case more than one single criterion has to
be considered valid and reasonable.

When different criteria cannot be integrated into a solution, this
solution should not be offered as the absolutely just one. Rather, it should
be conceded that it is not more than a preference decision. As soon as
another criterion is applied or other weights are attached to the applied
ones the preferred solution will no longer be jugded the relatively best
one. Moreover, positive relativism implies that every attempt to reduce
injustice or to solve justice problems will create new injustices from the
perspective of unconsidered criteria (Ruethers, 1991). Decision makers
should be aware of this fact. The co-existence of multiple criteria
(principles) of distributive justice is but one of the complexities we have
to be aware of. Another one is the fact that the justice of every allocation
must be evaluated from the diverging perspectives of several affected
parties as well as several levels of a social system: various individuals
affected, social groups, social categories, and populations (Griffith,
Parker & Toernblom, 1993).

The debate about the justice of affirmative actions in favor of women
is a good example to illustrate the problem. There is little doubt that
women were disadvantaged in the past with respect to opportunities for
a professional career. At the level of the gender categories "women" and
"men" affirmative actions in favor of women obviously seem to be just
corrections of still existing inequalities. Affirmative actions in favor of

single women might be justifiable if these social categories were primary social groups in which all members would enjoy the success of one member and possibly profit by it: undeserved advantages of one group would be balanced by assigning equal advantages to the hitherto disadvantaged group. Yet, is it reasonable to assume that the men constitute one group and the women another?

Men compete professionally not only with women but also with other men and women not only with men but also with other women. Most men and women build primary social groups with one another: partnerships, marriages, and families, where mothers are usually just as pleased about the professional success of their sons as of their daughters, and where wives worry about the professional success of their husbands more than about the success of their husbands' women competitors. Considered at the level of individuals affected, affirmative actions privilege individuals, usually young women by disadvantaging individuals, usually young men who compete for the same positions. The privileged individual women are not the ones who were disadvantaged in the past and the disadvantaged men are not the ones who profitted from the uncontested privileges of men during the history up to our days.

What would be just? Changing traditional, not justified inequalities is a just goal. Realizing more equality at the level of gender categories by discriminating against young men - and at the same time allowing the older generations of men to keep enjoying their traditional advantages - is that the just solution? Doubts appear as soon as one starts thinking at the level of individuals or at the level of groups (families) they belong to. Only at the level of gender categories -which do not constitute psychological entities - affirmative actions can be defended as just.

It might well be, however, that affirmative action is an efficient way to realize desirable social change: By providing more examples of successful women in career positions more women might be attracted to compete for such positions. And the goal to motivate more women to compete for career positions can be justified by common welfare arguments. It is in the public interest that important positions are assigned to the best qualified individuals available. Attracting more women will raise the number of qualified applicants and enhance the chances to recruit really good ones. Therefore, welfare arguments for affirmative actions seem less ambiguous to me than justice arguments. Moreover, I would consider affirmative actions in favor of women even more acceptable if the injustices implied (the advantaging of individual women and the disadvantaging of individual men) were conceded, meaning that welfare is given priority over justice for good reasons in this specific case.

Given the multifaceted nature of justice and given the complexities created by this fact I rather doubt if universally valid solutions for justice problems could be found. We need pragmatism to deal with diverging and competing views of justice. Examples of pragmatic approaches to justice are offered by research on "local justice" done, for instance, by Jon Elster (1992): "Local justice" research analyses decisions made at an institutional level, e.g., dismissals, the allocation of scarce positions in universities, the allocation of organs for transplants. Looking at the diversities in allocation criteria and procedures used in different institutions and in different societies, Elster concluded that no generalizations can be drawn from this intra-and interculturally comparative research. I don't agree with this conclusion.

Studying this research I became convinced that widely acceptable solutions are never based on one single criterion (or principle) of distributive justice but are always comprised of a mix of several principles. A mix is less than a convincing integration of conflicting notions which may not be achieved or not be achievable. For instance, in case of mass dismissals, a mix may simply mean that several principles are applied but not in the way that a specified combination of criteria (given stable weights) would be consistently applied to everybody. Such mixes or trade-offs may reflect the fact that discretionary elements in decision making and in the negotiations among conflicting parties may be unavoidable. What we need is not only tradeoffs between divergent notions of justice which are acceptable to all parties concerned but also tradeoffs between justice and other values such as common welfare and self-interest, which may interfere with justice conceptions. It might well be that the complexities of justice let common welfare and self-interest appear attractively simple criteria for the evaluation of social order, policies, and allocations. However, both welfare and self-interest are not more homogenous, nor less complex constructs than is justice.

2. Self-Interest and the Justice Motive

The dominant model of man in economic theories is homo oeconomicus - people act rationally according to self-interest (under conditions of scarcity and in competition with other actors of the same "nature"). The model of homo economicus was not intended to apply to single acts of individuals in every social context and every situation but to predict modal action tendencies of many actors. According to homo oeconomicus , behavior in (moral) dilemma situations (such as social traps or conflicts between solidarity and self-interest) does not necessarily have to appear overtly selfish or egoistic in the sense of maximizing own profits at the cost of others. Selfish behavior is expected to become likely in situations and contexts where some competing actors behave egoistically (e.g., aggressively competitive, exploitative, free rider like, and so forth), or where such behavior of competitors is expected. In principle, self-interest does not exclude solidarity, caring for others, responsibility for future generations (for instance, in the sense of concern for sustainable instead of exploitative use of resources) if such behavior serves their own best interests in the long run. This, of course, presupposes that other actors behave the same way. Social contract theories of social justice and social institutions refer to self-interest as the guiding motivation (Rawls, 1971, Buchanan, 1984).

There are alternative anthropological models assuming man to be a cooperative, solidarity oriented, responsible actor, in political science (Mulhall & Swift, 1993), in economics (e.g., Etzioni, 1988) and in psychology (Lerner, 1977). Doubts about the universal validity of the hypothesis that human nature is guided by self-interest are usually substantiated by observational examples that do not fit this motivational construct neatly (e.g., Mansbridge, 1990). Is it in the self-interest of adult childen to care for their needy parents? Is it in the self-interest of parents to care for their disabled child? Is it in the self-interest of a society to care for the mentally handicapped?

Of course, it can be argued that seemingly unselfish caring is a favorable self-presentation in public and is rewarded by social recognition, and that social welfare granted by the communities creates a feeling of security to all members thus increasing the common welfare, the well-being and maybe even the productivity of all. But what about anonymous contributions to impersonal charity? In contrast to public rewards they do not raise the donors' prestige nor will the donors be rewarded by a grateful recipient. Yet, one might argue that anonymous donors are interested in the survival of impersonal charity since they prefer help by such an institution in case of becoming needy themselves rather than being helped by individual others. And what about caring and helping out of love? Advocates of the self-interest model would argue that love is a condition where the wellbeing of the loved ones is rewarding the loving one. The argument with empathy motivated help is similar: Empathy means to suffer with the needy person and the suffering of the empathic helper ends with that of the needy person.

Thus, hypotheses of a hidden self-interest are conceivable in every case of apparently altruistic behavior. Let us look for other cases. What about people who do not cheat even when they are certain their cheating would not be detected? Defending the self-interest model, one might hypothesize that these apparently honest people either wish to avoid every risk of being punished or that they are convinced that cheating is a threat to interpersonal trust and/or common welfare. Since they expect to ultimately profit more by promoting common welfare than cheating, their decision can be portrayed as a form of self-interest. Observing laws and moral norms can be "explained" rationally as ultimately self-serving according to the postulates of social contract theories. To mention as a last case "irrationally" costly and risky revenges of suffered injustices: Would it not be in the interest of victims to avoid further costs and harm? It would not if retaliation is their dominant interest.

What I tried to demonstrate by these examples is that the construct self-interest can only be applied universally if it is defined sufficiently abstract to subsume every motive: altruistic, and moral ones, as well as patently self-interested ones. Considering every motive basically as an implementation of self-interest negates the scientific usefulness of distinct specific motivational constructs. With some ingenuity it is always possible to generate hypotheses that reduce every ("surface") motivation to an underlying self-interest or "unmask" it as ultimately serving self-interest. In my view, such a use of self-interest is scientifically unproductive. Conceived to explain everything it does in fact explain nothing. This is my critique of the quasi axiomatic use of the construct self-interest. We need motivational constructs with predictive and explanatory power. What should be predicted and explained? Interindividual and intraindividual differences in behavior, in judgements, in emotional reactions to specific events.

Self-interest should a priori not be conceived of as the motive but only as one motive among others. It needs alternative motivational constructs as hypotheses for human behavior, reliable and valid operationalizations to infer or to assess them, so that the hypotheses can be tested empirically. One of these constructs should be self-interest but not as the general driving force underlying every motivation but as one construct distinguishable from other motivational constructs which can be identified in empirical observations, preferably assessable by adequate measurement devices. Different motivational constructs are useful when they imply different meanings and when they explain different parts of the variance of criterion variables, when their distributions in populations vary and vary meaningfully, when their developmental trajectories can be distinguished, and so forth. Interpreting every motivation as self-interest is an anthropological, a pretheoretical decision which is theoretically not fruitful because it is not falsifiable empirically. Falsification would require alternative, well operationalized motivational constructs.

Dale Miller and Rebecca Ratner report highly intriguing observations which demonstrate that self-interest is a dominating motivational hypothesis in common sense. It is not only that people assume others to be motivated by self-interest, many present themselves in public as being guided by self-interest. Miller and Ratner report data that raises doubts concerning whether people's self-reported self-interest is their true motivation. Self-interest seems significantly overestimated, maybe because people find it easier to communicate self-interest as the reason for their behavior rather than altruistic or moral motivation. To "confess" self-interest avoids doubts about the truth of ones' self-presentation, doubts which might be expected, for instance, if other-centered motivations were reported.

This analysis suggests that self-interest has become an influential myth, a social construction of man that influences self-presentation, attributions, expectations, and actions. Spreading this myth will result in disguising alternative motivations. Tendencies to respond in socially expected or desirable ways may result in denying the true motivations, provided subjects are able at all to perceive their true motivations introspectively. Pretending self-interest seems to have become a "socially desirable" form of self-presentation. (Consequently, we have to control for tendencies of social desirability before we take self-reported self-interest for granted.) Again, what we need are valid methods to identify self-interest and other motivations empirically.

I will illustrate this request by referring to the contribution by Karen Cook and Shawn Donnelly in this volume. They are dealing with the question why the generation contract is continued inspite of the heavy burden it puts on the currently productive generation. They argue on the basis of a version of the exchange theory considering all relationships to be governed by the participants' rewards and costs: People engage in specific relationships when their exchanges are relatively profitable compared with what they might expect to obtain in others. Cook and Donnelly's analysis of the dynamics involved in intergenerational relations contains a highly fruitful extension of the social exchange model by including "generalized" exchanges. The social system as a frame for exchange processes is extended beyond the directly exchanging parties. Indirect exchanges become countable in the general balance (e.g., A is compensated by C for his or her service in favor of B). Applying this model to intergenerational relations, the authors hypothesize: Although the younger generations may engage in clearly unprofitable direct exchanges with their parent generation, they continue because they anticipate later reciprocity for themselves by future generations. They accumulate credit to be paid back by the next generation(s). The question now is: How does justice come into this model? The prototype for exchange relations is the contract. The ideal contract is one that the parties expect (ex ante) to be mutually, if not equally advantageous. This ideal is jeopardized by power inequalities, or by informational, economic, or social inequalities of the parties involved at the time the contract is concluded. It might turn out (ex post) that the contract is not as advantageous as expected for one of the parties but already in the tradition of Roman law it was a common sense of justice that pacta sunt servanda provided the contracts were signed up freely and informed. On the basis of this obligation all parties may expect the fulfillment of the contract.

However, it can be argued that "the generation contract" is actually not a contract since "the generations" were not the parties negotiating it consenting freely and informed. Instead, it is imposed on them by law(s) binding currently living and future generations that did not even had voice when the contract was agreed upon! Nevertheless, every living generation has already profited by the contract and is therefore obligated to reciprocal performance. What would happen if a working generation would attempt to terminate the burden imposed upon them and to negotiate a more profitable contract? This would cause a number of justice problems. We doubt that the main reason offered by this generation could be that the "contract" (simulated by laws and practiced by tradition) is not profitable for them. The generation proposing termination would be reminded of the investments the parent generation had made both in this younger one and in the grandparent generation. Certainly, the older generation has acquired entitlements against the younger one. My guess is the following: If the younger generation would attempt to terminate the contract an outburst of outrage would be the answer, at least if termination were based upon reasons of self-interest. That would only be acceptable if convincing justice arguments were forwarded, e.g., if a currently unjust balance of costs and profits could be proven compared to the parent generation. But even then, termination of the contract would not be a tolerable option. Only a modification in the direction of more justice would be acceptable.

In fact, we do not have empirical data proving that the younger generation is more guided by self-interest than by justice considerations. Why, then, should the observed continuation of the contract be explained by self-interest and not by the motives of the younger generation to do justice to the older one, to meet their justified entitlements? This alternative hypothesis seems just as plausible to me. However, is it not an arbitrary replacing of self-interest by the justice motives? It is indeed arbitrary as long as the impact of alternative motivational hypotheses is not assumed to be different and as long as alternative hypotheses are not made empirically testable.

Let us propose, then, two alternative versions of the justice motive, a primary and a secondary one. Karen Cook and Shawn Donnelly''s hypotheses that were derived from the general exchange model I would like to call the secondary version: Giving justice priority over current profit maximization will possibly pay off provided it can be assumed that the next generation will make their decisions according to the same priorities. The justice motive is merely instrumental for self-interest. The primary version of the justice motive means that the working generation will do justice to the parent generation without consideration of what will be reciprocated to them by future filial generations. Subsuming justice motives a priori under benefit maximation motives (by assuming that justice pays off in the long run), however, seems of limited scientific fruitfulness if one expects that both versions of the justice motive (the primary and the secondary) can be operationalized and made testable. I plead for differentiations that make sense theoretically and empirically.

The usefulness of such differentiations is illustrated in Elisabeth Kals' contribution. She presents data from two large scale multivariate studies designed to test a variety of hypothesized predictors of proenvironmental commitments derived from a complex heuristic model. In the extended list of predictors she assessed, various motivational variables were included representing self-interest, freedom rights, economic welfare, moral responsibilities, and evaluations of the justice or injustice of various environmental policies. One replicated result of these studies is that proenvironmental commitments and readiness for personal renunciations in favor of a sound ecology are morally motivated, they are not motivated by self-interest in the sense of protecting personal or familial health. Kals was able to identify self-interests (economic welfare, employment opportunities, individual freedom rights, fun by car driving) which interfere with proenvironmental commitments; yet, looking at various heterogenous samples it may be concluded that it is anything but uncommon that moral and justice motives trump these conflicting self-interests. And, we have to expect large individual differences.

Contrasting the justice motive with altruism and self-interest, Batson, too, favors a "not reductionistic" approach. Self-interest is not the only motive that might interfere with the justice motive. In line with his well known research on prosocial motivation and behavior, Batson discusses another motive: altruism. Whereas justice requires impartiality in decision making, altruism and self-interest imply partiality - altruism in favor of specific others. Analyzing distribution conflicts, Batson is successful in distinguishing three competing motivations:

altruism, collective welfare orientation and self-interest. In his experiments, both self-interest and altruism (in favor of single others) interfere with collective welfare insofar as they reduce the shares allocated to an anonymous group.

Dealing with leadership, Jim Meindl and Karen Thompson offer some new perspectives to the arena of social construction. Analyzing leadership as the social construction of a relationship between leaders and followers, they distinguish two forms of leadership with differing associations to distributive and procedural justice. What is most interesting to me is the authors' assumption that justice conceptions are essential features of two types of leadership. However, they considers the third type, the charismatic leaders, to have the personal power to suspend the justice conceptions and motives of their followers. This hypothesis is compelling. It is, however, not the only reasonable one. Applying a social interactionist's view one might hypothesize that leaders gain their power by adopting (or presenting) specific concepts of justice that are shared by their followers. Of course, historical examples reveal that charismatic political leaders are able to suspend traditional views of justice and to establish new ones. However, this does not mean that these leaders disregard all existing justice motives. There are numerous historical examples that charismatic leaders take advantage of them; they recruit their followers and gain their power over them by pointing to social injustices and promising to abolish them. This promise is only credible, of course, when it comes from leaders who feature persuasiveness, control, and power. Yet, are followers not attracted by a leader who puts their views of justice or injustice in his or her center of the political combat? At least in the formative stage of leadership, leaders, even charismatic ones, may care about the justice concepts of their followers.

3. Linking Justice and Welfare Criteria

In the tradition of Pareto's welfare theory, collective welfare is considered the welfare of all individual members who have their own individual views about welfare and their own individual preferences for material or non-material goods. Not every increase in available material goods means an uncontestable increase in collective welfare, because there are large individual differences in preferences for these goods and because their production and consumption have costs: losses of immaterial goods (e.g., beauty and diversity of nature, side effects of pollution, noise) as well as material costs in the long run as a result of poisening soil and water, by wasting natural resources, and by destroying living conditions. Collective welfare is easy to assess only in terms of currently available quantities of material goods or income. It is much more difficult to predict the long term consequences of productive and consumptive processes.

Collective welfare becomes a much more multifaceted construct when immaterial goods and the variance of individual preferences are considered and included in the definition. Thus, what welfare is, is not less divergent and conflictful than what justice is within a pluralistic society. And, justice is one of the immaterial values (such as solidarity, peace, beauty of nature, religion etc.) that may become salient in individual and social constructions of welfare. Having this view in mind we can look at the proposed relationships between justice and welfare. As Hardin (in this volume states in his analysis of moral and political theories: "Backed to the wall by the real world, virtually every moral and political theorist is a mutual advantage pragmatist." ... "The core concern of mutual advantage theories is to allow for making our world better for us, not only fairer." This sentence could be reversed "... to allow for making our world fairer, not only better for us."

Mutual advantage is a formula to harmonize welfare and justice. The utilitarian principle "maximization of common wealth" is chained linked to the justice principle that common wealth may not be increased at the cost of single members or subgroups of a community or society (Pareto) or that every member of a social system is entitled to receive a share when common wealth is increased (Rawls). Mutual advantage implies at the same time that justice is linked to welfare: The establishment of justice (more precisely: a specific notion of justice) is morally contestable if it is not commonly advantagous, if it jeopardizes common welfare.

One could ask whether justice notions could be evaluated according to their impact on productivity. Vobruba (1994) distinguished productivistic conceptions of distributive justice (such as allocations according to performance criteria) from nonproductivity conceptions (like equality). Of course, productivity conceptions of justice are not antagonistic to welfare conceptions. Equal poverty is not less equal than equal welfare, but is poverty just(ifiable) at all if we would be able to overcome it at the cost of accepting some inequality? The world of ideas about justice offers arguments to justify inequalities when they raise collective welfare.

Mutual advantage must not mean discounting justice. Instead, it may mean the integration of justice and welfare by linking both classes of criteria to each other. It remains open to question, however, how this can be realized best: What weights have to be assigned to these basic principles in concrete distribution problems and in specific policies is open to debate.

Linking justice and welfare does not imply giving priority to welfare whenever there is a conflict between welfare and justice. It is true, as Susan Clayton maintains in her contribution, that a single, one-sided "absolute" definition of what is fair can be a tyranny for those who do not share this specific conception of what is just and who do not give it priority in their individual ranking of values including their individual conceptions of welfare (of a good life). Yet, I hesitate to agree with her recommendation that thinking through the effects of any policy including several different justice perspectives allows people to "make decisions that will truly maximize the collective welfare". I hesitate to agree before it is clarified what exactly collective welfare means in this case. Should it mean the total of produced goods available, we have to expect protest against this "tyranny of material goods" by all those who are committed to a sound ecology priority. Again, we need a trade-off between justice principles and welfare criteria.

Referring to the arguments given above, both justice and common welfare cannot be defined absolutely or a priori. We have to deal with conflicting views, with diverging options. We observe historical changes and ongoing efforts to change the common sense about these constructs. Shared views of what welfare means may be the result of a process of social construction, and the same is true for shared views about what is just and unjust. Maybe justice and welfare conceptions converge or maybe they do not. Examples of ongoing conflicts and ongoing efforts to change the common sense about justice and welfare are provided in several chapters of this volume.

In dealing with environmental issues, Susan Opotow discusses the issue that rules of justice are applied within social systems. Distributions of resources, rights and duties are realized within the borderlines of a social system. Distributive justice is conceivable only within these borderlines (Cohen, 1986), which, of course, can be drawn wider or narrower, subjectively or culturally or by law. Just distributions of natural resources and of profits, of risks and of impediments by pollution can be striven for within a community, a society, neighboring societies, the presently living humanity, present and future generations, the totality of all living organisms, or our planet as a whole. Susan Opotow speaks of the scope of justice, the scope of the system where justice is to be established.

Extending her previous work on "moral exclusion", she describes stages of "environmental inclusion" emerging within the environmental movement where egocentric views are surpassed by other-centered, anthropocentric views, and "ecocentric" philosophies. Opotow starts from such a stage typology of environmental value orientations to sketch an enlarging scope of justice as a developmental task. This task, however, is impeded by barriers that need to be identified such as situational constraints (like economic recessions) and perceptual biases, e.g., by comparing the current eco-protective conventions with (even) less effective previous ones instead of with optimal ones. Opotows conceptualizations stress the importance of values. Self-centered values might interfere with ecological justice. Ecological desasters as well as ecological enlightment may help to revise people's views about what best serves their interests. Protection of environment can be motivated by long term self-interest or by moral oughts which basically imply concern for justice. It might well be that to convince people that it is in their own interest to protect ecology is effective with a part of the population, for another part justice-related arguments might be necessary or more convincing. But typically the risks and costs of pollution and exploitation of nature are vague and expected in the distant future whereas the profits are certain and immediate. Therefore, moral and justice arguments seem indispensable.

The issue "scope of justice" is also discussed in my own chapter on unemployment and occupational policies, namely the insider-outsider problem. One of the barriers against the integration of outsiders (the unemployed) into the labor market is the selfishness of insiders (those who have a job) and policies that favor insiders (like protective laws against dismissals). For instance, it is well known that the number of jobs offered by the economy depends on the labor costs. In regulated economies with strong unions as the European ones the labor costs are not adapted quickly to changing conditions on the labor market. The insiders - the jobholders, respectively the unions - pushing for increases in wages and other costly entitlements also raises the total labor costs and reduces the chances of the "outsiders" seeking employment. Claims by the insiders to improve or, at least, to preserve the status quo (the "justly acquired" status quo!; in Germany the term is "Besitzstandswahrung") are the most frequent justice claims in the public debate about occupational policies.

Fortunately, conflicting justice orientations can be observed, more frequently within the general population than among the officials in the unions. In fact, significant parts of the population experience problems with their own relatively advantageous working and living conditions when confronted with the fate of less fortunate others. We called this "existential guilt" (Montada & Schneider, 1989). Existential guilt feelings about own advantages as well as moral resentment about undeserved disadvantages of others are not rare "exotic" feelings but normally distributed emotional reactions about the fate of less fortunate others demonstrating that the scope of justice reaches beyond self-interest and the interests of one's own primary group. Existential guilt and resentment because of the unemployed can motivate more fortunate workers to accept redistributions. Most likely, to have redistributions in working time and working income accepted, they have to be considered just in the sense that all equals have to contribute equal shares. Of course, there are several ways to cope with one's own relatively privileged living conditions. Derogation of the disadvantaged is one coping strategy, sharing and helping is another. Individual differences in emotional reactions to relatively less fortunate others and in ways of coping with these feelings are large and they are related to beliefs and views about justice: Belief in Just World, preferences for certain distribution principles, centrality of justice in one's life, etc.

Lerner, in his chapter, provides more persuasive examples of the fact that not everybody is happy with his or her relative welfare. Describing injustices caused by "corporate restructuring" he identifies not only the dismissed individuals as victimized and suffering, but reports problems and guilt feelings of those who keep their jobs (the survivors), and of the managers who have to execute the dismissals. Guilt feelings of the survivors, existential guilt because of more or less fortunate own advantages give strong evidence for the existence of a justice motive.

Another strong evidence for the power of justice motives is the fact of social movements that gain momentum by protesting against perceived injustices. The first battles of a social movement are aimed at changing the dominant social constructions of justice (if the claimed changes are not profitable for everybody). It would not require a social movement if it were easy to reach a consensus about what is just and what is unjust and to realize changes in accordance with these consensual views.

There are multiple reasons why the vigor of a movement may decrease over time. One of them might be that activists gain insight into the complexities of justice. As Ruethers (1991) stated, there is no measure aiming at reducing injustice that does not create new injustices. Another hypothesis that activists experience in various ways may be the difficulties in establishing social change so that their personal effort-outcome balance is less than rewarding. If, however, the commitment is continued in spite of it, it would prove that the justice motive is powerful.

Faye Crosby, Janet Todd, and Judith Worrell explored whether the commitment of feminist Psychology professors commitment declined as the movement came to age. The results of their study confirm that the feminist movement is "alive and flourishing", working within as well as outside the social and political systems " to increase the "civil rights of all women". It would be interesting to find out who continues to be committed and why, and who has given up engagement over time and why. Analyzing interindividual differences with respect to the stability of commitments would be an opportunity to test the relative impact of justice motives and self-concern.

That is what Barbara Reichle did in her longitudinal study of young couples struggling with the redistribution of duties, privileges, costs and benefits after the birth of their first child. These distributions usually disadvantage the young mothers who end or interrupt their professional careers and bear a significantly higher share of the new burdens. Individually varying views about justice, both procedural and distributive, affect the way in which couples experience the distribution problems and the outcomes. Significant gender-related inequalities in the distribution of duties and rights are still the rule. Perceiving these inequalitites as unjust turned out to be a powerful determinant of dissatisfaction with the partnership and to bear the risk of separation and divorce. Assuming that separation and divorce quite often mean a drop in economic welfare, these data indicate that some people, at least, are not willing to compensate their frustrated justice motive by personal or familial welfare but follow the directives of their justice motives.

4. Procedural Fairness in Value Conflicts and the Social Construction of Value Orientations

Coming back to the myth of self-interest, I would like to say I share the assumption that much of the motivational "equipment" of humans is socially shaped. The spreading of myths is one of the contributions in the process of social construction. The myth of self-interest can shape human motivation when it becomes the guiding idea in education and socialization, when it guides public self-presentation, when it motivates skepticisms about the honesty of self-reported moral motives, when everybody who does not act according to self-interest is considered irrational, when it becomes dominant in scientific modelling. There is, however, no doubt in my mind that a myth cannot be victorious in the sense of shaping reality perfectly. At some point in time a movement of critiques will spread "enlightenment" about the "mistakes of the myths", as can currently be observed with the communitarians who doubt the ubiquity and universal dominance of self-interest. So, I am convinced that altruism and the justice motive, value orientations and other motivations will survive in human nature and human cultures. Therefore, a variety of competing options will be available for the social construction of values, shaping value oriented motivations. Consequently, the debate about what is and what should be will be continued. What is true for widely held myths is also true for vigorously held subjective intuitions about what is just and what is valuable: They are usally onesided and cannot claim to be the truth even if strong beliefs and emotional attitudes support them.

Given as a matter of fact that views about justices, self-interests and common welfare are varying and may be conflicting, the question is, how to come to solutions, how to arrive at broadly accepted, possibly even shared solutions. The more familiar strategies include the use of one-sided arguments, selective information, efforts to impose one's views and preferences on others by using legal, illegal, charismatic power, creating facts with the expectation that they will be accepted, even justified in the long run. Procedural justice (Thibaut & Walker, 1975; Luhmann, 1975, Lind & Tyler, 1988) and discourse ethics (Ackerman, 1980; Habermas, 1983; Apel, 1976) have specified ideal rules and personal conditions (favorable attitudes, basic necessary knowledge, communication and empathic capacities, presence of an important mediator) which are helpful in reaching consensus. This is not the occasion to review this literature but it is an occasion to cite research which proves that people are ready to accept laws, administrative prescriptions, sentences by courts, if they judge the applied procedure as fair even of the outcomes of the laws, prescriptions, and sentences were not profitable for them. (e.g., Tyler, 1990).

References

Ackermann, B. (1980). Justice in the liberal state. New Haven: Yale University Press.

Apel, K. O. (1976). Transformation der Philosophie. Das Apriori der Kommunikationsgemeinschaft. Bd. 2. Frankfurt: Suhrkamp.

Buchanan, J. (1984). Die Grenzen der Freiheit. Tübingen: Mohr.

Cohen, R. L. (1986). Membership, intergroup relations, and justice. In M. J. Lerner & R.Vermunt (Eds.), Social justice in human relations I (pp 239-258). New York: Plenum Press.

Cook, K.S. & Emerson, R. M. (1978). Power, equity, and commitment in exchange networks. American Sociological Review 43, 721-739.

Elster, J. (1992). Local justice. New York: Russel Sage Foundation.

Etzioni, A. 1988). The moral dimension: Toward a new economics. New York: Free Press.

Griffith, W. I., Parker, M. J. & Törnblom, K.Y. (1993). Putting the group back into intergroup justice studies. Social Justice Reserarch 6, 331-342.

Habermas, J. (1976). Moralentwicklung und Ich-Identität. In J. Habermas (Hrsg.), Zur Rekonstruktion des historischen Materialismus (S. 63-91). Frankfurt: Suhrkamp.

Lerner, M. J. (1977). The justice motive. Some hypotheses as to its origins and forms. Journal of Personality 45, 1-32.

Lind, E. A. & Tyler, T.R. (1988). The social psychology of procedural justice. New York: Plenum Press.

Luhmann, (1975). Legitimation durch Verfahren. Darmstadt: Luchterhand.

Mansbridge, J. J. (Ed.). (1990). Beyond self-interest. Chicago: The University of Chicago Press.

Mansbridge, J. J. (1990). The rise and fall of self-interest in the explanation of political life. In J. J. Mansbridge (Ed.), Beyond self-interest (pp. 3-22). Chicago: The University of Chicago Press.

Montada, L. & Schneider, A. (1989). Justice and emotional reactions to the disadvantaged. Social Justice Research 3, No. 4, 313-344.

Montada, L. & Schneider, A. (1991). Justice and prosocial commitments. In L. Montada & H.W. Bierhoff (Eds.), Altruism in social systems (pp. 58-81). Toronto: Hogrefe.

Mulhall, S. & Swift, A. (1993). Liberals and communitarians. Oxford: Blackwell.

Rawls, J. (1971). A theory of justice. Cambridge, MA: Belknap.

Ruethers, B. (1991). Das Ungerechte an der Gerechtigkeit. Zuerich: Edition Interfrom.

Thibaut, J. & Walker, L. (1975). Procedural Justice. A psychological analysis. Hillsdale, NJ.:Lawrence Erlbaum.

Tyler, T. R. (1990). Justice, self-interest, and the legitimacy of legal and political authority. In J. J. Mansbridge (Ed.), Beyond self-interest (pp. 171-179). Chicago: The University of Chicago Press.

Vobruba, G. (1994). Die Faktizität der Geltung. Gerechtigkeit im sozialpolitischen Umbau-Diskurs. In L. Clausen (Hrsg.), Gesellschaften im Umbruch. Verhandlungen des 27. Kongreß der Deutschen Gesellschaft für Soziologie in Halle.

Walzer, M. (1983). Spheres of justice: A defense of pluralism and equality. New York: Basic Books.

Author Index

Subject Index